2   The Republican Experiment, 1848–1852

The Republican Experiment, 1848–1852

MAURICE AGULHON

Professor of Contemporary History, University of Paris I

Translated by
JANET LLOYD

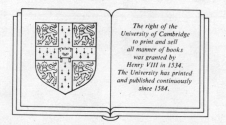

The right of the
University of Cambridge
to print and sell
all manner of books
was granted by
Henry VIII in 1534.
The University has printed
and published continuously
since 1584.

CAMBRIDGE UNIVERSITY PRESS

Cambridge
New York   Port Chester   Melbourne   Sydney

EDITIONS DE
LA MAISON DES SCIENCES DE L'HOMME

Paris

Published by the Press Syndicate of the University of Cambridge
The Pitt Building, Trumpington Street, Cambridge CB2 1RP
32 East 57th Street, New York, NY 10022, USA
296 Beaconsfield Parade, Middle Park, Melbourne 3206, Australia
and
Éditions de la Maison des Sciences de l'Homme
54 Boulevard Raspail, 75270 Paris Cedex 06

Originally published in French as *1848 ou l'Apprentissage de la République 1848–1852*
by Editions du Seuil, Paris 1973 and © Editions du Seuil, 1973

English translation © Maison des Sciences de l'Homme and
Cambridge University Press 1983

First published in English by Maison des Sciences de l'Homme and
Cambridge University Press 1983 as *The Republican Experiment, 1848–1852*
Reprinted 1989

Printed in Great Britain at the University Press, Cambridge

Library of Congress catalogue card number: 82-23461

British Library Cataloguing in Publication Data

Agulhon, Maurice
The republican experiment, 1848–1852. – (Cambridge history of modern
France; 2)
1. France – History – Second Republic, 1848–1852
I. Title   II. 1848 ou l'apprentissage de la république 1848–1852.
944.07   DC272

ISBN 0 521 24829 9 hard covers
ISBN 0 521 28988 2 paperback
ISBN 2 7351 0028 6 hard covers (France only)
ISBN 2 7351 0029 4 paperback (France only)

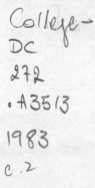

Contents

The great economic initiatives   178
Social policy. The affair of the Orléans fortune. Industrial
expansion. The new capitalism. Agricultural policies.

The return to imperial monarchy   183
The session of the Legislative Body. The tour of Provence. The
speech in Bordeaux. The restoration of the Empire.

Conclusion   187

The Republic of the 'forty-eighters'   188

The official Republic   191

The Bonapartist dictatorship   192

*Appendix: Statistics of the repression of the insurrection of
December 1851*   196
Notes   199
Bibliography   204
Index of names   209

Chronology

1789: beginning of the Revolution. Establishment of a *Constitutional Monarchy*
1792: (10 August to 21 September) New Revolution. Establishment of the *Republic*.
Three periods may be distinguished:
1. the 'Revolutionary Government' by the Convention, 1792–5
2. government by the Constitution of Year II, known as the Directory, 1795–9
3. the dictatorship of Napoleon Bonaparte, known as the Consulate, 1799–1804.
1804: establishment of the *Empire*: Emperor Napoleon I.
Abdicates in 1814, seizes power again during the '100 Days' of 1815, then abdicates definitively.
1814–15: *Restoration* of the monarchy. Openly counter-revolutionary. Symbolised by the white flag.
Louis XVIII (1814–24)
Charles X (1824–1830)
1830: (end of July) Revolution which topples the Restoration and establishes a new constitutional monarchy (following the principles of 1789). Symbolised by the tricolour flag, known as the *July Monarchy*: Louis-Philippe I (1830–48).

The following list naturally contains more dates than we have cited in the chapters of this book. Perhaps they will suggest other lines of research that our own synthesis has not emphasised. With a few exceptions, it contains only dates in the national and (which often comes to the same thing) Parisian chronology. The inclusion of episodes in the various departments (which would inevitably have been incomplete anyhow) would have made it much too long. The calendar given below is only intended as one of general reference for those who, whether as general readers or as scholars, might wish to study the history of particular regions or localities in greater depth.

1848

2 January	Michelet's course of lectures is suspended.
14 January	The banquet in the 12^e *arrondissement* is banned.
21 February	It is banned again. The banquet is cancelled.
22 February	Street demonstrations in Paris.
	The Bourse closes.
23 February	The National Guard goes over to the opposition.
	The king dismisses the ministry.
	Shooting in the boulevard des Capucines.
24 February	Street fighting. Abdication and departure of the king. Formation of the provisional government which declares itself in favour of the Republic.

25 February	The sacking of the chateaux of Neuilly and Suresnes. Lamartine is successful in retaining the tricolour rather than adopting the red flag.
	Cavaignac governor of Algeria.
	Proclamation of the right to work (the principle underlying the national workshops and aid for the associations).
26 February	Abolition of the death penalty for political offences.
	Creation of the mobile National Guard.
28 February	Demonstration demanding a Ministry of Work.
	Creation of the Luxembourg Commission.
29 February	Principle of the abolition of the *octrois* and of the salt tax.
2 March	Abolition of 'sweated labour' (through sub-contractors).
	Limitation of the working day to 10 hours (Paris) and 11 hours (provinces).
	Principle of universal suffrage.
4 March	Lamartine's circular to diplomatic agents.
	Total liberty for the press and for meetings.
	Principle of the abolition of slavery.
5 March	Decree organising methods to be followed in elections and fixing 9 April as the date for the elections.
6 March	Michelet reinstated at the Collège de France. Organisation of the national workshops in the Seine.
7 March	Reopening of the Paris Bourse.
	Creation of discount banks.
8 March	The National Guard opened to all citizens.
	Creation of a school of administration.
14 March	Dissolution of the elite companies of the National Guard.
15 March	Increased circulation of Banque de France banknotes, creation of paper money of small denominations.
16 March	Demonstration by the so-called '*bonnets-à-poil*'.
	Decree creating the '45 centimes' tax.
17 March	Popular counter-demonstration. Elections postponed from 9 to 23 April.
19 March	Abolition of imprisonment for debt.
24–25 March	Restrictive regulations on work in prisons and asylums.
30 March	Defeat of the Belgian Legion at Risquons-tout.
31 March	Reform of the tax on alcohol.
	Publication of the Taschereau document.
3 April	Failure of the Voraces' aid to Savoy.
4 April	Sequestration of two railway companies.
8 April	Ledru-Rollin's circular on the elections.
16 April	Popular demonstration and counter-demonstration in favour of the government.
April	Reform of regulations relating to the *octroi* and the salt tax.
23 April	Election of the Constituent Assembly.
26–28 April	Bloody disturbances in Rouen.
27 April	Definitive decree on the abolition of slavery.
4 May	First meeting of the Constituent Assembly.
	Official proclamation of the Republic.
9–10 May	Election of the Executive Commission, followed by the formation of the ministry (on 17 May Cavaignac becomes Minister of War).

15 May	Popular demonstration. Invasion of the Assembly. Repression and counter-revolutionary scenes of violence.
17 May	Lacordaire resigns from National Assembly. Duclerc proposes the nationalisation of the railways.
20 May and days following	The Assembly begins to call into question the fate of the national workshops. Militant workers arrested.
4 June	By-elections to the Constituent Assembly (Thiers, Proudhon, Victor Hugo, L.-N. Bonaparte).
5–10 June	Popular unrest in Paris, seditious cries, arrests.
6 June	Sénard president of the Assembly.
13 June	Debate in the Assembly on the admission of L.-N. Bonaparte. He is admitted but resigns.
21 June	Decree on the national workshops. Reimposition of the tax on alcohol.
22 June	Workers' demonstrations in Paris.
23 June	Beginning of the workers' insurrection in Paris.
22–3 June	Riots in Marseilles.
24 June	State of siege in Paris. Resignation of the Executive Commission.
25 June	Offensive by the forces of order. Death of Mgr Affre.
26 June	End of the insurrection.
28 June	Cavaignac is appointed President of the Council and forms a new ministry. National workshops abolished. Retraction of the proposal to buy back the railways.
5 July	Carnot loses the Ministry of Public Instruction.
28 July	Decree on the clubs.
31 July	Debate in the Assembly on Proudhon's proposition. Municipal elections.
9–11 August	Decrees on the press.
24 August	Decree on the postal system.
27 August–3 September	Cantonal elections.
End of August	Under threat from the Commission of Enquiry for the Assembly, Louis Blanc and Caussidière go into exile. Debate on the working day which is eventually (9 September) fixed at 12 hours (instead of 10).
4 September	Beginning of the discussion on the Constitution.
17 September	By-elections. Louis-Napoleon Bonaparte re-elected.
21 September	Anniversary of the First Republic (1792). Democratic banquets.
15 October	Ministry reshuffle. The party of order gains a foothold.
31 October	Second reading for the constitutional debate.
4 November	Assembly votes on the Constitution. Ledru-Rollin founds Republican Solidarity.
21 November	Solemn promulgation of the Constitution.
10 December	Election of the President of the Republic.
20 December	Proclamation of the result. Swearing in of the president. Formation of the Barrot–Falloux ministry.
26 December	Changarnier appointed commander of the army in Paris.

27 December	The Assembly reimposes the salt tax.
End of December	The Assembly sets up a programme of organic laws.
29 December	The Rateau proposition which leads to the early dissolution of the Constituent Assembly.

1849

29 January	Military preparations on the part of the government to bring pressure upon the Assembly. Vote on the Rateau proposition.
March	Trial of the affair of 15 May.
16 April	Decision on the Rome expedition, sent to effect mediation. Lesseps' mission.
30 April	Oudinot's first attack against republican Rome.
7 May	The Constituent Assembly protests against the attack.
13 May	Election of the Legislative Assembly.
16 May	The tax on alcohol abolished once again (in the last sitting of the Constituent Assembly).
28 May	The Legislative Assembly meets. Dupin is elected as its president.
1 June	Lesseps' mission to Rome recalled.
3 June	Oudinot's second attack against Rome.
11 June	The Assembly rejects Ledru-Rollin's demand for a vote of no confidence in the ministers.
13 June	Demonstration on the boulevards by representatives of the left.
15 June	Street fighting in Lyons. The first and sixth military regions declared to be in a state of siege.
19 June	New law on the clubs.
30 June–3 July	Rome is taken.
27 July	New law on the press.
18 August	President's letter to Edgar Ney.
7 September	Publication of the letter.
October	High court trial of the affair of 13 June. Difficulties between the president and the ministers.
31 October	President's message to the Assembly. The Hautpoul ministry.
20 December	The tax on alcohol reimposed once again.

1850

11 January	Vote on the Parieu law on primary school teaching.
10 March	By-elections for the Legislative Assembly.
15 March	Vote on the Falloux law.
28 April	By-elections for the Legislative Assembly in Paris.
May	Commission for the revision of electoral law. Democratic petitions throughout the country.
31 May	Law restricting universal suffrage.
8 June	New law on the press.
16 July	Prorogation of the law on the clubs.
July	The president's tour of the provinces of the north-east and east.

August	The general councils in session. Hopes for revision of the Constitution are expressed.
26 August	Death of Louis-Philippe. The problem of dynastic fusion is posed.
September	The president's tour of Normandy.
20 September	Circular by the comte de Chambord (failure for fusion).
10 October	Review of troops at Sabory. Neumayer dismissed.
24 October	Gent arrested. 'The south-eastern plot'.
2 November	Changarnier's order of the day.

1851

3 January	Changarnier dismissed. Ministerial crisis.
24 January	New ministry known as 'the little ministry'.
February	The Assembly rejects the president's claim for entertainment expenses, amnesty for the republicans, Creton proposal (on the exile of the princes).
Spring	Unofficial popular petitions in favour of revision. Republican counter-petitions against the law of 31 May. Saint-Arnaud's expedition to Kabylia.
10 April	Ministerial reshuffle.
28 May	Beginning of the legal period of time for discussing revision.
19 July	The Assembly rejects constitutional revision.
4 October	The president declares himself in favour of abrogating the law of 31 May.
27 October	Ministerial crisis (Léon Faucher resigns).
4 November	President's message to the Assembly, proposing the abolition of the law of 31 May. The Assembly temporises.
Beginning of November	Saint-Arnaud's circular on passive resistance.
6 November	The *Proposition des questeurs*.
13 November	The Assembly rejects the presidential proposal to abrogate the law of 31 May.
17 November	The Assembly rejects the *Proposition des questeurs*.
2 December	*Coup d'Etat*.
3 December	Attempt at resistance on the part of the Assembly. Beginning of popular resistance in Paris.
4 December	Resistance in Paris is crushed. Resistance begins in the provinces.
5–10 December	The development and failure of resistance in the provinces.
December	Expulsion of representatives. Arrests.
21 December	Plebiscite.

1852

5 January	The State cedes the Paris–Lyons line.
14 January	Promulgation of the Constitution.
January	More decrees expelling representatives hostile to the *coup d'Etat*.

23 January	Nationalisation of the property of the Orléans family.
2 February	Decree on the elections.
3 February	Decree setting up the mixed commissions.
17 February	Decree on the press.
19 February	Prolongation of the concession of the *Compagnie de chemins de fer du Nord*.
29 February	Elections for the Legislative Body.
26 March	Decree on mutual aid societies.
28 March	Suppression of the state of siege.
29 March	First meeting of the Legislative Body.
June	The fusion of the Lyons–Marseilles railways.
September	Foundation of the *Crédit mobilier*.
September–October	The prince-president's tour of central France and the south (26 September: Marseilles; 9 October: Bordeaux).
7 November	*Senatus-consultum* revising the Constitution.
21 November	Second plebiscite.
2 December	Beginning of the Second Empire.

1

Why the Republic?

The year 1848 in French history stands for a new kind of change in the political regime: that is its salient characteristic. The Republic took the place of the Monarchy, or of a monarchy. An anonymous power, more or less collective or at any rate in the main depersonalised and securalised, now replaced the rule of a single man, a sovereign designated and set above his peers by sole virtue of his birth.

But what did this form of power mean? Was it an expedient to ensure the functioning of the State in the temporary absence of a monarch; was it, in short, a kind of regency? Or was it a system chosen for itself and credited with positive merits of its own? The first concept, that of a temporary republic in the expectation of a restoration of the monarchy, is not one that is foreign to French history. To anticipate a little: we find just such a republic in existence from February 1871 to January 1879. And there can be no doubt that even as early as 1848 a very large number of French politicians would only accept the idea of the Republic seen in that particular light. However, these passive republicans – republicans merely through force of circumstance – known as 'latter-day republicans' (*républicains du lendemain*), that is, 'in the aftermath of the Revolution', were initially not the strongest. On 25 February 1848, the Republic was proclaimed in Paris by republicans 'of long-standing' (*de la veille*), committed and convinced men who desired it for its own sake.

A historical and political struggle

What were their aspirations? One cannot attach much importance to foreign influences, schoolboy memories of the free cities of Athens and Rome or knowledge of the United States of America.

To be sure, the former still featured large in bourgeois education and the latter too was accessible to the educated public. But Demosthenes, Brutus and Washington provided models of personal behaviour rather than constitutional or political examples. Such examples were now mainly national ones. In 1848 thinking about the Republic meant thinking about

1

the French Revolution. As Henri Guillemin[1] put it a few years ago, 1848 was to be, as it were, 'the first resurrection of the Republic' (*la première résurrection de la République*).

The image and memory of the Revolution

What we must discover is what the idea of the first French Republic meant to the young men of 1848 and how they came to love it. It is no simple matter: the spirit of the Age of Enlightenment, political liberty and civil equality, together with modernised institutions and a generalised national pride were all points already gained in 1789 and which could be reconciled to a monarchical regime. Such a regime had existed from 1789 to 1792, from 1804 to 1814 and, again, since 1830, under the symbol of the tricolour flag and the titular leadership of a king (or emperor) 'of the French'. It was possible to be a genuine *philosophe*, a liberal and a patriot, without pressing for more. So to identify, as a republican, with the period 1792–1804 was to want something else. Let us leave aside the years of the Consulate (1800–4), when the Imperial monarchy was already in gestation; and also the Directorial Republic (1795–1800), which was patently a political and social failure. We are left with the key period from 10 August, the period of the Commune and the Convention. Now, it is easy to argue that, without the excess of revolutionary energy deployed during that period, even the gains made by the reasonable wing of the revolution would have been threatened and that '93 was necessary to complete and salvage '89. But although this is nowadays the common view, it was not the one immediately recognised at the time. For many years it continued to be masked by another, more striking, historical fact, namely that the Republic, from 1792 to the Year II, had forced democracy to the point of popular dictatorship and propelled radicalism into the Terror. Being a republican meant being a supporter of the guillotine, of going to the limit of the oppression of individuals and property by the police; it meant, in short, being 'a man of blood'.

Around 1815, this was the grossly simplistic and strongly repellent image of the Republic in the minds of the vast majority of French people. At this date, those who were capable, primarily by example, of testifying to the positive values of the Jacobin revolution (those, at least, who were neither dead nor won over to the opportunism of the constitutional monarchies nor immersed in a somewhat shamefaced scepticism which induced them to condemn their own pasts quite spontaneously) – such men now numbered no more than a handful; and the republican party consisted, essentially, of them and their scattered and un-coordinated families: that is, of old men and their descendants. Before the Republic could attempt a reappearance in 1830 and do so successfully in 1848, it was necessary for this amorphous group to win over new members and acquire a measure of coordination. The obscure progress made by the republican idea in the course of the successive reigns of the Restoration and of Orleanism must be counted as the first of the political causes of the 1848 Revolution.

We do not know enough about the later lives and influence of those who had fought for the First Republic. In comparison with the vast body of literature inspired by the Napoleonic legend, the bibliography of the republican legend is very meagre. Everyone remembers the veteran soldier created by Balzac in his *Médecin de campagne*, but Victor Hugo's former member of the Convention in *Les Misérables* (the 'bishop visited by a hitherto unexperienced enlightenment') enjoys no such fame. It is true that Victor Hugo invests his characters with such symbolic significance and distorts their images so boldly that they can hardly be considered as representative social types. All the same, there *were* erstwhile Jacobins who resumed their roles as notaries, artisans or men of private means in their own little towns, just as there were classic veteran soldiers on half-pay from the Imperial army, and they too must have told their tales of an evening, dispensed advice to their neighbours and (after 1831) taken part in municipal politics. Quite apart from their own personal influence and that of their families, we must also bear in mind the impact they may have had within associations such as masonic lodges, secret societies or even plain *cercles*.* The former partisans of the Republic who rubbed shoulders there with other free-thinkers, other supporters of political liberty and other patriots may well have won over to their own ideal more than a few disenchanted Orleanists or even Bonapartists.

The role of historians and of history

However, the overall impact of these individual memories would not have been sufficiently strong had not literature evoked a collective memory. If the Republic was better known during the forties and able to win supporters from beyond the restricted circle of republican survivors and their immediate intimates, this was the achievement of History. The History of the Revolution had come into being many years earlier, under the Restoration, during the period when those who rallied to the white flag were in power. It was against them that liberals such as Thiers and Mignet were obliged to defend the great choice made in 1789; namely the adoption of the tricolour flag and the values of modern and rational policies. In this defence of the Revolution as a whole, constitutional monarchy was exalted and the republican parenthesis excused as the fruit of an inevitable sequence of events, chief of which was the war that had

*The equivalent of the English club, in the most general sense of the term. (In France, 'club' has two specific accepted meanings: (1) a political association at the time of the French revolution; (2) more recently, a sports association.

been foisted upon France by outside powers. But once the course of reconstituting and meditating upon the recent national past was embarked upon, there was no checking it and it led inevitably to deeper, more emotional and less politically circumspect historical studies. Thus, within less than two years (1847–8) four separate books appeared almost simultaneously: Michelet's *Histoire de la Révolution*, Lamartine's *Histoire des Girondins*, Louis Blanc's *Histoire de la Révolution* and Alphonse Esquiros' *Histoire des montagnards*. Although Louis Blanc generally associated praise of Robespierrism with socialist convictions, the others were less exclusive; which is what made them new and important. For in Michelet or in Lamartine we do not find the Republic identified only – or even essentially – with those few months of the tense, dark and sometimes cruel dictatorship of the spring and summer of the Year II. For them, it had at first in 1792 been the party of those men who picked up the torch of 1789 just when the king and most of the constitutionalists were setting it down. In short, the Republic was not a shameful and short-lived parenthesis, but rather, a new revolution, the revolution of 1792, as exalting and noble as that of 1789. And this is what was said by the most renowned poet of the age, Lamartine of the Académie française, as well as by France's most eminent scholar, Michelet, professor at the Collège de France. There was no need for the republican party's writers to declare their explicit support for it. Whether they liked it or not, they were regarded as its moral guarantors.

In every domain, furthermore, History, as mobilised by the July revolution against the out-moded or retrograde spirit of the monarchy of the Restoration, was now opposed to its own former conservatism. In the first years of his reign, Louis-Philippe had erected a column in the place de la Bastille in commemoration of the July struggles; it was a way of paying homage to popular struggles: those of 1830 which were referred to explicitly and those of 1789 which were implied by the choice of the column's location. The tradition of taking up arms was thus officially commemorated right in the centre of working-class Paris. Furthermore, on the other side of the capital, at the top of the Champs-Elysées, the hub of the newly developed part of the city, the regime had at the same date completed the decoration of the Arc de Triomphe at the Etoile. Here Rude had sculpted the *Departure of the volunteers* in glorification of the national fervour of 1792. For obvious reasons there is nothing at all to commemorate the constitutional monarchy in this famous sculpture. In theory, the woman leading the marching column represents the spirit of war. But she could also be seen as an allegory of the Republic. It was no mere chance that the *Departure of the volunteers* was to be more commonly known as the *Marseillaise*, after the title of an anthem still, at this date, regarded as revolutionary. For the worthy Rouget de l'Isle, the 'tyranny' raising its 'bloody standard' was the tyranny of Austria and Prussia, but it was not long before the circumstances of the Revolution made it possible to interpret it equally well in terms of internal politics. Here too, the patriotic struggle had become the republican one. It was certainly extremely difficult to honour the militant Revolution without at the same time exalting the Republic. In its earliest days the July Monarchy had naïvely taken that risk and, by raising these two monuments, had committed two acts of iconographical imprudence within its capital. And, as is well known, in those days the general attitude towards monuments and symbols was far from being blasé.

Of course, the point we are demonstrating by way of these monuments is also only a symbolic one: put simply, that given what the French Revolution represented, namely the birth of modern France, the romantic dynamism of its exaltation was bound to mirror the trajectory of its rise. Just as 1792 had followed 1789, History, which had prepared the way for 1830, was now leading up to 1848 and the July regime was to perish at the hand of History, despite having initially been presented as the historians' own creation and a golden age. So it was that, on the eve of 1848, the Republic, unknown or derided though it had been thirty years earlier, could boast an honourable past, its own partisans and an audience which it could reach through the press, through public opinion and from its own public rostrum; in short, it had won credibility.

The decline of the dynasties

It goes without saying that its chances were increasing along with the discredit that attached to the alternative solutions. France had no less than three dynasties from which to choose. But the first, that of the senior branch of the Bourbons, had become too closely identified with the counter-revolution, the negation of liberalism and the pre-eminence of the Church for it to enjoy the support of the country's most vital forces. It was, furthermore, represented by a prince – the comte de Chambord – who, although in his early youth (he was born in 1820), had left France while still a child and been brought up in a foreign court in an archaic atmosphere. The chances of the second dynasty, that of the Bonapartes, were greater, since the Empire stemmed from the tricolour flag and had extended the life of the Republic. It could thus lay claim to some measure of glory and to the patriotic tradition. Nevertheless, true lovers of liberty could not but feel some misgivings where a Napoleon was concerned. Moreover, here again, the dynasty was not well served by its representative, Prince Louis (born in 1808), a man now in the prime of life but about whom little was known apart from a couple of military scuffles, one or two non-conformist pamphlets, his inglorious escape and impecunious life in London. Far from considering him, the survivors and successors of the

great military and civil groups representing imperial power had long been
in the service of Louis-Philippe. As for the third dynasty, that selfsame
house of Orléans, its disadvantages were obvious: the advanced years of
the king and the decline of his political aptitude; an heir who was still no
more than a child, with the consequent prospect of a regency under a
prince neither well known nor popular; the usury and attendant corrup-
tion connected with its power; the politics of Guizot, who in the 1846
elections had chosen to draw his strength from the right by wooing a
handful of legitimists, rather than from the left by making concessions to
the party of reform. In its evolution, the regime was thus turning its back
upon its quasi-revolutionary origins and becoming purely conservative.
But this was a pragmatic conservatism devoid even of the dignity of any
theory, since the philosophy of order was monopolised by legitimism and
the Church. We must thus conclude from our political analysis that, as a
possible solution, the Republic was in a strong position because it could
appeal to an audience of its own; and because the prestige of its rivals was
on the wane.

A society in crisis

However, these political considerations do not exhaust the field of possible
causes. The 1848 Revolution in France remains very much more than a
mere successful repetition of the revolution of 1830. The hopes vested in it
were not simply liberal and patriotic, but social too. The aim was to
correct the workings not just of the political machine but of human society
as a whole.

The problem of the workers

The problem of the working classes came to the fore during the
1840s. It is difficult to give a precise date to the beginnings of such
objective processes as the introduction of machinery in French industry,
the concentration of the working force in large workshops, the lengthening
of the working day and all the new forms of 'pauperism' that resulted from
these factors; nor is it easy to trace the first instances of strikes or pre-
syndicalist organisations. On the other hand there is no problem in
establishing when public opinion became aware of these various factors: it
was between 1830 and 1840. They were first drawn to its attention
through the efforts of men of the opposition. Republicans such as Doctor
Guépin or legitimists such as Villeneuve-Bargemon were naturally
inclined to pity by their respective philosophical doctrines – humanitarian
in the one case, Christian in the other. Furthermore, standing as they did
in opposition to the regime, they were naturally inclined to ascribe all
known ills to it, all the more so since they were concerned with the ills of

the working class, while the existing regime claimed to represent the 'middle class'; industry and business. However, it was not at all the case that the only denunciators of social evils came from the opposition. Neither Villermé nor Adolphe Blanqui belonged to it; indeed, they had been encouraged to make a study of pauperism by that very Academy of Moral and Political Sciences that the July Monarchy had hoped to turn into a centre of advanced studies, a veritable laboratory for reflection and advice. We have suggested that history rebounded against the regime of the historians. It could equally be said that the social economy rebounded against the regime of the economists. It is customary to represent Louis-Philippe in the late 1840s as having been the victim of the impetus that his reign had given to national history and to patriotism during the early 1830s. In a similar fashion we now find him to be the victim of another of his initial impulses: the boost that he gave to studies of all kinds, as well as to a positivist administration which observed and made records of everything, from the figures relating to land assessments to those relating to foundlings, or to the number of needy receiving public assistance – in short, to Statistics. One fact emerges quite clearly: around 1830–1, at the time of the first 'Saint-Simonian' missions, the time when Charles Fourier* was growing old in lonely isolation and the young Auguste Blanqui† was just beginning to move away from the Jacobinism of the *quartier latin*, the socialist idea was already accepted by a small minority of eccentrics. Ten years later both the press and literature in general were full of the social question. Five years after that, a general strike mounted by the carpenters of Paris was regarded as a major event, and the opposition's greatest orator, Berryer, once a champion of the duchesse de Berry, defended a number of obscure comrades charged before the courts with unlawfully forming *coalitions*.

The problem of the peasants

The proletariat was certainly too much of a minority and the workers' movement too embryonic to pose a real threat to the established institutions. But the social question was not confined to the *faubourgs* of industrial towns; it existed in the countryside too. At the end of the century a remark made by Jules Ferry, a striking historical aphorism, was much quoted: 'the first Republic gave us the land; the second, suffrage; the third, knowledge'.

*(1772–1837). After Saint-Simon, the foremost French theoretician of utopian socialism. A particular feature of his theories was the idea that all the passions are good and must be put to good use by harmonising them in such a way that they all contribute to the common weal within an ideal social whole, known as a *phalanstère*.
†(1805–81). One of the most tenacious republican and 'communist' secret society militants, the prototype of the activist alternately fighting as an insurgent and imprisoned for his activities.

But the impression – an incomplete one anyway – that the France of 1900 may have given of a democracy of land-owning peasants was in part a result of the effects of the Revolution (i.e. the total expropriation of the clergy and the partial expropriation of the émigrés) and also, in part, of a whole series of processes that had evolved over the nineteenth century: many of the existing large properties were eroded and the poorest of the peasants left the land. Now, these two decisive evolutions had hardly begun in 1848: there were still many large domains, whether they belonged to former noble families or to new owners, and there were still many proletarians in the villages. Indeed, there had perhaps never been so many, for the beginnings of the migration towards the large industrial centres did not offset the demographic increase which was the continuing result of the surge in the birth rate in the eighteenth century. There is no doubt that the rural departments of France that are most deserted today were then more highly populated than ever before or since.

Nor had the Revolution eliminated all or even the most archaic of conflicts between rich and poor, landowners and those who worked the land, 'masters' and day labourers. It may have abolished 'feudalism' but it had not yet had time to elaborate a rural code. Thus the problem of common grazing was still unsolved; the mode of exploitation of communal property was an apple of discord; and lastly, perhaps most importantly, the eminently secular problem of users' rights in the hitherto feudal forests of rural communes continued to give rise to all kinds of conflicts: lawsuits here, a rash of thefts of firewood there, elsewhere bullets whistling past the ears of the forestry guard. There is even reason to wonder whether, in some regions at least, such bitter altercations did not reach their peak during this period. In order to survive, the poor peasants still as much as ever needed the resources offered them by the woods or 'communal or waste lands': for pasturage, for gathering various types of produce, for the free use of dead wood or for wood for making tools and the like. Now, the exercise of such rights was becoming even more unacceptable to the large landowners, who were increasingly attracted by ideas of rational agronomy and profit, especially at this time when – before the establishment of any easy and general distribution of coal by means of the railway – anything that could be burnt that could be found locally had a ready market. It was not without good reason that Balzac, in *Les Paysans*, located the class struggle in its pure state in the forests.

The poor peasants coveted State- or communally-owned forests as much as the private ones. Now here, the Revolution, albeit involuntarily, had justified their ancestors by in effect suppressing any form of repression. A new forestry code voted in at the end of the Restoration had re-established a rigorous rural police, and the July regime had been at pains to ensure it was respected. This was one more aspect to the peasant question in 1848: while rural pauperism and archaism had diminished scarcely at all, there were many causes for complaint and they were all the more exasperating given that they were directed against those who loomed large in the lives of the peasants: the big landowner, the guard and the tax-collector.

To this list we should add the moneylender, for capitalism, which was still in its early stages and had not yet established any satisfactory network of credit for urban industry and commerce, was – understandably – even more unknown in the rural areas. A man would borrow from his better-off neighbour or from the wholesaler who bought up his harvests, or else he would fall into debt with a mortgage.

But unlike the ills of the urban proletariat which – it should be repeated – were well known or even almost fashionable, rural unrest, which was more diffuse, less immediately felt and above all infinitely diversified, was only to make itself generally known through its consequences. In *Le Peuple* (written in 1845–6), Michelet expresses his feeling of running against the general tide of opinion when he claims – in explicit disagreement with the socialists – that it is not so much the worker but the peasant who is the social pariah.

Romanticism and the education of the people

However, the point was that the general attitude towards 'the People', whether workers or peasants, was favourable; and in this climate of opinion the pessimism of a writer such as Balzac struck a discordant note. Within the thinking world the prevailing atmosphere was humanitarian. Indeed, this humanitarianism also represented an aspect to the origins of the Revolution.

Romanticism and populism

Romanticism was everywhere. It is fair to say that by the 1840s the great poets – Hugo, Lamartine, Vigny, Musset – whether still active or not, had shot their bolts or were changing their attitudes and that even the fashionable Parisian world was turning against the author of *Les Burgraves*.* Who, at this juncture, could have predicted that within a few years Vicomte Hugo, member of the upper house, would be discovering a new popular source of inspiration and a new poetical point of departure? But this was the moment when – with the inevitable historical delay – the Romantics' triumph was penetrating deep into the rest of France. Among the provincial intelligentsia where amateur poets proliferated, the genera-tion of Béranger's emulators, the *chansonniers* (songwriters) of the *caveaux*

*Romantic drama with a medieval subject by Victor Hugo. It was a total flop in 1843.

(drinking cellars) – sybarites and admirers of Voltaire – had been super-
seded by a generation of serious young men who poured out their feelings
in Lamartinian tirades in Alexandrine metre. There were even a few
young workers among these poets – craftsmen rather than factory workers, admittedly – who seemed to have discovered their vocation through
the stirrings of an interest in the social question. But in reality, the
working-class poetry of the 1840s stemmed more probably from the
upsurge of sociability, the more widespread reading of newspapers in the
cafés and even from the first effects of Guizot's law on primary education.
It was, in short, a result of this confused ascent towards culture on the
part of the masses which represented the major achievement of the age
and perhaps, to some extent, of the regime too. At all events, in Paris, the
Romantic and socialist writers grouped around Michelet, George Sand
and Pierre Leroux were greatly moved by the proletarian muse, hailing it
as a sign of the people's accession to adulthood.

Besides, there was every reason why the intellectual elite should present
the people as a reservoir of new and healthy energy. In their stand against
the courts and aristocracies of cosmopolitan culture, the inspirers and
leaders of national movements in central and eastern Europe were
readopting themes originally launched at the end of the preceding century
by German Ro..anticism. They sang the praises of the national virtues of
folklore, of popular songs and poetry and of the masses with all their
primitive wholesomeness. France was not of course in a comparable
situation: the problem of nationalism there was considered settled once
and for all. But those peoples and nationalities engaged in protest, from
Greece to Ireland, from Poland to Italy, were dear to the hearts of French
liberals and republicans and so, naturally, the vaguely populist ideology
that underlay the European struggles did not fail to leave its mark upon
their friends in France.

The discovery of France

Furthermore, whether or not direct political or national conclu-
sions should be drawn, folklore had now been discovered in France as
well, and a taste for it was developing. It would seem that folklore in itself
reached a kind of peak of popularity during the first half of the nineteenth
century; but above all there can be no doubt that it was during this period
that the cultivated classes discovered it, along with their own country.
Between 1830 and 1840, long journeys through the French provinces
ceased to be a rarity, an exceptional kind of expedition, and instead
became a form of cultivated leisure. It was a far cry from modern tourism,
needless to say, but it nevertheless represented an early stage in the
evolution of the latter. This discovery of the land of France by the cream of
the intellectual elite was passionately undertaken and of passionate inter-

est to those who undertook it; and it was in the main a felicitous discovery. It was an accompaniment to Romanticism, fuelling – and fuelled by – the latter and doubtless instrumental in steering it towards a diffuse populism. In 1820 there were many bourgeois who still saw France as a minority of enlightened elite circles composed of educated groups of bourgeois, together with the wholesale businessmen of the large towns within a framework constituted by country squires and the clergy, all in great danger of being submerged by the France of the masses. A quarter of a century later, this simplistic black-and-white view which was used to justify – among other things – electoral laws of an extraordinarily oligarchical nature, was no longer considered acceptable. The richness and diversity of the nation were by then a thousand times better known and so it was possible to envisage its future with more confidence.

It thus seems that there were a number of great political and intellectual currents leading up to the Republic of 1848: the progress made by the republican idea, the desire for social improvements, in short the opening up of people's minds and the tolerance and generosity of spirit which were Romanticism's own particular contributions to collective life.

Uncertainty and confusions

But we must not be misled by these analyses that rest upon hindsight. We can find causes because we know what happened. We must, above all, take care not to attribute to all those who encouraged these currents of thought a clear awareness of their implications, let alone of the outcome to which they were leading.

Not all the Romantic writers inclined to populism or even to political criticism. Not all republicans were convinced of the need for social change. As his book *Le Peuple* shows, Michelet was a friend of the people, a Romantic, virtually a republican, despite his explicit anti-socialism. In contrast Proudhon, for example, was socialist but not particularly concerned with the question of the political regime, and averse to most of the emotional trends of Romanticism. At a less elevated intellectual level, one might cite a similar antithesis: the non-socialist republicanism of a Cavaignac and the non-republican socialism[2] of one such as Louis-Napoleon Bonaparte.

Plenty of trends (republicanism, socialism, Romanticism) which nowadays from a distance, and with our bird's-eye perspective, seem logically and obviously convergent, are in reality only seen to be complementary after the event. On the eve of the establishment of the Republic, towards the end of 1847, what ideas can have been common to all those who were about to welcome the Revolution? The knowledge that Guizot's resolute conservatism was unsuited to the prodigious complexity of the

economic, social and political situation; and no doubt also the notion that
the remedy should be sought in a widening of the bases of power.

At other periods, a government and a chamber deemed incapable and
corrupt would provoke the temptation of an 18 Brumaire.* But in the
effervescent atmosphere of the winter of 1847–8, nobody appears to have
envisaged an authoritarian solution. Authoritarianism was already associated with the men who were in power; and the consensus of opinion that
was forming against them in the country was in favour of resuming and
strengthening the liberal movement to which the July Monarchy had
owed its origin eighteen years earlier.

Widespread support for the idea of democracy, however

It was well known that universal suffrage was to be introduced as
soon as the Republic was proclaimed and that it was this that would give
it its essential political character. Universal suffrage was the logical end of
all the trends mentioned above. It was the legal expression of the general
diffuse desire to give 'the People' its voice, to acknowledge its dignity and
maturity. It was the normal outcome of the republican principle that
considered not just the well-to-do and powerful owner of property to be a
citizen, but each and every man. And why should not universal suffrage at
long last prove to be the social panacea? The people were suffering from
an egoistical and unjust society protected by uniformly bourgeois legislation. How could it be otherwise, given that only the bourgeois could vote?
But if the great majority of workers and peasants now acquired the right
to vote, it would follow logically that genuine representatives of the people
would take their places in the chambers of government; the voice of work
would be heard alongside that of wealth, and it would at last be possible to
establish harmony between these opposing interests.

The fact that in historical praxis this line of reasoning was disproved
within a few weeks, as we shall see, should not allow us to forget that it
was more or less upon just such a line that the great threefold aspirations
(social, political and moral) of 1848 rested.

Let us return for a moment to the purely political demands that were
made with increasing force throughout the reign of Louis-Philippe. The
reign had opened with a revision of the Charter, the decisive ruling being
to lower the qualification to vote in national elections to 200 f. But, in
strictly logical and moral terms, what was the point of this barrier of 200 f
and why should there be any more justification for it than for barriers of
1000 or 300 f or for more ancient ones such as the '*marc d'argent*'† or the

*On 18 Brumaire, Year VIII (9 November 1799), General Napoleon Bonaparte seized
power with the help of the army, abolished the Republican Constitution and did away with
the parliamentary deputies.
† The sum of money it was necessary to be able to pay to have the right to be elected deputy
according to the 1791 Constitution.

'three working days'? Its value was no more than that of a trial-and-error standard and, as everybody knows, those kinds of standards, always open to the accusation of opportunism, are by their very nature less attractive than the principles of rigorous extremism. The principle of authority or, in contrast, that of universal suffrage, or similarly tradition or democracy, can be played off against one another more brilliantly and overcome resistance infinitely more easily than the prudent and practical compromise policy of suffrage by census qualification. The prosaic aspect of the middle way is the classic intellectual handicap of all moderate liberalism, the more so when the latter sets up its old pragmatic compromises as dogma and refuses to evolve. Time and again during the reign, this was made quite clear: this regime of professors and academicians ended up with most of the young intelligentsia in opposition to it.

But we must be careful not to reduce the country's growing aspirations towards democracy to these considerations which are, after all, of a fairly unexceptional nature. The 1830 Revolution had not only abolished article 14,* reduced the census qualification for the national legislature and suppressed the hereditary peerage; it had also, in 1831, passed two laws of fundamental importance. The one resurrected the National Guard; the other instituted elections to determine the composition of municipal councils. Now, in both these cases, political participation reached down the social scale well below the census rating of 200 f. The whole of the *petite bourgeoisie* and the most comfortably-off of the popular classes, all of whom were excluded from the election of deputies, became initiated into political life, since they could now elect their local administrators and also the officers of the 'citizen militia'. Of course, the level of such politics was lower, but it was enough to wrench them from their state of ignorance and passivity. Now these gains were irreversible. It is true that, from 1834 onwards, the regime had been successful in almost totally stifling the intense life of the associations and the press that had been generated by the liberal explosion of 1830. However, this spectacular 'reaction' should not make us forget those institutional achievements of 1831 that were maintained and the general effect of progressive democratisation that they were eventually to have in the life of the nation.

In short, in this domain, as in so many others already mentioned – patriotism and administrative work, the introduction of public primary schooling, the advances made in communications and the first spurts of industrial growth – the regime born in 1830 had instigated or accelerated a veritable maturation (one might almost say acculturation) at the deeper

---

*Article in the Charter of 1814 which gave the king the right to govern by issuing decrees if the 'safety of the State' – a vague notion – required it. It was on the strength of this article that on 26 July 1830, Charles X issued the Four Decrees (*Les Quatre Ordonnances*) which provoked the uprising of the July Revolution.

levels of French society; and this development was now rebounding against that regime or at least against what it had become under Guizot. The desire for reform in 1847 corresponded in a wider, stronger, more popularised form to the aspiration to resuscitate and prolong the 'movement' initiated in 1830 and abruptly arrested from 1832 onwards. In a similar fashion, the spirit of 1848 was a desire to resurrect the spirit of the 1789, 1792 and 1830 revolutions, with the realisation that the full human potential of those revolutions had not yet fully emerged.

A 'republican party'

The end result of all these developments was the creation of a 'republican party'.

'A republican party' – the expression has become a hallowed one, particularly since the appearance, half a century ago, of Georges Weill's classic *Histoire du parti républicain en France (1814–1870)*.[3] But let us not be misled! It is only a history of the Republic's partisans and those partisans were a far cry from constituting a 'party' in the sense that the word has acquired in our own day and age. There was no stable, common organisation to group together those who shared the same political ideal. That may have been because the idea of concerted and disciplined action was judged incompatible with a political concept that set a high value upon the responsibility and conscience of the individual; or it may quite simply have been that the legal obstacles were considered too great, for the freedom of association did not yet exist. So any concerted action that did take place was occasional, informal and partial only.

There were three possible centres of attraction or of impetus: the Chamber of Deputies, the newspapers, and the associations (or what remained of them). We may attempt to evaluate them but it will not be so easy to evaluate the scope or the manner of their influence.

The deputies

In the Chamber of Deputies there were no more than half a dozen republicans; furthermore they could not style themselves as such for fear of prosecution, since any allusion to the Republic was considered subversive to the principles upon which the existing institutions rested. It was, in fact, in order to get around this difficulty that they were sometimes called 'radicals', a term borrowed from Anglo-Saxon political vocabulary, in which it referred to the most extreme version of political liberalism which – as the etymology suggests – aimed to suppress the old evils and initiate progress, starting with the very roots instead of proceeding prudently by means of pruning or grafting. Of these radicals the man most in the public eye was Alexandre-Auguste Ledru-Rollin (b. 1807), who had been elected deputy for Le Mans in 1841 after the death of Garnier-Pagès (the elder). It is not surprising to find that the most solid pocket of republican voters was to be found in the *chef-lieu* (chief town) of the Sarthe district. In the bourgeois world of the electorate qualified by the census, political positions would still frequently be determined by the conflicts of the past. Thus here, on the borders of the Breton west, confronted with the rural masses amongst whom *chouannerie** had again appeared to rear its head in the aftermath of 1830, the towns became stalwart bastions of the blue party.† The transition from advanced liberalism to the Republic had been an easy one to make once the monarch's lukewarm will to put down the white opponent had become clear. So it was that Le Mans faithfully elected all the great men selected by Liberty as her spokesmen in the Palais-Bourbon, from Benjamin Constant from Geneva to Garnier-Pagès from Marseilles and the worthy bourgeois of Paris, Ledru-Rollin. Ledru-Rollin was a lawyer, a good speaker and as generous in his feeling as he was with his fortune, which was to suffer considerably from the support he gave to the republican press. His politics were sincerely and 'radically' liberal. His economic policies were equally so, to the extent that, although he never formally adhered to the principles of socialism, he was liberal in the moral sense of the word: that is being generous and humanitarian, he at least recognised the need for the State to intervene to legislate against poverty; and this interventionism was, at the time, enough to make him clash with the sacred egoism of the orthodox bourgeois economy. In short, Ledru-Rollin's heart lay on the left and certain of his solidly held principles and an implacable and mutual hostility set him against the conservatives. And, although the fact is less well known in his case, he – like Victor Hugo – was to pay for his loyalty to the Republic with a twenty-year exile. To this day, his memory remains burdened with the sarcasms of Marx, and with the adulation of more modern radicals who are seldom worthy of their eminent ancestor. It surely deserves better than this double misfortune.

While Ledru-Rollin lent the Republic his eloquence, François Arago brought to it the prestige of a renowned scholar. Already old (he was born in 1786), he was the most illustrious of the French physicists and astronomers and occupied a chair at the Institut. He was the head of a large bourgeois family from Estagel (in the east Pyrenees), and unlike Ledru-Rollin he was deeply-rooted in his constituency. As deputy for his native town, he was a prime example (frequent among conservatives of every shade but less common among republicans) of the great provincial

*The name given, at the end of the Revolutionary period (1793–1804, approximately) to the royalist insurrections in western France, composed mostly of peasants.
†The party supporting the Revolution, the Republic (as opposed to the whites, who supported the monarchy of the *Ancien Regime*).

bourgeois who is the 'natural' electoral choice of his 'home town', deter-
mining its political opinion rather than being determined by it. However,
it should be repeated that, over and above this, François Arago enjoyed a
renown in the capital that was due solely to his scholarship.

The other deputies of the extreme left were not so well-known, although
some bore names that were already famous: Hippolyte Carnot was the son
of the great Lazare Carnot,* Louis-Antoine Garnier-Pagès was the younger brother of the old republican leader of the thirties. We should also
mention Marie, who had made his name as Counsel for the Defence in
countless prosecutions against republican newspapers and militants.
Carnot, Marie and Ledru-Rollin were all lawyers, a profession typical of
the rich, educated families of the established bourgeoisie. Only Garnier-
Pagès was in business, as a result of a division of tasks common at the time
in families whose promotion from the world of production to that of
private means and cultivated leisure was not yet totally assured. He had
continued to make money as a businessman while his elder brother was
making a name for himself at the Bar. That brother's death had made him
the undisputed head of the family and had subsequently projected him
into politics. Although he did not offer the party the voice and talent of a
lawyer (which is why his brother's seat had been allocated to Ledru-
Rollin), he nevertheless brought with him considerable financial skills,
and at that time it was still believed that national economics and those of
the private banker did not require very different kinds of training.

Although too few to play a very appreciable role in the voting of the
Chamber, this handful of men was nevertheless not isolated. They constituted a possible pole of attraction for those deputies who were moving
away from the regime. Some of these came from the dynastic opposition –
for example, André Crémieux who was a Jewish lawyer instinctively
faithful to the liberal principles of 1789 and 1830. Others – Alphonse de
Lamartine, for instance – came from the traditional right by the way of
Romanticism. Whatever the case, their chief role in the Palais-Bourbon
was to proclaim their principles, and this served to orchestrate the great
campaigns which were being organised elsewhere.

The newspapers

The fact was that, all in all, the role closest to that of the offices,
committees and headquarters of the twentieth-century political 'parties'
was played throughout the nineteenth century by the editorial offices of
the newspapers: permanent arenas of discussion and sometimes of organisation, as had been quite clear in 1830.

*(1753–1823). A revolutionary, member of the Convention and of the *Comité du Salut publique*.
A specialist on military matters and, as such, the leader most responsible for the French
victories of Year II.

However, the republican press comprised two principal newspapers and the lines that they adopted were not quite the same. *Le National* was the great veteran organ founded by Armand Carrel, with Thiers and Mignet, just before the 1830 Revolution, with the purpose of giving the movement the decisive push it needed. It had become republican under Carrel, now remained so under Armand Marrast, and could be said to be the principal opponent of the July regime. The latter, for its part, recognised its combative powers by heaping it with lawsuits – from many of which, incidentally, the newspaper emerged victorious in the courts.

Le National was a formidable publication. Skilfully edited and stimulatingly polemical and ironical, it enjoyed the kind of success that always belongs to this type of newspaper, and a large readership remained faithful to the regular ration of amusement and emotion that it provided. It was also formidable because of the very moderation of its politics: liberal republican rather than socialist, it shared enough common principles with the liberal supporters of dynastic monarchy for it to establish a tactical alliance with them. Universal suffrage was what it advocated in principle, but in the short term it was not above supporting monarchists of the left and centre-left in their campaigns for much more limited electoral reform, since, in practical terms, this was where the opposition could prove effective and where the regime stood threatened.

As for the fundamental bases of society, these were not contested by *Le National*. Far from renouncing economic and social liberalism, it was rather of the opinion that the principles of liberalism had not yet been fully applied (which, by and large, was perfectly true) and that if freedom to form coalitions and associations was eventually granted to the workers, that in itself would mark an advance against social injustice and poverty. This fell some way short of socialism.

This was precisely why many republicans had long been seeking a mouthpiece that was both more radical and more socially minded. In 1843, thanks to the efforts of Godefroy Cavaignac, they found such an organ in the shape of *La Réforme*. After Cavaignac's death in 1845, he was replaced by a rather obscure group of militants: Baune, Ribeyrolles and Flocon (the latter editor-in-chief in 1848). In contrast to *Le National, La Réforme* was truly a paper of uncompromising opposition and was much less given to forming tactical alliances with the dynastic opposition. And it was an opposition paper openly on the side of socialism, sympathetic to declarations of the right to work and to the organisation of labour, the implications of which were, in themselves, incompatible with free enterprise. It sometimes published articles by Louis Blanc.

The doctrinal rigour of *La Réforme* gave it a more theoretical, more solemn character than *Le National*, and it therefore perhaps lacked the latter's biting edge in everyday polemic.

We should however not see the distinctions between the two papers as too clear-cut. They are easier to discern from a distance than they were at the time. It was rather a matter of degree in the differences between their programmes and articles, a question of modes of expression and style and also of course of personalities, that set the two republican newspapers apart. There were not really two 'parties' within 'the party'; and deputies maintained their links with both of them at the same time.

The associations

As for the associations, these were more removed from the deputies' field of vision.

Formally, associations were still illegal, according to article 291 of the Penal Code. Immediately after the July revolution they had not only been numerous but also very much alive. After April 1834 they had once again been the object of energetic persecution and had been reduced to clandestine existence as secret societies. Following the clamp-down of 12 May 1839, they had been increasingly hounded and now only small fragments remained in existence. By the eve of 1848 the major rebels were in prison serving life sentences, in some cases broken men. One such was Auguste Blanqui who had had to be transferred from the dungeons of the Mont Saint-Michel to Tours hospital. Others had had their integrity destroyed as, for example, Aloysius Huber who had become a police protégé and informer. Others in prison included Armand Barbès and Martin Bernard, among many. A few leaders of second rank remained at liberty and these, particularly in Paris, were successful in maintaining their ties with the humble rank and file who had survived the riots. So there were certainly a few remaining revolutionary secret societies, though long inactive, since, apart from an irreproachable handful of militants such as Alexandre Martin, known as Albert (a mechanic), their leadership had been infiltrated by traitors who had become agents for the police: one such was Lucien Delahodde who later boasted of his success in neutralising the militants of Paris by preaching a policy of prudence and delay to them.

In the provinces, the associations suffered the same fate as in Paris, and were hounded by the authorities. One or two committed workers appear to have plunged into ventures which seemed to offer better and longer-term chances of success and set up professional mutual insurance companies. A few journalists occasionally attempted to launch or resuscitate local news-sheets, but they lacked funds and the police were constantly at their heels.

Nevertheless, even if the political associations appear to have been effectively contained by the repression, it sometimes happened that politics infiltrated associations not originally geared to them. We shall never know exactly how many republican bourgeois in small provincial towns

managed to remain in contact in *cercles* established under the cover of
friendship and sociability for conversation after drinking together or discussing the newspapers. There is slightly more evidence that freemasonry
also, in a few places, succeeded in providing shelter and a common
meeting-place for republicans in localities where they were numerous.
Freemasonry was not currently very flourishing, and was tolerated because
it was non-political. However, it was as always mainly liberal, a powerful
potential source of rationalist thought and shared critical attitudes. Thus
many future republican militants were freemasons and some of them – at
Beaune, Chalon-sur-Saône, Le Mans and Toulon, for instance – were the
leaders of their lodges.

All the same, there was no organisation covering a complete and
coherent network for France as a whole or capable of establishing links
between all republicans. Here again the press was the closest thing to a
modern political party, not only at the level of its editorship (as we have
already mentioned), but also at that of employees in subordinate positions.

Many of the former militants from the secret societies had instinctively
turned to the press as to the sole remaining effective force. It was thus that
Marc Caussidière, the old militant from Lyons, now found himself travelling salesman for *La Réforme* and in his tours through the provinces
(particularly in 1846), he may not only have sought out and collected
subscriptions, but also contributed towards establishing or re-establishing
liaisons of a more general kind. All in all, this role played by the press makes
one look ahead to that described by Lenin half a century later when, as yet
unable to found a party, he founded a newspaper and described his
periodical as a 'collective organiser'.

Such were the scattered elements of what could not yet be called 'the
apparatus' of the republican party.

How was influence exerted?

We have yet to determine the scope of its influence. As we have
already suggested, it was considerable within intellectual, literary and
artistic circles. One may mention as an example the *Revue indépendante* which
was produced by George Sand and Pierre Leroux. This was a periodical
that was not explicitly political, but that was none the less affected by all the
current trends in literary, moral and social discussion. It was eclectic in that
it extended a welcome to the emotional liberalism of Michelet as well as to
Louis Blanc's socialism. But over and above such divergencies, it was
profoundly committed to the opposition and to the people. There were also
many republicans in the world of the press and of publishing. One of the
great publishers of Paris, Pagnerre, was an old republican who had
acquired both a name and influence, even though he had by now turned his
back upon conspiracy.

The Republic had many supporters in the *quartier latin* among 'the younger generation in the schools'. Here, to call oneself 'republican' had exactly the same meaning as, at a later period, calling oneself 'leftist' or feeling oneself to be 'revolutionary'. It was something very confused and very diverse, but deeply felt and by now practically instinctive. One has, for example, only to think of the group of young people so different and yet so much in agreement that Flaubert describes at the beginning of his *Education sentimentale*.

Finally, the Republic was also the 'party' of the working class, but to what extent? There can be no doubt that in Paris the working population of the eastern districts of the city was politically very aware. It had fought in 1830, 1832, 1834 and 1839, to mention only the most serious riots. There can be no doubt that it was disenchanted with the monarchy. The republican press was familiar to and read by the workers of Paris. But in their minds it had already come into competition with the socialist or 'communist' press, in particular Victor Considérant's *Démocratie populaire* and Cabet's *Populaire*. Was there disagreement or agreement here? Certainly neither of these two newspapers could be described as 'monarchist'. However, they concentrated insistently upon problems of economic and social criticism to the virtual exclusion of the problem of the political regime and consequently can hardly be described as 'republican' either. Thus, while in the provinces there were still plenty of workers who had not yet reached the point of even the most elementary political consciousness or republicanism, in Paris a large proportion of the working class had already moved beyond such a point. There was just one publication, Buchez's *Atelier*, edited – we should point out – by authentic workers and marked by a number of Christian influences, which was striving to make its contribution to the Republic and to socialism and was, in this respect, close to the spirit of *La Réforme*.

Workers and republicans

Within the Parisian working class, then, there was plenty of potential but there were many divisions. Moreover, there was also much archaism. We should be on our guard against giving an over-modern impression of the class consciousness of the workers at this period and must, for instance, bear in mind their relations with the bourgeois republicans. The latter, in many cases products of the liberal professions, were well-to-do or even, quite simply, rich in comparison with the working class, for this was the period when considerably greater disparity between incomes and living standards was possible than is today. They were rich, but at the same time humanitarian and therefore naturally given to philanthropy and good works. It would be patently anachronistic to regard charity and paternalism at this time as 'right wing'. They were not hailed as the social panacea by conservative circles until later on.

Equally, it was not until later that the left, in contrast, sought to identify itself only with justice, social improvement on an institutional level and independence in respect of the organisation of the masses. In 1848 a republican did not consider himself as falling short of his principles when he engaged in good works. Doctors in particular, who found themselves closest to the worst conditions of poverty, often charged nothing for their services to the poor. And many of those doctors were republicans. In Paris, men such as Trélat and Raspail owed their popularity as much to the fact that they were 'doctors to the poor' as to their pasts as political militants during the 1830s. The fact is that the working classes were much affected by such behaviour and responded to it. Using a term very much in keeping with the age, which may reflect the influence of the life of the *compagnonniques*,* they felt no compunction in adulating the bourgeois who had become 'a father to the workers'; they were well aware that conservatives of this period, especially in Paris, were to be regarded more often as 'the police' than as 'fathers'. Even the important bourgeois republicans in the Chamber of Deputies sometimes benefited from this devotion if they but vouchsafed a word of pity for the people, or indicated some support for the idea of social legislation. Thus Arago on one occasion received a delegation of workers who had come to congratulate him; and Ledru-Rollin, whose attacks upon the regime in power were extremely vigorous, was familiarly referred to in the populous districts of Paris as '*le dru*' ('the toughie').

In the provinces the situation was much more varied. Lyons was probably just as politicised as Paris. But elsewhere you could still find populations, for the most part working class, which were dominated by the Church (in Marseilles, for instance), or else totally unaroused, while others were politically awakened, but still followed in the footsteps of the local philanthropic notables (as in Toulon). Meanwhile, scattered here and there were tiny groups of 'communists', for the most part Icarians (the disciples of Cabet).†

As for the peasant masses, the subject of politics was even less familiar to them. All the evidence suggests that their intellectual emancipation was infinitely more retarded. In a few areas the social influence of the notables, which was the accepted rule at the time, operated to the advantage of the Republic. Were there any regions where subterranean advances were made by the republican or revolutionary spirit in despite of the local notables (rather than through them)? If so, they were certainly even more exceptional, as became clear, first as liberty came to be experienced and subsequently on the evidence of the ballot-box.

*An ancient working men's association, which combined apprenticeship, mutual help, secrecy and some mystical doctrine.
†Cabet's theories were detailed in a book entitled *Voyage en Icarie*, Icarie being the name of the ideal city.

2

The trial and failure of a kind of socialism (24 February–4 May 1848)

In contemporary France every political regime sets up rules regarding its functioning, in the form of a Constitution. But as it takes considerably longer to elaborate a new constitution than it does to topple the preceding regime, it is impossible for the new regime to operate regularly, legitimately, and according to a set constitution until it has done so provisionally for a period longer or shorter as the case may be. This was the case with the constitutional monarchy from June/July 1789 to October 1791 and with the First Republic from 10 August 1792 to October 1795; and so it was to be with the Third Republic from 4 September 1870 to December 1875 and with the Fourth from August 1944 to December 1946. The Second Republic, which is our concern at present, was no exception. It acquired its duly voted and promulgated Constitution in November 1848, the essential apparatus for which was set up by the end of December, following the presidential election.

Thus the greater part of the year 1848 ran its course under the aegis of a provisional form of government in the process of setting up a constitution, and this stands in contrast to its three years of regular political life: 1849, 1850 and 1851. It is a legalistic and formal contrast that is eclipsed by the major political contrast with which it coincides (1848: a Republic without a Bonaparte; 1849–51: a Republic with a Bonaparte as its president), but we would do well not to lose sight of it altogether.

We can give greater precision to our analysis if we focus upon these months of 1848 which – as is often the case during these pre-constitutional phases that are still close to the initial Revolution – are also the most eventful.

In the aftermath of a democratic revolution it is impossible to improvise a constitution in an arbitrary fashion as one does immediately after a *coup d'état*; the people must be called upon to elect an assembly. This too takes time, so that, with the constituent and governing assembly not yet in operation, a short purely provisional interlude necessarily ensues – a period during which the only source of power is that which emerges from the Revolution itself. So it was in the First Republic between 10 August and 21 September 1792 and in the Third between 4 September 1870 and 8 February 1871.

The Second Republic, with which we are concerned, existed in this fashion from 24 February 1848 until 4 May, the day upon which the Constituent Assembly elected on 23 April met and the provisional government immediately laid down its powers.

Is that too formalistic an analysis, or to impose too artificial a break? Is not the more traditional view that of an acceleration in the popular conflict up until the June confrontation, followed by the long-drawn-out agony of democracy and popular hopes that lasted from June 1848 to December 1851? Are we not forcing these historical events into an over-revolutionary perspective?

That is by no means certain, for even the most political or politico-social considerations coincide well enough with the legal phases we have just set out. The fact is that in the aftermath of the February days there were two eminently revolutionary aspects to the situation: the provisional government, the sole organ of power, included two proponents of socialism; they were both very young and one was even a worker. These were hitherto unheard-of innovations. Furthermore, the only audience to which this government could possibly address itself was the people of Paris. It was a people aroused, up in arms, unrepresented but omnipresent beneath the walls of the Hôtel de Ville; a people occupying the place de Grève or reoccupying it in demonstrations of its sense of self-importance. This was the revolutionary situation that was to be brought to an end by the elections held in late April and early May. From that time on the Executive, in the classic manner, had at its disposal an Assembly with which to share its power, and the first concern of this Assembly was to purge the Executive of its socialist wing. When this came about the revolutionary phase of the Second Republic was well and truly over. It had lasted seventy days, which we should examine in more detail.

The change of regime

It took place in Paris.

The February days

The February days issued directly from the banquets campaign. As noted in the volume on France 1815–48 by Jardin and Tudesq (*Restoration and Reaction*), those who supported electoral and parliamentary reform (the dynastic and republican opposition, sometimes in coalition, sometimes in competition) had led the campaign, substituting for meetings (now banned by law) banquets which were attended by huge crowds and in which toasts took the place of speeches. In the climate of political exasperation and social tension produced by the failings of the Guizot administration, and by economic stagnation, this campaign had been highly successful. The last banquet, to be held in Paris, was awaited with high expectation; which was why, on 14 January 1848, Guizot decided to ban it. The organisers took up the challenge, decided that the banquet would nonetheless take place with an accompanying demonstration; and to have more time to prepare, fixed the date for 22 February. They were watchful to appearances: the demonstrators were only to be citizens 'accompanying' the diners to the banqueting hall! However, the government was not fooled and on 21 February repeated the ban. With their backs to the wall, the organising committee gave in and cancelled the banquet.

But it was too late. The workers and students, mobilising for the past few days, refused to capitulate. Spontaneously, or rather in answer to a call made by the self-appointed leaders of the movement and also, no doubt, by a few surviving leaders of secret societies, they flocked in on the appointed day from the eastern suburbs and the *quartier latin* towards the place de la Concorde. (The banquet was to have taken place in a hall in the Champs-Elysées). The size of this openly illicit demonstration and its popularity with the Parisian crowds made 22 February the first day of the Revolution even if, in the early scuffles which took place that evening, the troops gained the upper hand.

On 23 February, people were still in the streets. To restore order, the government decided to resort to the National Guard – which had put down riots in those same Parisian streets so often before. But on this 23 February the National Guardsmen could no longer assume the same role. They knew that now they would not be fighting to defend private property against 'communists', but Guizot against other citizens, just like themselves, who supported reform.[1] So they refused to fight; instead, fraternising with the crowd and shouting 'Long live reform!' and 'Guizot resign!', the citizen militia precipitated the crisis for the regime. And, in a flash, they opened the eyes of the king, Louis-Philippe, who had not realised hitherto quite how widespread was the discontent with his minister nor how unpopular he was. In the early afternoon of 23 February it was learned that the king 'had accepted' Guizot's resignation and had asked comte Molé to form a new government.

This substantial victory on the part of the campaigning reformers found expression in a joyful explosion. During the afternoon of 23 February the demonstrators crowded the streets, demanding the traditional street illuminations to celebrate their success. But that very success was to give rise to drama and reprisals. The demonstrators went off to clamour for 'illuminations' under the windows of Guizot himself, at the Ministry for Foreign Affairs, then situated in the boulevard des Capucines. The guards there believed themselves threatened; there were scuffles, fighting broke out, shots were fired. A number of demonstrators were killed. Anger had the effect of radicalising the crowd's demands. The dead were loaded on to carts which were then paraded through the streets of Paris in a spectacular call to arms ('the procession of the corpses') and those manning the new barricades that were erected during the night of 23–24 February were bent upon revolution.

During 24 February the conflict thus engaged upon was resolved by force of arms. The king no longer had a government: first Molé, then Thiers, stood down; Odilon Barrot had no time to form and install a team. Furthermore, prompted by contrary impulses, the king, while calling upon Barrot, whose name represented a considerable concession to the reformists, also appointed Marshal Bugeaud to command the troops of Paris; and *his* name spelled repression. As it turned out, Barrot's calming influence was less effective than Bugeaud's provocation. During the morning there was determined fighting in several parts of Paris (in particular at the place du Château-d'Eau, today the place de la République) and finally, towards noon, the palais de Tuileries, the king's residence, was attacked. At that point Louis-Philippe, by now totally demoralised by the idea of finishing up 'like Charles X', called off all resistance and abdicated in favour of his grandson, the comte de Paris.

The formation of the provisional government

A new reign, inaugurated under such conditions (and furthermore accompanied by a regency, for the young king was only nine years old), could not do without some kind of parliamentary investiture and this would, moreover, have been in line with the liberal principles of the duchesse d'Orléans. As regent presumptive she therefore marched bravely from the Tuileries towards the Palais-Bourbon, leading her son by the hand. By now, however, the deputies there were not alone. Following their victory at the Tuileries, a party of insurgents had invaded the meeting hall. In different circumstances the prestige of the handful of elected representatives of the opposition, such as Lamartine, might have supported the regency, but the wave of popular pressure represented by the insurgents was enough to make them incline definitively towards the Republic. The republican deputies soon became the centre of a group which set about drawing up a list for a provisional government.

However, news soon spread to the effect that another government was being formed in the Hôtel de Ville, that symbolic spot where the preceding regime had itself received its baptism in July 1830. Here, in the true heart of insurgent Paris, the government that was about to be formed stood a better chance of being more progressive than any that the parliamentary extreme left might produce. Lamartine, Ledru-Rollin and their colleagues therefore hastily left the Palais-Bourbon and went to the

Hôtel de Ville. So it was there, during the evening of 24 February, that the final list for the provisional government of the Republic was drawn up. It was the result of a compromise between the two possible tendencies in the republican party that we have already described: the non-socialist liberals who were deputies or editors of *Le National*; and the democrats, who were more or less receptive to socialist ideas and were better represented by *La Réforme*. The former group wished to limit itself to a list of deputies and former deputies (Dupont from the Eure, Arago, Lamartine, Crémieux, Ledru-Rollin, Marie and Garnier-Pagès) together with the editors-in-chief of the two large newspapers, Marrast of *Le National* and Flocon of *La Réforme*. The democrats were quite willing to be represented by Ledru-Rollin and Flocon, but they felt many misgivings about the other seven. However, as a counter-balance and to represent their own slant they added two new names highly charged with symbolism: Louis Blanc, the socialist theoretician, and Albert, the secret society leader. Thus was the list of eleven names drawn up.

But what exactly *is* a provisional government? Does it replace the king? Or his ministers? Or both at once?

The provisional government was incontestably a college invested with sovereign power; a Head of State with eleven heads. The eleven names appeared as signatories to its major decisions and, with two exceptions only, no titles were given. The exceptions were 'Arago, of the Institute' and 'Albert, worker', and they lend startling emphasis to the breadth of the unanimity that had been achieved. The provisional government was also a team of ministers, but power was unevenly distributed among its members. No decision was ever taken to choose any ministers other than the eleven, as had been done under the Directory of the First Republic, nor were the various ministerial posts divided up between the eleven, as they later were in the governments of the Third Republic.

The end result of the hybrid solution adopted on 24 February was thus to produce three categories of leaders: members of the government who were ministers, members of the government who were not ministers and ministers who were not members of the government. Those in the most favourable position were the members of the provisional government who were also ministers: Lamartine, responsible for Foreign Affairs; Crémieux, for Justice; Ledru-Rollin, for Home Affairs; Arago, for Marine Affairs and Marie for Public Works. This category could also include Garnier-Pagès, initially appointed Mayor of Paris but soon to take over the Ministry of Finance, and A. Marrast who took over from him as Mayor.

Those members of the provisional government who were not personally responsible for any ministry were in a less favoured position. Dupont (from the Eure department) was too elderly to assume any more than an honorific prominence; and Flocon, Louis Blanc and Albert were pushed aside on account of their political convictions. Here the inequality of forces established within the governing team, qualitatively as well as quantitively, was most glaringly apparent.

Lastly, there was the third category: the handful of ministers who were not members of the provisional government: Bethmont, responsible for Commerce; Carnot for Public Instruction; General Bedeau in the War Office, together with two Under-Secretaries of State appointed a little later: Colonel Charras also in the War Office and Victor Schoelcher in the department for Marine Affairs.

A number of other key posts were filled at this time. The directorship of the postal services, which opened up communications with the provinces, went to Etienne Arago, François' brother, and the *préfecture de police* was given to Marc Caussidière (or rather left with him as he had already taken over the post for himself). For moderate republican opinion the former of these two appointments was reassuring; the latter, by contrast, was rather alarming.

A Republic with a human face

On the crest of the same wave of feeling, during that evening of 24 February, in the same atmosphere of mixed enthusiasm and tension, the Hôtel de Ville was still so crammed with excited but vigilant crowds that the eleven had difficulty even in finding a room for their private discussions. Nevertheless, it was there that a number of decisions of principle were taken that were as crucial as the choice of men had been.

First, the Republic was proclaimed; or rather it was declared to be 'desired'. Did that follow automatically? Hardly. In 1792 the Republic had not been proclaimed on the evening of 10 August; the decision had been left to the representatives of the people and had only been taken on 21 September (at the first meeting of the Convention). The same procedure could have been followed now. The question of the type of regime could have been deferred until a Constituent Body was assembled. But the fact was that now such scruples would have been thought unacceptably indecisive and delaying. Too fresh in mens' minds, in Paris, was the memory of that other popular victory of 1830 when, as a result of the failure to impose the Republic, the Hôtel de Ville had witnessed the ascendancy of a new king. So now, while the smell of gunpowder still lingered in the air, the Republic would be announced without delay and ratified by the acclamations of the hundred thousand witnesses thronging the place de Grève.

This Republic would be democratic: there would be universal suffrage.

It would be generous-hearted or, more simply, human: within a few days slavery would be abolished in the colonies.

It would repudiate any system of terror or any attempt to impose such:

the death penalty for political offences was abolished. And this decision was not simply an indirect reproach levelled against the three preceding reigns which had seen the martyrdom of the four sergeants of La Rochelle* and had come close to executing Armand Barbès,† whose pardon had been won only after a long public campaign. The abolition of the political scaffold was more a repudiation of the revolutionary tribunal of 1793, Year II, whose obsessive image still obscured that of the Republic for most French people at this time. To make the new Republic acceptable, they swore that it would be '*girondin*' or, more simply, liberal. To this extent the decision reflected political calculation. But was that its chief motivation? In the last analysis did it not stem principally from a sincere humanitarianism? Was not that the source of all the victors' vague and widely shared aspirations: democracy, pity and generosity towards the humble, social justice through conciliation, fraternity realised at last?

The reception in the provinces. Political acceptability?

The news soon reached the provinces. The visual telegraph system made it possible to reach the principal towns within a few hours. On the other hand, the emissaries of the new authorities needed much longer to install themselves in the *préfectures*. Appointments had first to be made and Ledru-Rollin had no ready-made list of civil servants of the Republic to be sent out to the departments. Next, those appointed had to make the journey, usually by nothing more rapid than the steady trot of the mail coach. Emile Ollivier arrived in Marseilles on 29 February, Marion in Grenoble on 1 March, Chevallier in Bordeaux not until 7 March. So everywhere a period of hours or days elapsed between the proclamation of the new regime and the moment when its new officials took up their new posts. During this interlude power could only be exercised by the prefects and sub-prefects who were now virtually under dismissal, or by bourgeois municipal authorities elected only by those qualified by the census. That means that power was in effect hardly exercised at all. The authorities not yet replaced in some cases effaced themselves completely, in others they prudently declared themselves won over to the Republic; in most they appealed for calm, order and unity. At all events, they could hardly assume any active responsibility, let alone act repressively.

There were *some* movements, though not movements of resistance on the part of the partisans of the monarchy that had fallen. Orleanism was pragmatic rather than a true system of principles and convictions, and as

---

*Four non-commissioned officers executed at La Rochelle in 1822 for having taken part in a conspiracy against the monarchy of the Restoration.
†(1809–70). He was condemned to death for his part in the republican insurrection of 13 May 1839 against the July Monarchy.

such could hardly arouse any fanatical defenders. Those who supported it came from the most circumspect middle-class circles for whom disorder was the ultimate threat – a state of mind hardly conducive to belligerence. There were certainly some legitimists – at least, those whom Guizot had not succeeded in winning over. They were people of principle and might have put up more of a fight. But they loathed Louis-Philippe and, on the spur of the moment, their delight at his fall was greater than their apprehension at the reappearance of the Republic. The republicans were of course delighted; power had fallen into their hands. They had no need of demonstrations, save of a euphoric, ritual kind ('processions', illuminations, 'serenades') or to ensure – without resistance in the event – that the doors of the prisons where militants were confined be opened. This all took place within what could be termed the 'political classes'.

Social difficulties?

As for working people, they were much more agitated but, essentially, their agitation was connected with the economic and social struggle. In the suburbs of Paris itself two symbolic fortresses of wealth, Louis-Philippe's château at Neuilly and the Rothschild château at Suresnes, were looted. These were really as much political as social symbols and perhaps we should view these incidents as echoes or repetitions of the sacking of the Tuileries, which was more an expression of outrage and derision, rather than a calculated looting operation.

In the provinces, however, it was not a political matter at all, rather one of settling old material scores.

In Lyons, the silk weavers attacked the monasteries, because they were suffering from the competition of low-paid labour from those who had found asylum there (old people living on assistance, orphans, and the like). In Limoges, workers on strike rose up against their employers. Elsewhere new machinery, said to be a cause of unemployment, was destroyed. However, this typically working-class unrest was less widespread than the classic type of popular (or as we might call it today, archaic) action. Here, an *octroi* barrier was set alight, because that kind of municipal taxation on consumer goods was irksome from a practical point of view, and instrumental in raising the cost of living; there, an indirect taxation office was broken into and its registers for the tax upon alcohol destroyed; elsewhere, sailors or carters attempted to destroy railway workyards, seeing them as a source of competition, soon to be a cause of unemployment.

Of even greater significance were the rural movements. The hostilities aroused by the forestry code, which had already reached flash-point following July 1830 in similar circumstances, but had since been more or less contained, were once again sparked off. In Alsace, in the southern

Alps, in the Pyrenees and elsewhere, villagers went off to 'get some wood' in the State or communal forests, in some cases molesting the forestry guards and driving them away. In other regions, private forests which had been the focus of conflicts over users' rights came under attack. In villages over most of France, from Seine-et-Marne to the Var, groups of poor peasants went so far as to attack the property of wealthy individuals (not just the State and its officials). Sometimes the large rural landowner himself became a focus of hostility, especially if he had lent money: the explanation for the aggression shown towards the Jews in Alsace, for instance.

Problems of interpretation

It would assuredly be wrong to exaggerate the importance of these disturbances and imagine a France given over to fire and bloodshed. The incidents were sporadic and, in the main, minor ones. Further, there were very few incidents of aggression against individuals, although rather more against material objects, institutions and property. In the provinces, the change of regime was generally peaceful, but it was not a peace in which the people were entirely passive. On the contrary: the climate was one of excited expectancy. This should help remind us that in the short term the Republic came into being against a background of grave economic depression and, in the long term, in a France that was still an 'ancient' land: the countryside was burdened with agrarian problems as yet unresolved, and humble folk were still resisting the fiscal institutions of the age. These are problems that tend to be overshadowed by the presence, in Paris, of a working-class problem with an already modern look to it.

One may also wonder, at a deeper level, what the relation really was between these popular movements of a seemingly infra-political kind and the events of 24 February. The movements certainly followed and were sparked off by the events. In this case the social reaction came on the rebound from the political; far from the social struggles being crowned by political victory as if by their natural end, this was a political victory (the Republic of 24 February) that brought social conflict in its wake, acting both as a signal and a licence. In a similar fashion, in times closer to our own, the political victory of the Popular Front at the beginning of May 1936 provoked – rather than followed – the strikes of June.

Now we must discover what tendencies and what type of collective reasoning were at work.

It could be that the poor, resentful masses of 1848 were simply conscious of the conditions of the interregnum: the authorities were on vacation or at least very weakened, so it was a good time to settle old scores or to secure new advantages with comparatively little risk. According to this hypothesis, the first days of the Republic can be seen simply as a welcomed period of weakness on the part of the State.

But there is another possibility, one which a detailed study of the workers' movements and even of certain peasant riots supports. It is that, in some cases, the concept of the Republic contained more positive, albeit confused, ideas: namely, that a regime that was in principle good and just was on the way in; such a regime would necessarily be favourable to the humble folk and would bring certain satisfactions upon which, in the euphoria of the moment, one could anticipate a little.

Moreover, there were plenty of republican officials who, in order to calm down the disturbances, felt no hesitation in promising, in the name of the Republic, that good laws would surely soon be passed and that it was therefore best to await them calmly as befitted Frenchmen newly promoted to the dignity of full citizenship. And, true enough, calm was quickly restored almost everywhere during the first days of March.

The rallying of Algiers and its prospects

Overseas, however, Algeria might well have been a subject of concern for the new regime. A strong army was stationed there under the command of Louis-Philippe's fourth son, the duc d'Aumale, who had replaced Bugeaud as Governor-General six months earlier. But such fears were unfounded. Aumale turned out to be more military than royalist and conformed with the general loyalty of the army, satisfied that there was no threat to the tricolour flag. Thus Aumale, like his admiral brother, the prince de Joinville, made a dignified departure for England after presenting his report and handing over his office. As early as 25 February, the provisional government appointed Cavaignac as his successor: he was on the spot and, in addition to being a sincere republican, had the advantage of 'African' experience which was entirely to his comrades' taste. Another 'African', General Bedeau, was appointed War Minister. Right from the start, then, the French Republic appears to have placed its military and Algerian policies in the hands of generals, or at least its 'native policy', for the negro slaves (a few existed as servants to the wealthy families) were to be given their freedom and the *colons* (colonials) were to win universal suffrage. Towards the Arabs, however, Cavaignac and his like were not, nor would ever be, any less harsh than Bugeaud and his men. On this point it must be recognised that it was not Lamartine who set the tone for the provisional government. In parliamentary debate before 1848, the poet had denounced the atrocities of the Algerian army and had embraced a humanitarian defence of the Arabs. This explains why, early in March 1848, the most Lamartinian of the Republic commissioners, the young Emile Ollivier, appointed to the Bouches-du-Rhône and the Var, went to Toulon where Abd el-Kader was still held prisoner in a fortress, despite promises for his release. Ollivier believed that he could assure el-Kader that the new regime would be magnanimous or, more simply, that it would keep its word. He was mistaken. Abd el-Kader remained in detention until 1852 when the prince-president, having overthrown the Republic, proved himself the more just in this matter. Twelve years later the memory of this may well have had something to do with why Emile Ollivier rallied to the Empire.[2]

However, let us not anticipate. For the moment we should just mention that there were already indications, at the heart of the Republic, that the spirit of Cavaignac was liable to clash with that of Lamartine.

The provisional government in action

Let us return to Paris where we left the Hôtel de Ville on the evening of 24 February. The provisional government proceeded to continue more or less permanently in session there, working in a not particularly methodical fashion and constantly interrupted by visiting delegations coming either to declare solemn support for the Republic or to present demands and complaints. These groups could be alarming, particularly if the delegation was large enough to resemble a demonstration. The visit then became a kind of political incident. This series of delegations, becoming increasingly irregular but also better organised and bigger, came more and more to resemble the classic 'days' of revolution in the old Parisian tradition.

But what kind of a figure was cut by the government they came to confront?

Diverse tendencies in the provisional government

The provisional government was not homogeneous.

Its most progressive members were the two socialists, Louis Blanc, the theoretician, and Albert, the worker; they were also the youngest. Perhaps Flocon could also be associated with them despite his legendary silence. (For the purposes of caricature, which was quick to fasten upon the new leaders of the hour, Flocon appeared as a pipe!) As we have already mentioned, none of these held a ministerial portfolio. On the other hand, during the early days they wielded a power of a different kind: they commanded the confidence of the masses for, at the very heart of the government, Louis Blanc could be regarded as their spokesman and ambassador. It was a link which most of his colleagues must have found sometimes threatening and sometimes extremely useful, depending on the circumstances.

At the other end of the spectrum Marie, Crémieux, Arago, Garnier-Pagès and Marrast, the '*National* men' as they were called, formed a more or less homogeneous block. They were liberal republicans, decidedly opposed to socialism and resolved to make no concessions where the interests of order, property and what was at the time regarded as economic orthodoxy were concerned. They were, moreover, in a position to keep a close watch on the situation given that two of them were in charge of ministries with authority over economic matters, namely those of Finance and Public Works.

Sandwiched between these two wings of the government, the right and the left, the combination of Lamartine and Ledru-Rollin formed a centre. Not that they were particularly close, or even friendly. But they had a common desire for reconciliation, and a determination not to cut themselves off from democratic opinion or to clash with the popular masses. They also wanted if possible to prevent the class clash that they sensed to be imminent behind the appearance of republican unanimity. Ever since Karl Marx, who was one of the first to analyse this period in a book which we would today describe as 'instant' history [*The Class Struggles in France*], this centre position has been harshly judged. It has been interpreted as the inevitable outcome of *petit bourgeois* tendencies to oscillate between the great social forces that confront each other, and these conciliatory policies have sometimes been denounced as deliberately aiming to fragment the working-class struggle, blocking its progress in a particularly insidious fashion. The fact that Ledru-Rollin was subsequently publicly recognised by the radical party as its precursor, ancestor and model reinforces this interpretation, an unfavourable one in the eyes of large sectors of contemporary opinion. We should perhaps be less severe both in respect of the reformist Republic, whose contribution to the common good was not inconsiderable, and also of Lamartine and Ledru-Rollin who devoted themselves wholeheartedly to this cause, thereby eventually losing much more than they gained in terms of immediate reputation, fortune and personal satisfaction.

Lamartine, peace and the flag

In addition to the advantages they gained from being in an intermediate position in the government, Lamartine and Ledru-Rollin also benefited from the fact that they had been appointed to the two principal ministries, the Interior and Foreign Affairs. The latter post, traditionally the most prestigious of all, made Lamartine the effective leader of the government, despite the official pre-eminence of Dupont of the Eure, exactly as Guizot, Minister for Foreign Affairs, had long been the real leader of the government whose president was the aged Marshal Soult. Quite apart from the importance of his office, Lamartine enjoyed a purely personal prestige. Apart from the scholar Arago, he was the only one of all his colleagues who enjoyed a reputation not entirely owed to politics. He was a diplomat by profession, an aristocrat, a man of the world and an academician. He was the great writer, read with emotion by the educated public, and he could not have wished for a more devoted following among the then innumerable young poetry-fanciers of the provinces; not least because the facile style of Béranger was now a little dated, while the powerful originality of Hugo had not yet made its mark. Thus, sandwiched in between two such eminences, the one belonging to the beginning of the century, the other to the end, this surely was the hour – albeit a more transient one – of Lamartine. Perhaps he was also appreciated because he had made his way to the Republic from an originally distant position. Under the Restoration, up until 1830 or a little beyond, he had been a royalist. He had then been won round by the arguments for Orleanism, although he had never been deeply committed to the values of strict rationalism or to the liberal economic orthodoxy upon which it rested. Like many others with a traditionalist upbringing, Lamartine was the more inclined to take up a critical position towards the bourgeois system given that his own intellectual formation had taken place outslde it. There was in this poet a measure of what Marx had recently termed 'feudal socialism', that is to say traces of anti-capitalism which, even if archaic, had more chance than an attitude of inveterate pro-capitalism of one day being converted to humanitarian reformism. Henri Guillemin is quite correct when, in his many works on this period of French history, he implies that Lamartine was the exact antithesis to the unadulterated Orleanist bourgeois, Adolphe Thiers.

At all events Lamartine, diplomat and deputy, was an old hand at politics. It would be mistaken to pigeonhole him as, so to speak, 'a lost poet' in the corridors of power. He lacked neither experience nor skill. Like Ledru-Rollin, he was able to steer a careful course between Louis Blanc and the group centred on Marie and Arago, but also to exploit extra-governmental forces and, for example, to capitalise or attempt to capitalise (his own personal inclination) on Blanqui's hostility towards Louis Blanc. We cannot here go into the details of all these extremely complex manoeuvres, but they all tended towards the same end: to maintain the February Republic in the ambiguous form that it had assumed: no socialism pure and simple (Lamartine considered it utopian) and no conservative reaction (which he judged inhuman). And no Jacobinism either.

It fell to Lamartine, as diplomatic leader of the Republic, to define the principles of French foreign policy. This he did in the famous circular of 4 March, on the whole a pacific and reassuring document. France would win respect, and maintain vigilance with regard to the balance of influences in Italy. But it would not export the Revolution, neither was it committed to supporting all other revolts. It thus disowned a small political uprising on the Belgian border; and although the Poles of Paris were permitted to form a legion and set off with much pomp for the East, they did so peacefully, and it was with the aid of the German patriots that they crossed the Rhine. All this was somewhat removed from the policies traditionally urged by *Le National*; above all, it reflected a realistic appreciation of the kind of means open to a France still uncertain of its internal equilibrium. It can also be regarded as a second exorcism of the demons of Year II: just as France had renounced the guillotine, it also renounced wars of conquest; it would create a Republic with clean hands.

With an explicit condemnation of violence and of the bloodshed of a day of rioting, expressed in a now famous passage of eloquence,* Lamartine was also successful in rejecting the red flag which demonstrators sought to set in the place of the tricolour. Why a red flag? It was only recently and for reasons that remained obscure that this brilliant colour had become identified with the social revolution. On the other hand, the idea of changing flags when one changed regimes seemed perfectly natural at the time. It had happened in 1789, in 1814, twice in 1815 and again in 1830. So why not in 1848, since the monarchy had just been replaced by a republic? Today, there is nothing new about the idea that Lamartine was putting forward but at the time it was relatively new: it was that the tricolour was not the emblem of a regime, but of a nation in all its continuity. As for the regime that had been born in February, all that was necessary to indicate its popular intentions was to pin a red rosette to the flagstaff! Thus with Lamartine as its spokesman, the provisional government managed to channel together all the confused waves of popular opinion and keep the State on its feet.

The whole affair provides a fair example of the succession of difficult exchanges that took place at this time between those in power and the Parisian masses. To get a clearer idea of the situation we may focus upon a series of problems which we shall examine synthetically, even though this may lead us somewhat astray from a strictly chronological position.

The great economic decisions

To a great extent, the Revolution was born of the industrial and commercial crisis and this continued and was even aggravated by the events. Fearing disorders or even 'socialism', 'communism' or 'anarchy', contractors were as hesitant to reopen their building sites and workshops as their customers were to place orders. As the saying then went, 'the rich were becoming tighter with their capital'. These difficulties were merely the paroxysm of the general – or, as we would call it, structural – *malaise* of

*'the red flag was only paraded around the Champ de Mars, dragged through the blood of the people, whereas the tricolour flag has been paraded right round the world together with the glory and liberty of the Motherland'. These words became famous and have often been quoted since.

the existing economy, which was so deficient in means of payment and credit facilities. This was the area where the provisional government decided to act first. The circulation of banknotes was compulsory. The Banque de France issued banknotes in smaller units (100 f; up until then the smallest note had been 500 f). Meanwhile the setting up of discount banks in the towns of the provinces was encouraged. On the whole, these were useful measures.

But the economic crisis was also an indirect threat to the State resources. The public exchequer was in difficulties. To cope with this, the provisional government chose a solution which, although technically easy, was to prove politically dangerous: it increased all direct taxation by 45 per cent (these were the famous 'forty-five centimes', 0.45 per franc of tax imposed).

The national workshops

Lastly and most important, the economic crisis was reflected in the unemployment which – after the excitement over prices had died down – was the principal cause of poverty among the people. In Paris, tens of thousands of men were out of work. Here too it was necessary to take action. There were two possible solutions: one, familiar to all the preceding regimes, lay in 'charity workshops', the organisation of public works of secondary importance, such as road mending or the levelling and planting of waste land. This was to provide the unemployed with work and State remuneration until they could return to their normal private occupations. The other solution was to set up 'social workshops'. Louis Blanc had made the suggestion some time ago and was now pressing for its implementation: in the face of the failure of private industry, the State would encourage workers to take economic activity in hand, sector by sector, by forming production cooperatives. This was in fact the theory, set out by Blanc, which had been adopted and sometimes put into practice by workers during the strikes of 1830 and 1840. When an employer refused to grant his workers' demands, the workers sometimes agreed to do without him and form an 'association'. At all events, 'the social workshop' had the advantage of being in principle applicable to all workers (whereas the charity workshop reduced them all to navvies). But the drawback was that it represented a threat to private property. For this reason it was the charity workshops, known as 'national workshops', that predominated. Since the organisation of these workshops was in the hands of Marie, in his capacity as Minister for Public Works, the undertaking was guaranteed not to be a socialist one. Marie and his collaborator, Emile Thomas, signed up a large proportion of the unemployed and strictly contained them under group leaders recruited from the students of the Ecole Centrale.* It was thought that it would thus be possible to palliate most of the social evils of the crisis and to pin down workers who might be tempted to hang about the streets, haunt the clubs and swell the demonstrations.

The question of socialism

It was a disappointment, a failure even, for the partisans of socialism. Would the new Republic do something decisive for the working people or not? It was to insist that it should do so that, as early as 28 February, the first large demonstration took place outside the Hôtel de Ville. Its first demand was the creation of a Ministry of Work, and the meaning of this was clear: seeing that there were already two ministries with economic responsibilities (Commerce and Agriculture, and Public Works), the purpose of the new one could only be social. Its creation would mean that the State explicitly recognised social well-being or at least social protection and amelioration among its responsibilities. The idea seems beyond dispute to us today, but then it was regarded as the very principle of socialism, betokening immediate revolution.

There was a bitter dispute which ended in a compromise. There would not be any Ministry of Work but a 'Government Commission for the Workers' would be created to make a study of the problem. It would have the participation of delegates elected from various bodies of workers and would be presided over by Louis Blanc assisted by Albert, both of them high-ranking Statesmen as well as convinced specialists on the subject. For the workers it seemed both a promise and a moral victory, further emphasised by the fact that this Chamber of Work, with its worker majority, would sit in the Palais de Luxembourg, occupying the seats of the erstwhile peers of the realm. Was it just a promise, an empty honour? Karl Marx was soon to use another, now famous, image to express the idea that it indeed was: 'While they were seeking the philosopher's stone in the Luxembourg, others were minting the valid currency at the Hôtel de Ville.'

It was, in effect, up to posterity to decide whether the creation of the Luxembourg Commission was a manoeuvre to buy time or a starting-point for the longed-for progress. The die was not yet cast. And meanwhile the workers had won considerable satisfaction from a moral, practical and social point of view: a decree issued by the provisional government fixed the maximum length of the working day in factories to ten hours (in Paris) and eleven hours (in the provinces). It had not hitherto either been regulated by law or limited in practice in any way. As for the Luxembourg,

*L'Ecole Centrale des Arts et Manufactures in Paris was, after the Ecole Polytechnique, the principal school for students of engineering at the time.

it immediately set to work, settling a number of social conflicts through arbitration and making a serious examination of various possible socialist systems. So in certain respects it resembled a club, or even a super club, that enjoyed official authorisation.

The great political decisions. Liberty and equality

These disagreements between liberal and socialist republicans (or, to put it another way, between men of *Le National* and men of *La Réforme*) over the flag, the national workshops and the 'organisation of work' should not obscure the deeply unanimous welcome that was extended to the re-found liberty.

On a political level the very first action of the provisional government had been a liberation. The historian Georges Weill writes that, on the evening of 25 February, 'the director of the prison [of Doullens] came, in a state of deep emotion, to speak with Martin Bernard; through the wall a prisoner asked the purpose of the visit and his next-door neighbour replied: "The one and indivisible [republic] has arrived ..."'[3]

As soon as they were set at liberty, the militants poured into Paris. They came from the dungeons of Doullens, the *hôpital* of Tours and the fortresses of Belle-Ile. At the same time, conversely, scores of young men, students or former students, who had fled from the stifling atmosphere of the provinces to lead a doubtless poorer but less constricted life in Paris, saw this as the moment to return to emancipate their home towns, and rushed to do so. The highways of France were thus thronged with a *chassé-croisé* of citizens all hurrying to their battle positions, their posts of public service, or even to their hoped-for careers.

On the level of protocol and symbolism, equality was born anew. Men addressed each other as 'citizen'; official letters were brought to a close with the expression 'Fraternal greetings'. In the army, general officers were no longer known as *maréchal de camp* and *lieutenant-général* as they had been during the monarchies, but as *général de brigade* and *général de division* as at the time of the Revolution and under the Empire.

The spectacular measures of repression which Guizot had introduced at the end of his 'reign', which had contributed in no mean fashion to exasperating public opinion, were hastily revoked. Michelet, suspended from his post on 2 January 1848, was triumphantly restored to his chair at the Collège de France on 6 March. And Karl Marx, expelled and living in Brussels since December 1845, also returned to Paris during March.

Free Paris.[4] The clubs

In a more general sense too, the whole system of constraint that had been set up in 1835 was presumed to be abolished. Anyone could open a club or launch a newspaper, without formalities. For Paris, this was a time of permanent meetings, of a fervent passion for reading and discussion, a time of relaxation and joy. This is how Flaubert describes it:

> As business was in abeyance, anxiety and a desire to stroll about brought everybody out of doors. The informality of dress masked the differences of social rank, hatreds were hidden, hopes took wing, the crowd was full of good will. Faces shone with the pride of rights won. There was a carnival gaiety, a bivouac feeling; there could be nothing such fun as the aspect of Paris on those first days.
>
> Frédéric would give the Maréchale his arm and they would stroll together through the streets. She was amused by the rosettes adorning every buttonhole, by the flags hung out at every window, by the many-coloured posters on the walls and from time to time she would toss a few coins into a chest for the wounded set up on a chair in the middle of the path. Then she would pause in front of the caricatures showing Louis-Philippe as a pastry-cook, a juggler, a dog, a leech. But Caussidière's men, with their swords and sashes, rather frightened her. In the old days what people used to do was plant trees of liberty.
>
> The worthy clerics played their parts in the ceremony, giving the Republic their blessing, escorted by their gold-braided attendants; and the crowds approved of it all. The most common spectacle was that of deputations of every kind bringing their demands to the Hôtel de Ville — for every trade, every industry expected the government to find a radical solution to its wretchedness. Some, it is true, came to give it their advice or to congratulate it or even just to visit and see the machine in action.

And in the evening the spectacle continued in the clubs. The reader will forgive us if we borrow another long passage from Flaubert. This one relates to a few weeks later. There is no better way of appreciating the atmosphere than listening to the words of a witness, one with such an admirable style and to be admired all the more for his ability, even after twenty years of political disappointment, to perceive behind the naivety that caused him so much distress the genuine flashes of exaltation that had moved him so much at the time.

> They visited all, or almost all, of them [the clubs], the red and the blue, the frenetic and the severe, the puritanical and the bohemian, the mystical and the boozy, the ones that insisted on death to all kings and those that criticised the sharp practice of grocers; and everywhere tenants cursed landlords, those in overalls attacked those in fine clothes and the rich plotted against the poor. Some, as former martyrs at the hands of the police, wanted compensation, others begged for money to develop their inventions or else it was a matter of Phalansterian plans,* projects for local markets, systems to promote public well-being; now and then there would be a flash of intelligence amid these clouds of foolishness, sudden spatters of exhortation, rights declared with an oath, flowers of eloquence on the lips of some apprentice-lad wearing his sword sash next to the skin of his shirtless chest. Sometimes there would be a humble-looking aristocrat making plebeian-sounding remarks and with

*An allusion to the theories of Fourier (see above, p. 7, note).

hands unwashed so as to appear calloused. He would be recognised by a patriot and jostled by those beyond reproach; and out he would go, eaten up with rage. To appear reasonable, it was necessary always to speak scathingly of lawyers and to make use of the following expressions as frequently as possible: 'every man must contribute his stone to the edifice ... social problems ... workshops ...'

All this in an atmosphere of the most total freedom of expression. It is worth repeating that absolute freedom of speech was the first and most important proposition in the provisional government's political platform.

The reappearance of the class struggle. Blanqui

But within a few weeks this liberty bore fruit. As Flaubert noted, it did not take long for it to dissipate the conciliatory euphoria of the early days. The revolutionary views that were disseminated by the clubs alarmed bourgeois opinion and soon provoked a reactionary swing. But, at the same time, they made definite inroads among the Parisian proletariat. At the beginning of March it was fair to say that the dominant influence upon the popular masses was that of Louis Blanc and the socialists of the palais de Luxembourg. By the end of the month, however, this no longer seemed so certain: it was now the hour of the club men – of Cabet, Raspail and, perhaps above all, Blanqui.

Auguste Blanqui in effect made his mark through the prestige he derived from his sufferings and through the striking originality of his behaviour. This struck a complete contrast with the lyrical effusions that were so much in vogue. Victor Hugo has left us the following description of him during this period:[5]

> He had reached the point of no longer wearing a shirt. His body was clad in the garments he had worn for the past twelve years: his prison clothes – rags which he displayed in his club with gloomy pride. The only items he ever replaced were his shoes, and his gloves which were invariably black ...
>
> The privations, the total poverty, the toil, the plotting and the dungeons had taken their toll. He was pale, of medium height, with a frail constitution. He was spitting blood. At forty, he looked like an old man. His lips were blanched, his brow furrowed, his hands trembled, but in his fierce eyes you could see the youth of an abiding inspiration ... [At club meetings] in the midst of the excited rumours, he maintained his contemplative attitude, his head a little bent, his hands dangling between his knees. In this position and without raising his voice, he demanded Lamartine's head, offering that of his brother [Adolphe Blanqui, the liberal economist and academician] in exchange ...

In the last phrase of this passage from his *Souvenirs*, Hugo, the great reporter and 'illustrator', stood aside to be replaced by the alarmed bourgeois that he also was at this time. And this too is significant. Hardly a month had elapsed since the fraternal embraces of February, and already the spectre of the class struggle had reappeared.

The problem of the armed forces. The March days

Thus it was not long before political tension began to mount again and the government was obliged to concern itself with ways of maintaining public order, if not (yet) of looking to its own defence. It was no longer possible to call upon the municipal police force, which was extremely unpopular and anyway not very strong; nor upon the army, which had withdrawn from Paris following the popular victory of 24 February. At the *préfecture*, Caussidière had improvised a police force from volunteers among fighters at the barricades, the '*montagnards*'. With the red sash that passed for a uniform, they were certainly somewhat alarming to the bourgeois, but they made an honest and spirited job of imposing law and order. And besides, their numbers were very small compared with the huge city that confronted them. The National Guard remained the essential force, the citizen militia more than ever at the command of the order of the day. Even from a theoretical point of view, it was natural that the Revolution should bring about a democratisation of its recruitment, and it was inevitable that it should reflect the spirit of the various quarters and classes from which it was drawn.

The government therefore deemed it advisable to create a 'mobile National Guard' which, unlike the normal companies of the National Guard, would be permanent and therefore salaried. Many of the young unemployed flocked to it, so that, as well as playing a policing role, it also took on one comparable to that of the national workshops: here the unemployed were paid, relieved of their poverty and at the same time removed from the attractive influence of the clubs. Naturally enough, the mobile National Guard attracted all the youngest and least skilled of the workers, and the least responsible too. Faced with this phenomenon, Marx and Engels, both good observers ever given to elaborating their observations into theories, developed the idea of the 'lumpenproletariat', 'the proletariat in rags' as distinct from the proletariat pure and simple, the proletariat destined to be a reserve fighting force for the counter-revolution rather than for the Revolution. The month of June was to confirm this pessimistic view.

But the government did not give up the idea of democratising the National Guard itself. On 14 March it decreed the dissolution of the elite companies which, before the Revolution, had been recruited from bourgeois districts and had been better equipped. These companies protested, and their demonstration on 16 March, known as the demonstration of the '*bonnets à poil*,'* was the first street demonstration made by the opposition of the right. It was countered, on 17 March, by the popular

*The distinctive headgear of the elite companies of the National Guard before 1848. These were more bourgeois and conservative than the general run of the National Guard and so had, naturally, just been dissolved by the government.

masses who mounted a huge demonstration in support of the government and the spirit of the February Revolution. This provided an opportunity for the leaders of the demonstration, Blanqui among them, to present the government with another demand, namely that it should postpone the election date.

The problem of the elections. 16 April

This was the third great political problem of the period. Everyone was well aware that it would be the vote of the provinces that would arbitrate between the two camps, the liberal and the socialist or – if you prefer – the bourgeois and the popular, that divided Paris and even the government. It was not difficult to foresee that this vote would not be revolutionary, and that the decision against socialism would be given by a rural majority that was either quite uneducated or else subject to the guidance of the well-to-do. The order of the day for the Revolution thus became: to delay the elections in order to give the countryfolk time to become politically aware. The elections had been set for 9 April. Faced with the demands made by Blanqui's delegation, on 17 March the government accepted a postponement, but only one of a derisory duration: the date was set back to 23 April.

Blanqui returned to the attack. But as early as mid-March he had been recognised to be the most redoubtable of the revolutionary leaders. That is no doubt why the government, which had by now learned to make the fullest use of all the resources of the police, on 31 March unearthed from the files of the previous regime a document named after the publicist Taschereau. According to this document, one of the leaders imprisoned after the 1839 affair* had given information regarding the organisation of the republican secret societies. This famous individual, known only as 'number XXX', was identified as Blanqui by unofficial commentators and also, sad to say, by Barbès, who had fallen out with his former fighting comrade and had forfeited to him his own former popular prestige. Blanqui defended himself vigorously and his response convinced most subsequent historians and certainly the mass of Parisian workers at the time.

On 16 April, he was again in action as their leader. Was it again a question of pressing for a postponement to the elections? The fact is that the day of 16 April was one of the most complex of episodes, a combination of various meetings with different purposes and sometimes tortuous intrigues. The workers came out on the streets without any clear purpose, and this time the provisional government had taken precautions and had mobilised a sufficient number of National Guardsmen from the bourgeois

*Mentioned above in connection with Barbès (p. 28, note).

districts for the protection of the Hôtel de Ville. This force was exceptionally determined and declared its support for the Republic and the government. It claimed that both were under threat – although it was not too clear by whom – and it raised the cry of 'Down with the communists!' The workers were disconcerted and avoided a confrontation. The day ended, without bloodshed, in success for the provisional government. The latter now even considered itself sufficiently strong to begin to reintroduce a number of garrison groups into Paris. As for the elections, they would be held, as decided, on 23 April. The provinces were going to pass judgement on Paris, or at least force it to review its position.

The provinces under the commissioners for the Republic

During March and April, the departments had become the responsibility of the commissioners for the Republic. They were intended to replace the prefects of the monarchy but, on account of the circumstances, they enjoyed much wider powers, almost reminiscent of those of the *représentants en mission* of the *grande époque*.* Ledru-Rollin who, as Minister for the Interior, was mainly responsible for appointing them, was anxious to employ only convinced republicans. He thus found himself in many cases obliged to call upon men whose capabilities and experience fell somewhat short of the strength of their convictions. Emile Ollivier, who was sent to Marseilles, was barely twenty-three years of age. Not that this choice was in itself a bad one. This future minister of the liberal Empire was matched on the opposite side of France by Charles Delescluze, a future leader of the Commune, now appointed commissioner at Lille. These men were faced with the local situation described above; they had to take emergency measures to relieve the economic distress (many of them opened national workshops, on the Parisian model) and, above all, they had to introduce men of the Republic into the administration by appointing new sub-prefects and, at least in the principal communes, by replacing the existing municipal councils with provisional municipal committees recruited on a popular basis. In other branches of public administration such purges were not necessary. Besides, everybody involved there claimed to be republican. It was at this juncture that political terminology produced a distinction between 'long-standing republicans' (*républicains de la veille*) (those who had declared themselves and fought before the February revolution) and 'latter-day republicans' (*républicains du lendemain*). Foremost among the latter were the Catholic clergy, as was evident in the festivals that were held more or less everywhere to mark the installation of the Republic. One of the main features of these ceremonies was usually

*In Year II the Convention sent some of its members on a mission to the various departments to keep watch on the spot over the defence of the regime, the application of its laws, mobilisation and national defence.

the planting of a tree of liberty; there would be processions, songs and speeches and the local priest would give the emblem his blessing. This stands in stark contrast to the days following the July 1830 revolution, when trees had also been planted but without any priests and more as secular symbols consciously set up in opposition to the mission crosses that dated from before 1830. In 1848 the tree no longer stood in opposition to the cross but was, so to speak, a gesture or step towards one. There is an explanation for this change. In 1848 the Church derived a certain advantage from having suffered a measure of harassment under the July Monarchy. Some of its members had attacked the scandalous escalation of working-class poverty; and, above all, among young republicans who had gone through a phase of Romanticism, a vague deist spiritualism had in many cases overlaid the Voltairian influence of the preceding generation. A fair number of them would have been only too happy to follow up the surge of political fraternisation with a genuine ideological syncretism: a fleeting moment.

Social tensions in the provinces

However, the commissioners did not all react in the same way and, in the event, they turned out not to be a very homogeneous body. The first test came when they had to decide upon the role they should grant (or refuse) to the 'latter-day republicans', whoever these might be. In Marseilles, Emile Ollivier fraternised with the bishop and made as few administrative changes as possible; in Lyons, Emmanuel Arago (the son of the great Arago) adopted the behaviour of a popular dictator, expelled the Jesuit and Capuchin Orders and submitted wealth to requisitioning and taxation. The social domain provided the principal criterion. In towns with a working-class population and sizeable socialist clubs, the commissioner might either protect them as the active wings or favoured offspring of the new social republic or, alternatively, oppose them (still, at this point, in a discreet fashion, by encouraging competition to them) in the name of order, a key word already being frequently used. The result was a multitude of widely differing regional situations, a number of clashes and even some dismissals.

As in Paris, however, the dominant factor on the political horizon very soon became the approaching elections.

Ledru-Rollin's commissioners had more or less satisfactorily carried out their task of installing the Republic and now, in a famous circular dated 8 April, he extended their brief by requesting them to enlighten public opinion and, in effect, to promote the election of long-standing republicans. What the government wanted thus became quite clear: no socialism in the urban areas but equally no monarchist reaction in the rural provincial regions. Thus while for the workers' leaders in Paris Ledru-Rollin was a defender of the established order, for the bourgeois in the provinces he was a demagogic dictator. The ambiguity is significant. In the event, electoral campaigning proceeded quite freely. There was indeed a veritable profusion of electoral lists produced and circulated by any newspaper, club or group that wished to do so – lists on which, as it happened, the same names often recurred.

The beginnings of conflict

The election of the Constituent Assembly

To break away from the politics of parochialism and cliquishness, the new electoral law had abolished voting on the basis of single nominees at the level of the *arrondissements*. Voting was now to take place within a departmental framework and therefore for a list of names (but not a list drawn up on a 'block' basis: votes were cast for each individual name). The lists contained a large number of names, as the Assembly was to comprise 900 members as it had at the time of the Revolution. Another sign of its revolutionary spirit was that the elected member was no longer to be known as a 'deputy' but as a 'representative of the people'. And, above all, he would in practice be elected by the entire (male) population aged 21 and over. No one had yet dared suggest carrying the logic of democracy so far as to institute voting within the commune itself: voters had to travel to the *chef-lieu* of the canton (or at least to a commune designated as the *chef-lieu* of a cantonal section). But in those days men were great walkers and if there were a few complaints they were not on the score of having to walk for a couple of hours, but rather because here or there a bridge might be missing over some mountain stream. The distance was covered in company: this 23 April happened to be Easter Sunday, a day when high mass had gathered together the entire village. And in some cases the parish priest was to be found, together with the mayor, leading the procession of villagers to the *bourg* to make their first use of Liberty. Sometimes the lord of the manor would be with them, as in the case of Alexis de Tocqueville, who recalled having led 'his' Normandy peasants to the polling booths in this fashion. But during these still conciliatory days of spring, such social constraints were not, in general, felt to be too irksome. It is difficult to interpret the results, precisely because scarcely any clearly delineated parties had yet been formed, at least at the level of France as a whole. A number of minorities emerged in the new Assembly, known as the National or Constituent Assembly: on the right there were the conservatives, in many cases still monarchists, and many of them former deputies from the Assemblies elected on the basis of the census; and on the left were the socialists. But there had been some significant failures: Thiers, for the right; Raspail, Blanqui and Cabet for the left.

Barbès, it is true, had been elected, but in his native locality, the Aude, and more for his family name than for his ideas/ France as a whole voted in conformity with the majority position in the provisional government: for a liberal Republic but not for social revolution or for monarchical reaction. In the Seine, all the members of the government were elected. Lamartine received most votes, followed by his moderate colleagues who were themselves ahead of Ledru-Rollin and the socialists. As this was also the position adopted by *Le National*, its name was sometimes used to refer to the political group which thus emerged victorious from the elections and which proceeded to govern France for the next four months. It was noticeable that a large number of commissioners for the Republic were elected from the provinces, as was natural enough, since they – most of them, at least – represented both the existing administration and also the ideal of a reassuring Republic. In the unofficial lists that they had promoted, it had been thought necessary to include a number of workers to carry through the symbolism of triumphant fraternity. It was, however, a prudent symbolism. Hardly any lists included more than one member of the proletariat, and those who did appear had been chosen from those workers who had somehow distinguished themselves from their own class: perhaps the theoretician of some reconstituted comradely group, or a self-educated mechanic foreman, or a porter–poet – men whose notoriety stemmed from their self-advancement, not from their contribution to the class struggle. As Georges Duveau has already pointed out, in the Assembly elected on 23 April, most of the representatives of working-class origin were positioned on the centre-left (as we should put it today), in the company of the countless lawyers, doctors and journalists who had been only too willing to adopt them. The extreme left, in contrast, included far fewer workers than intellectuals, Lacordaire being briefly among the latter.

The first bloodshed (Rouen)

The days immediately after the elections saw the first instances of bloodshed. They occurred, not surprisingly, in a large industrial town ravaged by the crisis: Rouen, with its massive level of unemployment. The Commissioner for the Republic, Deschamps, had organised national workshops for the relief of the workers and was popular among them; he was a rare example of a commissioner who inclined towards socialism. The bourgeoisie, whose leader was the public prosecutor, Sénard, a republican of *National* inclinations, was exasperated by the new taxes imposed to defray the expense of the national workshops (an expense admittedly largely unproductive, except in charitable terms). They settled this account when the elections came round: Sénard and his men were elected, Deschamps and his friends defeated, for the votes of the depart-

ment as a whole had soon swamped those of the *chef-lieu* town. On 26
April, when the results were known, a demonstration of workers took
place in front of the town hall. Possibly the workers wanted to contest the
result, or even to insist upon Deschamps' election. But their intention was
more probably to remind people of their needs and make a preventative
protest against any suppression of the national workshops (their only
resource) – a suppression now rendered likely by the victory of the men of
order. They were repulsed roughly by the National Guard, still mainly
composed of members of the bourgeoisie: confused blows dealt in the
jostling, followed by cavalry charges, were regarded as provocative by the
workers who brought their main demonstration to a close, and drew back
to their local districts to erect barricades. That evening and the next day,
Sénard brought in troops, even cannon, and the barricades were swept
away. The forces of order suffered no casualties, but there were several
dozen dead among the workers.

The attention paid here to this incident is not as disproportionate as it
may appear. In the first place, it was not an isolated incident. In Limoges,
the political and social situation was altogether analogous and it too
simultaneously led to a riot, although without loss of life. The incidents
are important in themselves, not because they are the first clashes between
republicans (16 April in Paris had already been a notable example), but
because they represent the first instances of bloodshed that stemmed from
class conflict and they shattered the euphoria of the new spirit of
fraternity. They are also important – if we may anticipate a little –
because this clash arising from the question of national workshops pres-
ages the conflict which was about to erupt in Paris and which, except in
terms of scale, had a similar outcome. These late April days straight after
the elections certainly marked the end of one phase of the Republic, that of
happiness and conciliation.

4 May, the Republic's official birth

It marked another ending, too, that of the provisional regime. For
the universal, free elections established the foundations of a regular, even
legitimate, republican system. Thus, when the representatives elected on
23 April gathered for their first session in Paris on 4 May, they felt duty-
bound to reproclaim the Republic. As we have already mentioned, this
was entirely in line with the precedent set by the Convention. They
proclaimed the Republic unanimously in their meeting hall, a huge temporary building hastily erected in the courtyard of the Palais-Bourbon;
they even proclaimed it again on the steps of their palace 'out in the light
of day'. The story goes that the cry of 'Long live the Republic!' went up in
unison as many as seventeen times; a well-known anecdote. What is less
well known is the importance that this date was subsequently to acquire.

In 1849, 1850 and 1851 the official festival to celebrate the Republic was held on 4 May and not on 24 February. A whole political philosophy can be read into this substitution: the regime wanted to be born in a regularly elected assembly, not upon the barricades.

With hindsight, we can see this as indicative of the spirit of the new power.

3

The re-establishment of order (May 1848–June 1849)

As we have said, the meeting of the Constituent Assembly at the beginning of May 1848 marked the end of the truly revolutionary period and represented a set-back for the popular leaders. The Republic now installed was increasingly hostile towards socialism, and ended by becoming openly conservative, even reactionary. This progression which effectively led to the *coup d'Etat* of 2 December 1851 evidently passed through a number of different stages. So why select the episode of June 1849 to bring the present chapter to a close? Ledru-Rollin's disappearance from the scene could alone almost justify the choice; but it is rather because 13 June 1849 was the occasion of the last attempt by the leftist opposition to obtain a political result in Paris through action on the streets. When this last spasm failed, the left was obliged to abide by the normal institutional processes. Indeed, it even made a conscious appraisal of its long-term chances of success in doing so. Over-simplifying slightly, you could almost say that up till June 1849 it was the conservatives who, fearing an uprising, were insisting on strict legality in their stand against the democrats, while after June 1849 it was the latter who spent their time pleading for legality and the law against the conservatives who were increasingly inclined to ignore them. But we shall of course come to qualify such generalisations, where necessary.

From an institutional point of view, the thirteen months that we shall consider in this chapter fall into three clearly defined phases. The first two were still preconstitutional, the Constituent Assembly being the sole source of power from which the executive emanated. But owing to the political changes that took place, there were in effect two executives: the first was the Commission, the second Cavaignac. As for the third phase, this falls in contrast within the period of the constituted Republic functioning in a regular fashion; and it saw the beginnings of presidential government.

The Executive Commission (5 May–24 June 1848)

After its moment of emotion when it proudly proclaimed the Republic for the second time, the Assembly's first task was to organise and rationalise the power that the provisional government had handed over.

49

The Executive Commission and the new ministry

It was time, first and foremost, to do away with a confusion of functions that had existed in the provisional government, namely between the wielders of sovereign power and their ministers. The course taken was to return to the system of Year III, when a collective presidency had been established over seven or eight ministers. Now there were to be five ministers and they were to be known quite simply as the Executive Commission. It seemed natural and only fair to select them from among the members of the out-going provisional government and the reduction in numbers made it possible to make the choice among them one of political significance. On the strength of their personal standing as former members of the provisional government, Louis Blanc and Albert had both been elected as members of the Assembly. But now socialism as a whole had suffered a reverse and the majority of representatives no longer wished to see them in power. Most of them would even have liked to eliminate Ledru-Rollin, whom they held accountable either for the ill-contained disturbances in Paris, for his famous circular, or for the initiatives of one or other of 'his' commissioners. But at this point Lamartine intervened. The elections had been a great personal triumph for the famous poet, if one considers that he had been elected as representative by all ten departments, winning in the Seine more votes than any other candidate. It was impossible not to include him in the Executive Commission without making too open a renunciation of the events of February and the wishes of the people. Lamartine was conscious of his own strength and made use of it. He made the election of Ledru-Rollin the condition of his own acceptance. This action defined his position better than any speech could have done. He had never believed in the viability of socialism and so felt no compunction in diverging from the path followed by Louis Blanc. However, he did believe in democracy, in generous-hearted reform of a liberal and humanitarian kind and, for him, Ledru-Rollin was a good enough symbol of this quintessential 'progressivism' from which the Republic could not dissociate itself without reneging on its very principles and essential inspiration. So Lamartine won the day, although not without difficulty. The Assembly elected the five in the following (significant) order: Arago, Garnier-Pagès, Marie, then Lamartine and lastly Ledru-Rollin.

Armand Marrast who, as we have seen, followed the same tendencies as the first three, retained his position as Mayor of Paris, but above all as a representative in the Assembly he became increasingly influential as a leader and manipulator for the *National* group there: the quintessential party leader. The presidency of the Assembly went by majority vote to the ageing Buchez, a former *carbonaro*,*a genuine republican, vaguely socialist,

*A member of the Charbonnerie, a secret society of patriotic and liberal inspiration which conspired against the monarchy of the Restoration.

but a committed Catholic: a man of goodwill, more a symbol of the spirit of 1848 than a partisan. But among the vice-presidents who surrounded him was Sénard, the 'victor' of Rouen. So the triumph of the *National* men was evidently tinged with a symbolic nuance of anti-worker revenge.

The ministry was composed correspondingly as follows: Bastide at the Ministry of Foreign Affairs, Recurt at the Ministry for the Interior, Trélat at Public Works and Cavaignac at the Ministry of War. They replaced, respectively, Lamartine, Ledru-Rollin, Marie and Arago.[1] Crémieux retained Justice, Bethmont Commerce, Duclerc, who had been Under-Secretary of State under Garnier-Pagès, took over Finance. They were all *National* men of more or less anti-socialist persuasion, and the only concessions to the more progressive current of opinion was the retention of Carnot at Public Instruction and the appointment of Flocon to Agriculture.

15 May and its problems

This series of votes and appointments confirmed, even accentuated, the defeat that the 23 April elections represented for the revolutionaries. Should we assume that their leaders wished to return to the demands they had made in February or to purge and exert pressure upon the Constituent Assembly just as the *sans-culottes** of 31 May 1793 had when faced with the Convention with its Girondin majority?† Here we face the enigma of 15 May.

A number of extreme-left clubs called upon the Parisian populace to demonstrate in support of Poland. As in 1830 and 1831, the absence of aid for other oppressed European peoples was one of the grievances that revolutionaries held against those in power. Naturally enough, aspirations towards Justice and Liberty were considered universal, calling for a solidarity that reached beyond the frontiers of the State. And, equally naturally, those in power, conscious of both internal and external difficulties, acted with extreme caution. One of Lamartine's last diplomatic actions (on 7 May) had been to make a purely symbolic approach to the King of Prussia in favour of the Poles. His successor Bastide was to make no such moves and indeed was extremely reticent regarding the German nationalist movement, which was viewed with sympathy by the extreme left.

*The name given to the men of the people in Paris, usually republicans, at the time of the Revolution. They wore trousers instead of breeches (worn to the knee with fine stockings), which were part of the costume worn by the upper classes.
†The 'Girondins' were the most moderate members of the Convention, whose support came mostly from the provinces. Their opponents were the '*montagnards*', who had a more advanced social programme and more radical methods. The latter were supported by the people of Paris.

It also seems likely that, beyond the Poland issue, which was regarded as exemplary and symbolic, the demonstration was intended to express opposition to the retrograde tendency of the policies of May and support for a return to the aspirations of February. But to what lengths was it really intended to go in expressing these desires? Moral pressure? Physical pressure? Or even as far as the subversion of power?

The call to demonstrate was successful. A considerable crowd gathered and, after a parade, it made its way to the virtually unguarded Assembly meeting chamber. The crowd proceeded to invade, led by a small but determined *avant-garde*. Carried along or swept up by the masses, all the non-parliamentary leaders thus found themselves amid a jostling tumult of representatives (mostly indignant) and demonstrators. President Buchez, in total disarray, took a number of contradictory measures, first summoning the National Guard, then cancelling the summons. However, he omitted to vacate his seat, so that the Assembly continued, in principle, to be in formal session. Barbès, one of the few representatives prepared to come to peaceful terms with the invasion, saw this as an unexpected, even unhoped-for opportunity to relaunch the Revolution. He mounted the rostrum and began to call out a list of names, as if calling for support for a new provisional government.

At this point, with the offence now well and truly committed, indeed with sacrilege openly and glaringly perpetrated, the arrival of the forces of order brought the situation to a head. The troops, National Guardsmen drawn from the more respectable *quartiers*, surrounded the Chamber, expelled the invaders and arrested those leaders who were most prominent either by reason of their behaviour or of their personality.[2]

We have described this day's events as enigmatic – even more so than those of 16 April, when there had been an excess of police precautions against a non-existent movement of popular aggression. On 15 May there was by contrast a manifest lack of defensive measures against a demonstration that was all too real.

The more competent of the political leaders of 15 May do not appear really to have planned to turn their show of strength into a takeover of power. Blanqui merely followed the rest and when he did speak it was only of the poverty of the workers and the need to find means to remedy it. What is disputed is simply what interpretation should be put upon the affair. The immediate evidence suggests that those in power seriously under-estimated the danger: their defences were weak and disorder ensued with an attempted revolutionary *coup* improvised on the spur of the moment. A different interpretation emerges from the (undeniably forceful) reconstruction put forward by Henri Guillemin.[3] He maintains that the whole thing was a huge trap designed for the revolutionaries: the explanation for the absence of defensive measures to repel any attempts to beseige the Chamber of Representatives is much more likely to have been a deliberate stratagem than a genuine miscalculation. We now have evidence to show that one of those most active in the demonstration, the old revolutionary Aloysius Huber, had been secretly in the pay of the secret police even in the time of Louis-Philippe. Now it was he – and he alone – who, to general astonishment, set up the cry of 'The Assembly is dissolved!', which precipitated the demonstration into a *coup d'Etat*: it all fitted in so neatly with the designs of the conservatives. Louis Blanc, for instance, was seized by the rioters and, despite his protestations, carried along in triumph as victor of the day. He, unlike Barbès, had done nothing at all to compromise himself in the affair, but 'they' were perhaps keen that he should be compromised, with a thousand witnesses standing by to testify. In the event, Louis Blanc subsequently managed to prove (with difficulty) that he had acted in good faith. But his friend Albert had shown less prudence and had, like Barbès, allowed himself to be compromised with talk of a provisional government. Accordingly, he found himself under arrest that evening, together with Barbès and all the other leaders of the foremost clubs including, as expected, Blanqui, Huber (who continued to play his role to the bitter end), Raspail (who like Blanqui had taken part in the demonstration and then gone along with the crowd albeit with no desire to seize power) and many others besides.

Depending on the extent of one's inclination to perceive the hand of chance or that of deliberation in history, we may choose between the thesis of improvisation and that of provocation (for which there is no rigorous proof but which certainly seems highly plausible). At any rate, the result was clear: the extreme left lost its leaders. For the first time since February there were again political prisoners, among them a former member of the provisional government. In anti-socialist and anti-revolutionary circles and among the *National* men, reactionary tendencies can only have been increased by the episode, as was quickly and clearly manifested on the evening of 15 May by the wave of illegal counter-violence by certain bourgeois members of the National Guard. They molested Louis Blanc, searched the home of Sobrier (Caussidière's assistant) and forced a number of clubs to evacuate their premises. It was a state of mind shared by the hundreds of worthy republican representatives from the provinces who witnessed the episode without being privy to the secret manoeuvres taking place in the corridors of power, although they admittedly felt strong reservations with regard to the violence incurred. The dignity of the Assembly elected by universal suffrage had been violated and its legitimacy contested by the populace of Paris, a capricious dictator with a thousand faces. Vengeance was soon to follow and it fell upon the national workshops.

Public opinion at the beginning of June. Polarisation

Before embarking upon an account of this last phase in the history of the national workshops, which will lead on directly to the June days, we must pause to consider the climate of public opinion at this particular juncture. In most of the departments, the April elections had brought to power men who symbolised the new republic, a republic sincere and conciliatory in spirit. Neither the extremism of monarchist reaction nor that of social revolution had found favour. Power had been at a premium: all the members of the government as well as many of the commissioners had been elected. The various episodes of May 1848 were bound to alter this climate of opinion. The spirit of reconciliation failed; attitudes became polarised. The conciliators, regrettably, departed. When Ledru-Rollin lost his ministry, George Sand, who had hitherto been happy enough to play the role of a patron of republicanism, returned to the provinces; on 17 May, Lacordaire tendered his resignation from the Assembly. On 6 June, Buchez resigned the presidency and Sénard was promoted in his place. As for the political polarisation, it became increasingly manifest. As early as 4 June the by-elections, occasioned by the numerous multiple elections of 23 April, had given some indication of the way in which extremism of one kind or another was gaining strength. Lamartine had not been the only national celebrity to be chosen by several departments at once as their representative. Since each of these favoured candidates could only represent one department at a time, they had to resign from all but one of the seats they had won, leaving the rest vacant. The Seine department in particular had to choose eleven new representatives: significantly, not one of those now elected was a republican of *National* tendencies (or was friendly towards the government, which came to the same thing!). Success was shared between various groups of men with particularly 'pronounced' opinions, who had been rejected at the polls on 33 April for that very reason. Thus Adolphe Thiers was now elected; so was General Changarnier and many others less well known. Meanwhile on the revolutionary side there were Caussidière, Pierre Leroux and Proudhon.

The new-comers

Louis-Napoleon Bonaparte was also a new representative. He was as alien to the extreme right as he was to the extreme left, but was, like them, a sign of the anxiety felt by a public seeking new alternatives. Another noteworthy representative, finally, was Victor Hugo. It was not at the time clear whether he should be labelled independent, Bonapartist or Orleanist. What is certain is that he too was a 'latter-day' republican. In February he had been in favour of the regency of the duchesse d'Orléans. He had declined to express support for the new regime, despite the entreaties of his friend Lamartine, who was offering him the ministry of Public Instruction. On 4 June, he chose to sit on the right-hand side of the Assembly, from which position he acted as an anxious (even anguished), but lucid, observer, caught between the disdain that he felt as a cultivated Parisian for the loquacious little lawyers of the left, and the revulsion that, as a man of feeling, he felt for the brutal policies he saw emerging among his fellows, the haughty bourgeois of the right. It took several months for his decision to mature.

As for Louis-Napoleon Bonaparte, the other celebrity elected on 4 June, his case was debated on 13 June. There was no objection to admitting a member of an erstwhile ruling family among the representatives, since other Bonapartes, elected on 23 April, had already been accepted. But Louis-Napoleon was a well-known claimant to power and even prior to 1848 had made two attempts to seize it.* Furthermore, he was only half-French. In the Assembly both Lamartine and Ledru-Rollin urged that he be disqualified. The majority did not follow their lead and admitted him. However Bonaparte, on his own initiative, sent a letter of resignation (from London). Was it genuine hesitation or was he biding his time, waiting for the right moment?

A new climate, a new problem. The railways

There was another problem: it will be remembered that in March the moderates in the government had favoured the national workshops as an institution which sheltered the workers from the preaching of the clubs and the Luxembourg Commission. However, in practice, there were many breaches in this dyke. There was much talk and coming and going; a measure of popular unity was reconstituting itself in Paris. Since early June the boulevards had again been in a state of constant restlessness. Every evening gatherings of workers and passers-by formed, singing and shouting, now for the social Republic, now for ''Poléon' in general defiance of the forces of order and the government. These riotous gatherings were a superficial aspect of deeper changes in public opinion. Some observers attributed the 4 June election of Pierre Leroux, Proudhon and other socialists to an agreement concluded between committees of workers from the Luxembourg Commission and worker delegates from the national workshops.

It is true that others were meanwhile attributing a measure of Bonaparte's success to the workshops as well (not really a contradiction: after all there were a great many workers in Paris!). The fact is that all kinds of agitators were circulating among the groups of idle passers-by and unemployed, and as well as socialist slogans, cries of 'Long live 'Poléon! We want 'Poléon!' were also heard.

---

*At Strasbourg in 1836 and at Boulogne in 1840. Both attempts had failed despite a number of army-based conspiracies.

Finally, the conservatives faced another danger from the quarter of the Executive Commission where Lamartine, although now in a minority, remained influential. It is certainly correct to ascribe to him much of the responsibility for the plan that now emerged to link the question of the national workshops to that of the railways. Lamartine was well aware of the trend towards the liquidation of the workshops and foresaw that this would be a sudden and summary economic blow, at the worst even a bloody one. He felt it his duty to fend off the catastrophe. Perhaps it could be done by finding more rational work for those left unemployed by the closure of the workshops, and at the same time reflating the economy: if the State assumed ownership of the ailing railway system, it could employ this reservoir of labour there and all would be well: unemployment would fall, industry would be stimulated and trade would receive encouragement. In a number of respects the plan may seem utopian (although that need not concern us here), but Lamartine was not really as naive as might be thought. Although he had never been a Saint-Simonian, he had shared the Saint-Simonian desire for modernity, industry and peace. Being something of an expert on the subject, he had always championed the railways and placed more faith in any encouragement forthcoming from the State than in private capitalist initiative left to its own devices. In this matter, in short, his essentially humanitarian position was in line with bold economic policies of much longer standing. However, as can readily be imagined, this plan, which both saved the workers from repression and at the same time constituted a threat to capital, was doubly alarming to bourgeois or even, simply, to parliamentary opinion.

Meanwhile, Lamartine was making headway. Duclerc, the Minister of Finance, had adopted the idea and was in the process of converting it into a legal proposition. Emile Thomas, who had for a long time been running the national workshops in the spirit dictated by Marie, finally began to take his responsibilities seriously and was now also working out ways in which their brutal liquidation could be converted into economic profit.

The end of the workshops and the explosion of the working-class revolt

The matter had, finally, to be resolved. Since the Executive Commission found it easy neither to achieve unanimity nor even to feel confidence in itself, all the preparations were made unofficially by the ministers affected (Recurt and Trélat) in concert with leaders of the majority who ranged from Marrast to Falloux.

The details of the preliminary bargaining and manoeuvres need not concern us. On 21 June the Executive Commission finally succumbed to pressure from the Assembly and passed the decisive decree that obliged workers of less than twenty-five years of age to enlist in the army and advised the rest to be ready to leave for the provinces. Failure to comply would mean no more wages. In effect, the workshops were dissolved.

On 22 June, when the decree appeared in *Le Moniteur*, a delegation of workers went to protest to the Commission. Marie met it with threats. It was then that the workers became agitated: there were marches through the streets, meetings and discussions of every kind. On 23 June the agitation culminated in a large dawn gathering around the July column in the place de la Bastille. It was presided over by a militant by the name of Pujol, a worker's son who by way of the seminary and then the army had reached the position of leader of one of the secret societies. It was he who, with a cry of 'Liberty or death!', dispersed the crowds to the various *quartiers* to erect barricades.

The spontaneity of the workers' revolt, now known as the 'June days', was in fact its most striking characteristic. Despite Pujol's abstract and romantic cry, the motivation behind it was starkly social: workers reduced to unemployment by the crisis, and thereafter dependent for their livelihood upon public funds, found themselves literally driven to despair when those funds were abolished. It is with good reason that history retains the cry uttered by an anonymous worker in the place du Panthéon (addressed to Arago while he was attempting to reason with a crowd on 22 June): 'Ah! Monsieur Arago, you have never been hungry!' Although a few militants of minor reputation, such as Pujol, emerged, there was virtually no *political* leadership. The organisational efforts made during the weeks immediately preceding by no means offset the effects of the imprisonment, on 15 May, of the better-known leaders of the old secret societies and of the clubs. The June days, more than any other period before or since in French history, remain a class battle pure and simple. It was certainly no mere chance that Marx and Engels, following the developments of the revolution in France with the most rapt attention, now roughed out the bases of their theory that the class struggle was the most profound historical reality of all.

But before the June days unconsciously became the source of that grandiose extrapolation, much blood was to flow.

Public opinion and the June days

Another reason for the bloodshed was the equally impressive determination evinced in the 'bourgeois' camp. In those days the ideals of order, property and liberty still retained a freshness and brilliance that they were later to lose. They were credited with a value that was absolute; it was only much later that this was gradually perceived to be no more than relative. 'People believed in them', you might say, with a fervour perhaps no less intense than that of the socialist workers' belief in justice, happiness and life. Furthermore, even in the camp of the workers' enemies there were plenty of men who believed passionately in the Republic. Now, for the ordinary republican citizen, unaware of the manoeuvres and provocations of men like Marrast and Falloux, only one thing was abundantly clear: a decision about which there was nothing irregular, emanating from powers freely elected by universal suffrage, was being contested by rebels. They were just as shocked by this disobedience as they would have been (and were to be) by a military *coup d'Etat*.[4] The final phrase in the official communiqué which was soon to announce victory to the departments ('Order has triumphed over Anarchy, Long live the Republic') was not nearly as hypocritical or cynical as were similar phrases used in 1871 or at later dates.

This makes it easier to understand the unanimous resolution of the Assembly and the fact that there were many loyal democrats who agreed to resist the workers. One such was Flocon, and it is said that the memory that he had done so remained a source of regret to him for the rest of his life. It is also in this light that we should understand the provinces' unanimous support for the government that contributed so much to strengthen the resolution of those in power in Paris. Flaubert, once again, grasped the significance of this first reaction and he ascribes his personal perception to the purest of his heroes, although later he also makes him aware of the ambiguity of the situation. Dussardier, a National Guardsman loyal to the call of the Assembly – that is to say of the Republic – does his duty when faced with the barricades in the rue la Fayette:

> A lad wrapped in a tricolour flag was shouting to the national guardsmen: 'Are you going to fire on your brothers?' While they were still advancing, Dussardier flung away his rifle, pushed the others aside, leaped on to the barricade and, with a kick, laid the insurgent low, tearing the flag from his grasp. Later on he was found beneath the rubble, his thigh pierced by a copper spike.

But a few days later his fame became a source of embarrassment to him:

> He even confessed to Frédéric that his conscience was troubling him. Perhaps he should have aligned himself with the other side, with those in working clothes, for, after all, they had been promised a whole lot of things and the promises had never been kept. Their conquerors detested the Republic; and besides they had had a raw deal. No doubt they *were* in the wrong but, all the same, not entirely. And the worthy fellow was tormented by the idea that he might have been fighting against justice.

But to feel scruples of this kind, you had to be living in Paris, close to the people. The provinces had shown unanimous support for the government and this had helped to strengthen the determination of the central powers. Conservatives in the provinces, more than anywhere, wanted order and, confronted with the lack of discipline in the streets of Paris,

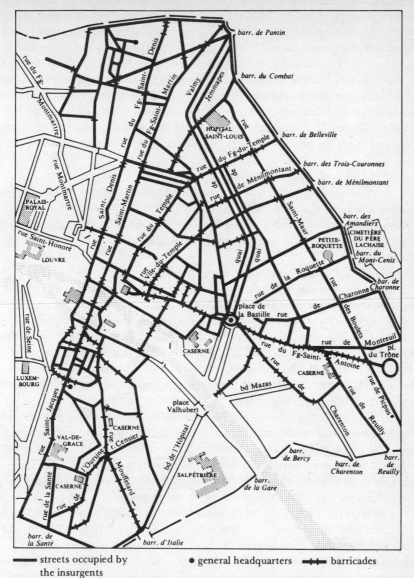

—— streets occupied by
     the insurgents   ● general headquarters   ╫╫╫ barricades

1 Insurgent Paris in June 1848

Note: This was eastern Paris and the contrast between it and the more bourgeois quarters
of western Paris was already clear. This Paris was still confined within its ancient limits; it
had not yet expanded to incorporate Belleville or Menilmontant; it was still the old
densely constructed Paris not yet penetrated by the larger boulevards.
(*Source*: *Histoire de France*, Georges Duby. Dynasties et révolutions from 1348 to 1852)

republicans upheld the legitimacy of the Assembly that they had elected. As for the workers, they were still too new to have formed any ties of organised or even conscious solidarity with the workers of the capital. They were only just starting to become aware of the benefits and merits of political democracy, whereas the Parisians had already become disenchanted with them.

So there was fighting in Paris on 23, 24 and 25 June; and it was intense, with the army and the bourgeois (the National Guard) ranged against the proletariat, in other words, the western quarters of the city against the eastern. Naturally enough, the major role in the confrontation passed to the minister most deeply involved, the Minister of War, General Cavaignac.

Cavaignac replaces the Five

Cavaignac waged war with cold determination, and took his time. Lamartine even suspected him (and told Victor Hugo so at the time) of having deliberately chosen not to disperse the first demonstrations on 23 June to allow the revolt to grow, so that his ultimate victory would be the more decisive.

As is clear, Lamartine was still hoping to hold the bloodshed in check. It was precisely because the Executive Commission was, on account of him, not in unanimous agreement that the Assembly, which was far less divided, first voted to declare a state of siege in Paris and then insisted upon the collective resignation of the Five. This happened on 24 June, the most critical day of the battle. From that moment on, the Executive became identified with the ministry; in effect, with Cavaignac, whose technical pre-eminence could not be denied. A few days later the general–minister was officially installed as leader of the executive power.

So the Five stepped down. For Lamartine and Ledru-Rollin this meant final retirement. Their departure marked the failure of conciliatory policies. But there was still a chance for conciliation in the future. Ledru-Rollin, whose star had not ceased to pale between February and June, was able a few months later to enter upon a new career, precisely because in June he had played no part in either the revolt or the repression.

In exactly the same way, thirty years later, Gambetta's success between 1875 and 1880 was in direct proportion to his failure in February 1871, thanks to which he became involved in neither the Commune nor Versailles. The caprices of History were at work and there is no reason to believe that the interested parties either foresaw them or consciously prepared for them.

The Cavaignac government (24 June–20 December 1848)

The crushing of the revolt and the subsequent reaction clearly reflected first and foremost the actions of the 'chief of the executive power' who took over quite naturally, having been the Minister of War of the previous system.

The crushing of the revolt

By the evening of 24 June, the workers' revolt could be said to be contained and doomed to failure. The Hôtel de Ville had not been taken by the insurgents. On the morning of 25 June it was possible to launch a counter-offensive by the army, with the support of the National Guardsmen and the mobile National Guard. After bloody fighting, the barricades were taken by assault. One dramatic episode followed upon another, fuelling hatred. General Bréa was invited for negotiations behind the barricades by the insurgents, only to be brutally slaughtered. Monsignor Affre, the Archbishop of Paris, tried to plead for peace in the place de la Bastille at the entrance of the Faubourg Saint-Antoine and was killed; not by the organised defenders of the barricade, who greeted him with respect and understanding, or by a stray bullet from where the troops were positioned (the topography of the place made that impossible), but at the hands of an isolated fanatical or over-excited inhabitant of the district.[5] Nevertheless not only the death of the archbishop but a thousand other horrors too (of which we shall have more to say later) were laid at the door of the insurgents. On the evening of 25 and on the morning of 26 June (it was all over by 11 a.m. on that day), the last barricades were taken and a number of summary executions and huge round-ups of suspects took place. About fifteen thousand men were arrested and literally piled into improvised prisons until they could be 'deported' to Algeria.

The conquest of this country had been the main preoccupation of the previous reign, and it was now beginning to pay off as Algeria came to play quite an important role in the internal policies of the French republics – as a training ground, a tough military school and a place of exile for rebels. It was also, we recall, Cavaignac's homeland.

Cavaignac and the Republic

However, it would be most unjust to see the new leader of France as a kind of warlike thug or, as he was unkindly dubbed in the *faubourgs*, a 'prince of blood'. This military man was the most authentic and loyal example imaginable of a 'long-standing' republican. Eugène Cavaignac was the son of a member of the Convention. He had scarcely known his father, but the memory of him had been passed on by his mother, whom he worshipped. He was the younger brother of Godefroy Cavaignac, who had been the passionate and disinterested leader of the republican party during the difficult 1830s. Eugène Cavaignac was as loyal to his political convictions as he was to his military vocation. The two were by no means incompatible in the ideology of *Le National*, which was patriotic to such a degree that the national humiliation suffered under Guizot had been one of the principal grievances with which the newspaper reproached him.

When Cavaignac became leader of the Executive, as a republican he showed extreme deference towards the institutions of the Republic, or at least towards the Constituent Assembly which, it should be remembered, was at this period the only depository of the national will as defined by popular suffrage. It was from this Assembly that Cavaignac held his brief, and he did not forget it. From June to December his provisional government remained strictly parliamentary, as it had been declared to be in May.

The governmental team that he set up on 28 June strove to be strictly republican (with a *National* slant). Cavaignac, who became president without ministerial portfolio, was replaced at the Ministry of War by General Lamoricière, while Goudchaux took over Finance and Sénard, the man of force, took the Ministry of the Interior. This left vacant the presidency of the Assembly: Armand Marrast was elected to it and remained for the full term of office. Cavaignac lost the collaboration of the worthy Flocon, who had been deeply shocked by the whole drama, but he would have liked to retain the services of the rest of the team including Hippolyte Carnot, like himself a pure republican, the son of a member of the Convention and a free-thinker. It was the Assembly that deemed his presence intolerable, especially at the Ministry of Public Instruction, and as early as 5 July it voted in defiance of Cavaignac to replace him by Vaulabelle, a figure less in the public eye. It was definitely a concession to the clerical right wing, now associated with the majority.

The Constituent Assembly and reaction

As can be seen, the Assembly, which had striven to outdo even the Executive in the fight against the rebel workers, was also more extreme than the latter in its reactionary inclinations.

The complete dissolution of the national workshops was announced, without concessions, as early as the beginning of July. The project of resuming State ownership of the railways was abandoned.

The representatives also set about restricting democracy. Not content to see the June episode as an explosion of socialism or an instance of disobedience to legally constituted government, they were also determined to interpret it as a consequence of the excessive liberty of propaganda introduced in February. To check such propaganda, the Assembly passed its first law designed to regulate the clubs and its first designed to erode the power of the popular press (by reintroducing stamp duty and caution money – measures which Lamennais, with painful irony, described as 'silencing the poor').

The press and the clubs did not suffer alone under this excessive implementation of the Assembly's responsibilities. A committee of enquiry into the events of 15 May and 23 June set about laying charges against anyone who had ever been tinged with socialism, declaring them to be responsible for all the plots and revolts. Albert, Blanqui and Raspail were already under lock and key, but Louis Blanc and Caussidière were at liberty and were even representatives of the people. They were attacked in debate with such venom and bitterness that they decided to avoid arrest and make their way to London. In April the Republic had acquired its first casualties; by May it had its first prisoners, and by June its first exiles.

These measures, encroachments upon the principles of democracy itself, did meet with some resistance in the Assembly. A minority intent on curbing the forces of reaction formed on the left wing. On 26 August, 252 representatives voted against authorising the arrest of Louis Blanc and Caussidière. But if liberty still found men to come to its defence, in the climate of drama and disarray of that summer of 1848 socialism could find few champions. The extraordinary struggle of 31 July made this quite clear.

Proudhon and socialism

Between February and June, with everybody else absorbed in their politics and demonstrations and finally in the barricades, there was one man who appeared indifferent to all the agitation, indeed who openly despised them all from Marie to Ledru-Rollin and from Louis Blanc to Raspail: Proudhon. He alone continued to disseminate socialist propaganda through a newspaper. He had already earned a certain notoriety before the Revolution, and by now his fame had grown. And so on 4 June he had won election. Dissociating himself profoundly and explicitly from the struggles of May and June, he refused to be alarmed and continued to argue that the social question should be resolved by organising free credit. This was to be done by creating an exchange bank with capital provided by automatic levies of one-third on all farm rents, rents and interests. So convinced was he of the correctness of his system that he preferred to describe himself as an 'economist' rather than as a 'socialist'. He spoke fearlessly from the rostrum of the Assembly on 31 July to put forward his plan, which he presented in the form of a legal proposal. His colleagues drowned his speech with their jeers and applauded loudly when it was refuted by Thiers, a veritable ghost from the monarchical past now posing as a Prudhommesque apostle of private property.* Socialism was rejected by 600 votes to 2! The other vote loyal to the ideal came from Louis Greppo, a cloth manufacturer from Lyons who was representative for the

*Monsieur Prudhomme, a fictional figure created by Henri Monnier after 1830, quickly came to represent a social type: the bourgeois convinced of both his values and his prejudices. In other respects, Thiers – a very real figure – was also taken to represent the typical bourgeois – strategically skilful, but extremely dogmatic in his doctrines, particularly his economic ones.

Rhône. Not that there were no other supporters of socialism at all on the benches of the Assembly – there were: Considérant for instance, and Pierre Leroux. But they decided to abstain on the grounds that it was not quite *their* system and that to their minds this was, in any case, not a political action, merely a theoretical debate.

But there were other debates that were of a less theoretical nature. For if socialism had never been any more than a dream, the reduction of working hours in March had been a very real benefit. In September a new law was passed which, although it did not deny the principle of the limitation of hours, fixed the working day at 12 hours (instead of 10 in Paris and 11 in the provinces).

Democracy lives on

But it would be wrong to describe Cavaignac's government (and period) as purely reactionary. That would be too Parisian, too parliamentary; in a word, too centralist a view of the situation. As we know, in the provinces the rhythm of life was quite different.

In the departments, the administrative officials remained republican. To be sure, they were moderates, for this was the hour of the almost total monopoly of the men of *Le National*, but they were as committed to the regime as Cavaignac himself. Emile Ollivier, the young commissioner for the Republic, later prefect for the Bouches-du-Rhône, is a good example. On 24 and 25 June, in Marseilles, he too had been faced with 'June days' of a sort: workers' riots which took place at the same time as those in Paris, but were not connected with, indeed were totally unaware of, them, and much less profoundly motivated besides. There had been bloodshed and Ollivier had taken repressive measures of a moderate nature only after he had done all he could to introduce calm. As a result he pleased nobody. If Cavaignac had recalled him, there would have been few objections. But Cavaignac contented himself with posting him elsewhere and Emile Ollivier remained prefect of the Haute-Marne until the end of that year. So, although an anti-socialist trend in the orientation of the prefectorial establishment was certainly detectable, there was no question of any anti-republican purge.

Above all, irrespective of intentions and personalities, the political system introduced in February was slowly taking effect.

It was altogether logical and had long been accepted that universal suffrage would be called upon to renew the general municipal and *arrondissement* councils that had earlier been returned by census-based elections (and, in some cases, in the towns and in the municipal councils designated in March by the commissioners for the Republic). In July and August these elections duly took place in a quiet atmosphere. With this second incidence of universal suffrage (the third, counting 4 June; but on that date voting did not take place everywhere), going to the polls was no longer the great post-revolutionary festival that it had been in April, no longer a solemn, exceptional occasion, but now a habitual practice, a normal institution, something everyone had learnt to do; the more so given that it was a matter of electing canton notables, municipal councillors, familiar people, neighbours, men to whom one might be linked by ties of friendship or hostility. It occasioned a birth of interest in public matters and, meanwhile, the struggle – now in many cases organised around new leaders – passed through a transition from the more ancient forms of noisy demonstration to expression through the ballot-box. In short, democracy had entered upon its apprenticeship and it was an apprenticeship of the only worthwhile kind – a practical one. The spectacular restrictions imposed upon the dissemination of republican views by clubs and newspapers were perhaps more than compensated for by the propagation of those views that universal suffrage as a part of daily life in effect represented.

The same spirit of discreet but effective progress presided over no less a matter than the introduction of the postage stamp. Before the Revolution, progressively-minded people had pressed in vain for the introduction of the English type of system: with a uniform and moderate rate, that is, one based upon the weight of the letter not upon the distance, payable by the sender not the recipient and manifested in the shape of an affixed stamp. Such a system was established in France by the law of 24 August 1848, which took effect on 1 January 1849. Thereafter, postal traffic rapidly became more intense and more widely used. Economic progress, social justice and the dissemination of culture all owed something to the little 20-centimes stamp.

The awakening of the provinces

Stirred though it was by the electoral process, provincial life was not yet in a state of upheaval. The departmental and local councils were still mostly dominated by the notables and many of the outgoing councillors elected by census-based suffrage were now re-elected. There were even – seemingly regressive – instances where the 'blue' mayors who had been supported by the Orleanist middle classes were replaced by 'whites', who were influential among the humble folk and therefore favoured by universal suffrage. The deeper effects of progress were to be long-term ones.

But at least it was becoming possible to distinguish in the vast sweep of the French provinces one or two regions already more alert than the rest, in which universal suffrage had brought about more changes in the town halls – changes for the most part favourable to the republicans and sometimes even to progressive ones. This was in particular the case in certain departments in the south and also, although more rarely, in central France.

It is already possible to detect regional differentiations in public opinion and perhaps also even in political structures. They were to become patently obvious in May 1849, and we shall describe the situation in greater detail in a later chapter.

We should note, then, that a popular awakening was definitely taking place in the provinces at the very moment when the proletariat in Paris itself appears to have had good reason to feel disenchanted. This is the reason why the June repression, experienced as a truly bludgeoning blow in Paris, was not felt nearly so painfully in the provinces.

Only those whose revolutionary consciousness was exceptionally alert could have felt as deeply stricken as the workers in the capital at that moment. To the provincial masses, even members of the populace, even democrats, Paris was another matter. Paris was isolated, Paris may even have been wrong; at all events, Paris was a long way away. Even the repression itself did not mean a great deal to the peasants at a time when there were no special squads of mobile police (except in Paris) and when regular troops and full-time National Guardsmen were hardly to be found except in the *chefs-lieux*. Besides, given the conditions of transport, all that was hours, or in some cases days, away. To a villager, repression meant charges preferred by the mayor or the *garde champêtre*, or the arrival of five or six *gendarmes* from the cantonal squad. Hardly enough to daunt a crowd, in the early days at any rate, although the time came when in serious cases the public forces of order made their presence felt. This is why, despite the events of June, the French provinces seem not to have felt cowed in the least.

That this was the case became clear in the autumn, when in some places order no longer prevailed. Tiny local conflicts involving the peasants' interests, citizens' grievances against the *octroi** and sporadic workers' strikes continued to be a part of everyday life; and between June and October, in the isolated and impoverished regions of the Massif Central and the South, from the Creuse (Guéret) to the Basses-Alpes, there were even a few instances of veritable rioting against the 45-centimes tax.

No doubt none of this was very serious or, if it was, then rarely. But it is important to visualise the situation correctly during this second half of 1848: on the one hand we find a traumatised Paris, on the other a provincial France more animated than agitated.

The Constitution

At the national level, however, the most important subject was the Constitution. It was the principal object, the *raison d'être*, of the national

*Local taxes on certain commodities that it was necessary to pay when entering towns (city tolls or dues).

Constituent Assembly and had been in the pipeline ever since May. A committee composed of representatives of every political inclination: men of *Le National*, foremost among them Marrast and Cormenin, latter-day republicans such as O. Barrot and Tocqueville, even socialists such as Corbon and Considérant, had been working at it since that time and had persevered with their task throughout the summer. It was possible to start debating it in the plenary session on 4 September and this first reading continued until the end of October. The second reading began on 31 October and a definitive vote took place on 4 November.

There were really only two models available to the Assembly on which to build a Republic: the French revolutionary tradition and the contemporary, stable and vigorous experience of American democracy. It made use of both. The first French Revolution inspired the preamble which consisted of eight articles of metaphysical and moral substance, before the exposition of the strictly constitutional measures. To quote from the most important passages:

> In the presence of God and in the name of the French people, the National Assembly proclaims:
> I.   France constitutes itself a Republic. In adopting this as its definitive form of government, it aims to follow more freely in the path of progress and civilisation, to work towards an increasingly equitable distribution of the responsibilities and advantages of society, to improve the material circumstances of every individual by the gradual reduction of public expenditure and taxation and, avoiding further commotion, to raise every citizen, through the progressive and constant action of the institutions and laws, to an ever higher level of morality, enlightenment and well-being.
> II.   The French Republic is democratic, united and indivisible ...
> IV.   Its principles are Liberty, Equality and Fraternity. Its bases are the Family, Work, Property and Public Order ...

So far as political organisation went, the principal contribution of the revolutionary tradition was the single Chamber. America, to be sure, had two Chambers but there the justification for the Senate was the confederal structure of the Union. In France, indeed in Europe generally, the establishment of a Higher Chamber had always been motivated by a desire to monitor or put a break upon the Lower Chamber elected by popular vote. So an Upper Chamber was not desirable and it was decided to have a single national Legislative Assembly consisting of 750 members (like the Assembly of 1791–2).

This Assembly was, furthermore, to be purely legislative, the executive power resting with the President of the Republic who was to be both Head of State and leader of the government and directly elected by universal suffrage. It was here, definitely, that the American system left its mark.

It would be over-fastidious to undertake a full description of the Constitution at this juncture. We will return to relevant points at a more appropriate time. Let us, for the moment, simply consider the issues that gave rise to most dissension.

A philosophical problem

The first concerned the preamble. Should the right to work be written into it? It was a phrase which at that time directly implied socialism, since it insisted that society should organise production in such a way as to ensure employment for all. It was deemed undesirable. The formula eventually retained (article 8 of the preamble) ran: 'by offering assistance in a fraternal spirit [the Republic should] ensure the existence of all citizens in need, either by providing them, so far as its resources allow, with work or providing succour for those unfit to work, in cases where their families are unable to do so.'

The extreme left, fighting passionately for the right to work, defended an amendment introduced by Mathieu (of the Drôme). It was rejected by 596 votes to 187.

A political problem

The second great debate was of a less philosophical nature. It concerned the very principle of the people's election of a president, and the outcome was to a large extent determined by the knowledge that candidates for the post were already coming forward. It seemed probable that the first president elected by the masses would be one who aspired to monarchy and the bearer of a name already renowned, to wit Bonaparte. What the Republic needed to consolidate itself was, rather, a kind of French Washington capable of duly relinquishing office when his term expired. Cavaignac seemed to possess the requisite qualities. But his friends and others, the purest and most egalitarian among the republicans, supported an amendment introduced by Grévy which in effect abolished the post of president. Lamartine, who was no friend of Cavaignac and who believed himself more popular than he really was, this time cast his vote with the right wing and managed to win over all those who were wavering or undecided. Election of a president by the people was carried by 643 votes to 158. The only republican precaution felt to be necessary was the stipulation that a president should not be eligible for re-election and the establishment of defensive and repressive procedures (article 68) to deal with the eventuality of a president perpetrating a *coup d'etat*.

Having thus coped with the major problems, the Assembly found itself, in a global and symbolic vote, once again in agreement almost as total as on the day of its inception. On 4 November the Constitution was carried by 739 votes to 30. It was solemnly promulgated on the 21 November.

By this date the campaign for the presidential election was already under way.

The presidential election. The candidates

There could be no doubt that Cavaignac, supported by the entire *National* 'party' and favoured by his fame, his reputation for disinterestedness and his actual position as Head of State, would be a candidate. It was also known that Louis-Napoleon Bonaparte would seek election. In the new by-elections held in mid-September he had had no difficulty in being elected as a representative, and thereupon had allowed himself to be persuaded to leave London for Paris to take his seat in person. He had also agreed to mumble on the rostrum words to the effect that he would never be a 'pretender'. Was the election going to be a two-cornered fight?

Much depended upon the forces of the right, the liberal or Catholic conservatives whose acceptance of the Republic had never been more than lip-service and who, since the summer, had – at any rate at a Parisian and parliamentary level – been openly regrouping. In a committee known by the name of 'rue de Poitiers' (where it met) those who yearned for the old monarchies sank their differences. Thiers, Molé, Berryer and O. Barrot reached agreement on a common policy. Their strength in the country, mediated through either the Church or the notables, was considerable. But it was an indirect influence, diffuse, social and anonymous: not one of them felt capable of making personal capital out of it, as a figurehead. We should remember that in those days there were no mass media. It would have taken many months of travelling to popularise the voice of a single man in the country regions and as many again to make an individual face familiar by producing lithographs and distributing them. In short, it was clearly not possible to mount a publicity campaign for Monsieur Thiers in the short time available and the rue de Poitiers group would have to seek votes for either Bonaparte or Cavaignac. Cavaignac attempted to woo the right wing. In October a minor ministerial crisis provided him with the opportunity of introducing two Orleanists into his government, Dufaure and Vivien; the following month he publicly offered refuge in France to the Pope who had been ejected from Rome by the Revolution. But he was too much of a puritan to carry this opportunism through to the limit and he refused to commit himself to the ex-royalist conservatives as fully as they would have liked. Bonaparte, on the other hand, promised Thiers anything he wanted and seemed to be a mediocre, simple-enough fellow whom it would be easy to manoeuvre in the corridors of power. So the rue de Poitiers group adopted him as their candidate.

Cavaignac was busy trying to consolidate his prestige. But although his majority in the Assembly agreed to raising the state of siege and went on to decree solemnly that 'he had served his country well', the leader of the executive had leaned too far to the right not to forfeit a few allies on the left. Furthermore, it almost goes without saying that in the aftermath of the June days he could expect nothing but hostility from those who favoured the working class and socialism. Republican intransigence and humanitarian aspirations thus found themselves in alliance. Ledru-Rollin made a come-back to play this particular card for a left-wing opposition that was unswervingly democratic from a political point of view and open to a measure of reformism from a social one. In doing so he was simply reverting to the spirit of *La Réforme* of pre-1848 and that probably encapsulated his deepest personal inclinations. He was not alone in believing it necessary to find some way of defending republicanism and establishing popular unity. Around 21 September, political banquets had taken place in many towns to commemorate the proclamation of the First Republic of 1792. The trend of opinion that this represented lent encouragement to the endeavours of the Assembly's extreme left in the foregoing constitutional struggle. In November, several dozen representatives of this persuasion banded together to publish a manifesto in which they baptised themselves the 'Mountain' party, desiring with this emotive name to perpetuate the spirit of Robespierre and of *L'ami du Peuple*.* More concrete efforts were made by Ledru-Rollin who, together with a few friends, tried to organise all the forces within an association known as 'republican solidarity'. It was short-lived, dying under the axe of the law passed against clubs. Nevertheless, it was the first in a long series of associations in French national history, reaching forward to the Bloc, the Cartel, the Popular Front and beyond: they all brought together the most advanced of the 'bourgeois' republicans with the most moderate partisans of socialism.

Naturally enough, from that moment another quite different socialist movement (inaugurating a tradition no less tenacious) also developed in defiance of this alliance. It was intransigent, revolutionary and resolutely '*Guesdiste*'† or leftist. Its recruits came mainly from amongst Cabet's former partisans, the Icarians, or the former members of the more egalitarian secret societies; in short, they came from groups generally described as 'communists' rather than 'socialists'. This movement decided to adopt Raspail as its figurehead.

Lamartine allowed his name to be put forward (he had, after all, been to some extent the subject of a plebiscite on 23 April); and a handful of intransigent legitimists produced the name of General Changarnier. The list of candidates was now complete.

The campaign took place in a peaceful atmosphere and was conducted,

*A newspaper published under the Revolution by the ultra-revolutionary *montagnard* Jean-Paul Marat, who was also often referred to as '*L'ami du peuple*' (the friend of the people).
†From the name of Jules Guesde; a socialist group which, under the Third Republic, became the most intransigent and critical with regard to the official institutions and the 'bourgeois' left.

in the main, by the press – a fact which seemed to point to victory for Cavaignac, who was supported by the largest number of newspapers.

The results

Bonaparte's crushing victory in the elections of 10 December, the results of which were generally known ten days later, came as a surprise.

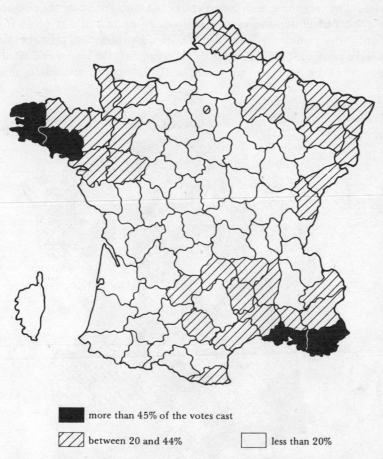

■ more than 45% of the votes cast

▨ between 20 and 44%   □ less than 20%

2 Votes obtained by Cavaignac in the election of 10 December 1848

Note: The peripheral location of votes cast for Cavaignac – that is, denied to Bonapartism – is striking. He was victorious in Basse-Provence and in Haute-Bretagne and obtained a large minority vote in almost all frontier or bilingual districts (with the exception of the Basque region). It is difficult to say whether or not this is pure coincidence. It is no doubt more rewarding to examine each local case separately (cf. Tudesq, *op. cit.*). At all events, this electoral geography was certainly of a fleeting nature. Cavaignac, who was absolutely typical of the 'blue' (centre-left) mentality obtained support in many regions which were very soon to declare themselves either white or red.

(Based on A.J. Tudesq, *L'Election présidentielle*, p. 252 (Biblio. no. 42))

He obtained more than 5,400,000 votes as against 1,400,000 for Cavaignac, less than 400,000 for Ledru-Rollin, 37,000 for Raspail, 8,000 for
Lamartine and even fewer for Changarnier.

It is difficult to interpret the grass-roots support for Bonaparte in terms
of class. Was it a peasant vote? Given the size of the majority obtained and
the composition of French society at that date, there can be no doubt that
there was a strong correlation between the Bonapartist and the rural vote.
But was it mainly the vote of conservative peasants led on by the notables,
voting for order, like the rue de Poitiers group? Or did it come from
peasants who confusedly wanted to register a protest and who, because
they were poor, cast their votes against Cavaignac, the leader and symbol
of power? A bit of both, no doubt; and distinctions should be made

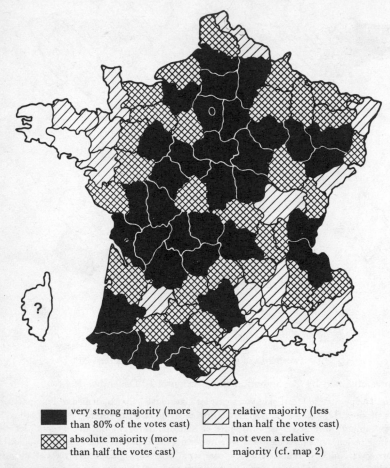

■ very strong majority (more
than 80% of the votes cast)

▨ absolute majority (more
than half the votes cast)

▨ relative majority (less
than half the votes cast)

☐ not even a relative
majority (cf. map 2)

3 Votes obtained by L.-N. Bonaparte in the election of 10 December 1848
(Based on A. J. Tudesq, *ibid.*)

between the different regions (a point to which we shall return). The immediate feeling was one of surprise. What we would today describe as the 'political class' (the great majority of representatives and journalists, the members of committees of every inclination ranging from the friends of Marrast to those of Blanqui, the educated, the city folk, the militant workers and so on) had been overwhelmingly defeated by a movement of irrational public opinion: it had no clearly defined programme, no really well-known leader, just a legend attached to a name.

For the next few decades, liberals and republicans of every shade regarded Bonapartism (at first in the strict sense of the term and – after 1880 – in the wider sense) as a direct reflection of political illiteracy. And perhaps that, in effect, is the least contentious diagnostic. But that is another problem which we shall discuss later.

The beginning of the presidency of Louis-Napoleon Bonaparte (20 December 1848–13 June 1849)

The oath

The date 20 December 1848 thus marked the beginning of the phase of normal functioning for the Second Republic, since an executive in accordance with the Constitution was now duly installed. Its titular head, Louis-Napoleon Bonaparte, the emperor's nephew, became the principal figure in this episode. He initially played his part with some discretion, so we will defer a more complete description of him until he begins to show his personal political hand. All the same, one element – perhaps the prime one – in his moral portrait is already detectable: this man, who had always presented himself in both word and deed as heir to the Empire, now went through the motions of a solemn oath-taking ceremony, swearing loyalty to a Constitution that was explicitly opposed to his own 'destiny'. The scene took place in the meeting chamber of the Constituent Assembly and Victor Hugo, in the account he has left us of it,[6] captured the atmosphere: the representatives were disturbed, not sure whether they were witnessing a conversion or a perjury. The applause for the new president was thin, as they preferred to reserve their acclaim for Cavaignac, who resigned his power with dignity, and to indulge once again in cries of 'Long live the Republic!' Lamartine was not present and thus avoided being insulted: when his derisory count of votes was declared there was a burst of spiteful laughter from the right-wing benches. Marrast presided. It was noticeable that he invited 'the citizen Louis Bonaparte' to take the oath ... but a week later, when Victor Hugo was invited to dine at the Elysée Palace, he noted that the citizen-president was being addressed by his guests as 'Monseigneur' or even 'Your Highness'. The rites of republicanism were already out of tune with the mores of the kind of society that was once again predominant.

The new political trend

Only a few days later, however, what was most striking in the political scene was not so much the arrival of this new figure but rather the overall victory of the rue de Poitiers group; the president formed a government of erstwhile royalist notables, headed by Odilon Barrot. Its most prominent member was the comte de Falloux at the Ministry of Public Instruction and Religion.

Far more than the days of June and the Cavaignac episode, it was this that marked the turning-point of the regime. It was the first time since February that a government had been formed that did not include any republicans; and its composition became even more right wing when, after no more than a few days in office, there was a clash with the president over responsibilities. This resulted in the liberal Malleville at the Ministry of the Interior being replaced there by Léon Faucher, later to be authoritarian and repressive in the summer of 1849.

There were repercussions to the new political trend throughout the country; these took the form of profound changes in the personnel of the *préfectures*. It is perhaps symbolic that a young civil servant, baron Haussmann, a Bonapartist by conviction and family tradition, who had been a sub-prefect under Louis-Philippe but left without authority for a year under the Republic, was now, in January 1849, appointed to his first *préfecture*. Conversely, the young Emile Ollivier, whom Cavaignac had been content simply to transfer from Marseilles to Chaumont, was now relieved of all duties. The step from anti-socialism to anti-republicanism had been well and truly taken.

Resistance and the end of the Constituent Assembly

Faced with this situation, the Constituent Assembly, with its large republican majority, radicalised its attitude. Even before 10 December, the electoral alliance between Bonaparte and the leaders of the old royalist parties had seemed threatening; reacting against this danger, even the most moderate of the long-standing republicans, the friends of Marrast, Marie and Cavaignac, had rediscovered their populist hearts, as was shown by the passing of two motions of importance. The first granted the peasants a long-sought-for economic respite by reducing the indirect taxation on salt and alcohol. The other aimed to consolidate republican-minded legislation by ruling that the Assembly should not go into recess until it had voted on a body of ten 'organic laws' which would bring a number of French institutions into line with the new Constitution. This represented a very wide interpretation of its duties as a constituent body. Some were in favour, others not. Foremost in people's minds were the political implications: for instance, the *National* men wanted to go along with the Palais-Bourbon to delay elections for the new Legislative Body, since, in the wake of the December vote, there was a danger that it would go over to royalist reaction.

The first weeks of 1849 were thus characterised by the efforts of the government and the right wing of the Constituent Assembly to force the Assembly to agree to curtail its mandate (the Rateau proposition). It was a confused struggle and there were aspects of intimidation to it: there were movements of armed forces within Paris, justified on the vague pretext of possible rioting (29 January). Eventually the Constituent Assembly gave in and reduced its ambitious programme of legislation so that the election could take place in the spring.

The legislative election of 13 May: the parties involved

The elections of 13 May 1849 were thus to install the second important institution of the constitutional system, a single Legislative Assembly elected for a period of three years by universal suffrage. The number of representatives was reduced to 750, but the electoral law remained unchanged.

However, an entirely new feature since the vote of April 1848 was the manifest political polarisation that had taken place since that date. Conciliatory euphoria was a thing of the past. So were the very real uncertainties which, in the early days of the Republic, had made possible in a large number of departments the election, from the same list and by the same electors, of republicans who, though enthusiastic, were ill-defined and whose real inclinations were only gradually revealed as time passed. Now, after a year of conflict, everyone knew of the policy disagreements that overshadowed the unity of the tricolour flag and the impersonality of the regime. Indeed, this was when each of those three colours was becoming a convenient party emblem for 'reds', 'whites' and 'blues'.

Those who were unwilling to countenance a Republic unconcerned with improving the lot of the populace, whether they were 'communist', like Raspail, 'socialist', like Pierre Leroux and Louis Blanc or 'vaguely humanitarian', like Ledru-Rollin, were uniformly and exaggeratedly regarded as revolutionaries by their adversaries; they were dubbed 'reds'. But as often happens, before long this nickname, given them by outsiders who intended it as an insult, was accepted and adopted by those concerned for whom the red flag and the red cap were anyway already associated. So the reds called themselves 'reds'; and so did the *montagnards*, though officially they were partisans of the 'democratic and social Republic'. Current slang shortened this to *démoc-soc* or even simplified it into 'socialist', widening the accepted meaning of the term. To all intents and purposes, all these terms now had the same meaning.

The reds returned the compliment by referring, equally sweepingly, to all conservatives as 'whites' or 'royalists'. Strictly speaking 'white' should really only have applied to former legitimists. But in point of fact the legitimist party, which often identified itself with the clerical party, did not fight under its own colours but rather under those of 'order'. There was an increasing tendency to use 'the party of order' to refer to the conservative coalition with all its different origins, centred on the rue de Poitiers committee in which the partisans of Louis-Philippe and those of Henri V* all forgot their differences. In truth, the party of order was a coalition between 'whites' and 'blues'.

But what *was* a 'blue'? The word had been used during the first Revolution in connection with the *chouans* of western France. A blue was a man who accepted the political philosophy of 1789 (which differentiated him from a white), but who refused to venture beyond liberty into social-ism (which differentiated him from a red). The fact is that the word could be applied just as well to Louis Bonaparte as to Thiers or to Cavaignac.

Results. The revelation of rural socialism

Now during this period when the class struggle was irrupting both in practice and in mens' minds (a subject to which we shall return in the next chapter), the abstract philosophy of liberalism pure and simple did not obviate a choice. There were to be a few instances of progressive republi-cans going over to the reds, while most Orleanists and Bonapartists joined the whites in the party of order. But throughout the country cases of moderate republicans wishing to maintain an intermediate position between, on the one hand, rejection of socialism and, on the other, rejection of reaction, were few and far between. The Legislative Assembly thus emerged from the ballot-box with the parties clearly defined. The victory of the party of order and the crushing defeat of the *National* party were, in sum, a repeat of Bonaparte's victory over Cavaignac in December 1848. Now there were almost 500 conservatives as against barely 100 *National* republi-cans. This was more or less the reverse of the proportions of the outgoing Assembly. On the extreme left was a block of about 200 *montagnards* (more than 200 in some votes, for the groups were, after all, not as fixed and clearly defined as they are today, and there was always a fringe of representatives who were undecided). That was a total no higher than that of the Constituent Assembly, and was still very much a minority.

*The comte de Chambord (1820–83), grandson of Charles X, who would have been heir to the throne had the 1830 Revolution not taken place. Those who hoped for his eventual restoration gave him this royal title in advance, although he never had the chance to assume it officially.

Nevertheless, this Mountain was considered alarming. In the first place it was realised that the election of these reds was by no means a surprise one as it had been in the euphoria of April 1848. They had been elected consciously, so to speak, after a year of experience and conflict, and notwithstanding the events of June and of December. More importantly, it was noticed that they did not come haphazardly from all over the place, but from a number of departments where they had been chosen by an electorate that knew what it was doing, and that a proportion of that electorate came from the peasantry. The reds represented the working-class quarters of Paris and Lyons, and that was understandable. But they also represented the Cher and the Allier, the Dordogne and the Lot-et-Garonne, the Var and the Basses-Alpes and many other districts besides.

We shall return to this 'geography of public opinion', this revelation of the political temperament of the French country regions. We know that it was indeed indicative and remained so constant that political commentators today are prone to detecting certain family resemblances between the geographical distribution of extreme-left areas in our own day and that of the famous map of May 1849.

However, we should not forget that at the time nobody knew what was to follow. Nobody realised that the geography of provincial red support was to remain more or less stable or change very little, that it would at any rate remain a minority phenomenon for several decades to come. The newness of the situation, the relative success of the left, was keenly felt (after all, there were more *démoc-soc* votes cast in May 1849 than Ledru-Rollin and Raspail together had managed to win in December). It was believed to be a beginning and that, since socialism had successfully spread beyond the town suburbs to win peasant electors, the hardest step had now been taken and an indefinite number of other peasants might follow this lead. It had not yet occurred to anyone that the mentality of a peasant in the Var might be closer to that of a worker than to another peasant in the Mayenne. Peasants were thought of *en bloc* and the idea that millions of French peasants could be potential reds caused fear and trembling – or hope and trembling, as the case might be. Add to this the fact that the Constitution had also granted the right to vote to soldiers serving under the flag and the 'reds' were already making some headway there[7], and it became easy to understand how it was that, apparently paradoxically, the election of May 1849 was received as a victory by the friends of Ledru-Rollin and as a source of anxiety by the conservatives.

The Rome expedition

At the end of the month, the Legislative Assembly held its first session. It adopted as its president a man of the party of order who came straight from the Orleanist political personnel: Dupin. However, it was very soon caught up in a grave problem of foreign policy.

By the authority of the Executive Commission and subsequently of Cavaignac, Bastide had remained responsible for Foreign Affairs. Adopting the line introduced by Lamartine, but with increasing emphasis, he devoted his efforts to the Italian sector. Together with liberal England (Palmerston), France, acting in a mediatory capacity, had been successful in mitigating the effects of the Austrian defeat inflicted upon Charles-Albert's kingdom of Piedmont.

In the Papal states the situation was more complicated. Pope Pius IX had been ejected from Rome by a national and democratic revolution, whose sympathy with the spirit of 1848 could not be in doubt. The much-celebrated Mazzini was involved in it, as was Garibaldi, whose fame was yet to come. Cavaignac had offered hospitality to the Pope (who had, however, preferred to accept the more classically reactionary invitation of the king of Naples, which was closer to home), but was hardly in a position to do any more. Furthermore, Austria, involved with the Hungarian revolt and the second Piedmontese war, was not yet regarded as a threat. The whole situation changed when, in March, Piedmont was once again defeated. By now Louis-Napoleon had replaced Cavaignac and Drouyn de Lhuys had replaced Bastide. As sometimes happens, Bonaparte was less reactionary in his foreign policies than he was at home. The decision in mid-April to send an expeditionary force to Italy had a traditionally national aim: to forestall an Austrian restoration. Meanwhile, a diplomatic mission led by Lesseps was in Rome trying to effect an acceptable compromise between the Pope and the republicans.

But Lesseps' mission was unsuccessful and – more importantly – in May the electoral victory of the French right persuaded Bonaparte to slant his policies in the direction favoured by the party of order, in other words to support the temporal power of the Pope.

From that point on, the presence of the French at the gates of Rome took on a different meaning. Lesseps was recalled, General Oudinot received new orders and eventually battle was engaged. The French army attacked Rome; within a few days it ousted the Mazzinian patriots and reopened the gates to the Pope or rather, in political terms, to the anachronistic temporal power of the cardinals.

13 June 1849

This action was in flagrant contradiction to the existing French Constitution which included the following statement (article V of the preamble): '[The Republic] respects foreign nationalities just as it expects its own nationality to be respected; it undertakes no war with a view to conquest and never employs its forces against the liberty of any people.'

Since this fine declaration was to be found in the preamble rather than in the positive measures, a failure to live up to the spirit of the Constitution was involved rather than a definite betrayal. But that is not important. Only the Mountain was now at one with the spirit of the Constitution. The majority and the government had certainly turned their backs upon it. Ledru-Rollin mounted the rostrum to denounce the Rome expedition and proposed a vote of no confidence in the government. His proposal was rejected.

The leader of the Mountain then had the idea of lending weight to the left's protest with a street demonstration. It was understood that 'the people of Paris' would stand behind the elected democrats and stage a peaceful march to persuade the Assembly and government to respect the Constitution. They were to meet on the boulevards on 13 June. It is not clear whether there was any idea, in the event of a massive rally, of turning the happening into a substantial show of force. What is certain is that there was no massive turn-out, that Ledru-Rollin and his friends hesitated between various alternative courses of action and that they soon found themselves cut off, isolated and pursued by the army.

Several representatives were arrested. Ledru-Rollin himself managed to go into hiding in time and then make his way secretly to London, where he lived in exile for more than twenty years. The leader of the Mountain was now no more than a leader of exiles.

It has often been said that, for a man who had restrained the popular revolution of April 1848 and stood passively by while the people were being massacred in June 1848, it was somewhat naive to hope to rally the survivors of the Parisian working class to fight under his leadership so soon. Perhaps; but we should also remember that it has always been more difficult to mobilise the masses to fight for a foreign people or for a violated principle than for their own survival.

A limited failure

However, it is remarkable that, even if Paris, traumatised by the events of June 1848, did not fight, the provinces in some cases reacted more sensitively. There were protest rallies in both the Allier and also in the Rhône. But in Lyons, that large working-class town where tensions were often greater and the class conflict more direct and undisguised than in Paris itself, Croix-Rousse actually erected barricades. Admittedly, it did so having been informed, falsely, that Paris had risen up in arms. (Whether or not it was the result of provocation this misunderstanding was a repeat, albeit a converse one, of the misunderstanding that had obtained between the two towns in April 1834.) Repression was brutal. The army brought in cannon against the barricades and there were scores of dead and hundreds of arrests.

And yet, the same can be said for June 1849 as for June 1848: it is important not to over-estimate the effect produced by this brutal repression in the large towns. These were isolated, separate incidents. Paris and Lyons were cowed, the leaders of social democracy were in exile, reaction held sway and the time for demonstrations was over. All the same, with Right on their side and universal suffrage, thanks to which the working people were beginning to acquire a sense of their peaceful strength, the militants were, despite everything, in an optimistic mood during that second summer of the Republic.

4

France faced with the great alternative: order or social democracy

Thus, at the point in time when the inglorious defeat of 13 June ushered in a period of regular functioning and conflict of only an ideological and parliamentary kind for the regime, public opinion appears to have been deeply divided. It was wooed by two important movements: one was the 'party of order', the other social democracy. We cannot at this point say that they represented two different concepts of the Republic, the one conservative, the other progressive. It is only too clear that at this date the *démoc-socs* were the only true partisans of the Republic, and that the formal acceptance of the regime by the party of order was merely a provisional cover for the immediate common interests of the partisans of the two or three possible forms of monarchy. Simultaneously, it is certainly worth noting that the idea of the Republic was beginning to become closely associated with that of humanitarian and social progress. But for the time being, given that the legality of the regime was not officially in question, the debate was taking place at both a higher and a lower level. At a lower level because, as was natural, the two parties clashed on the issues of every law proposed and every action of the executive. At a higher level, nevertheless, because the actions and declarations of each camp reveal an entire human and social philosophy. Should order be presented in the form in which it had been established over centuries of Christian tradition and in which, *most recently*, it had been endorsed, with amendments, by the liberal philosophy of 1789? Or should it be made to evolve in line with new needs, taking the philosophy of 1789 as, on the contrary, simply a model and a *point of departure*? And, at a deeper level, should one proceed with pragmatic prudence on the basis of a pessimistic view of man, or press confidently forward, adapting the optimism of the Age of Enlightenment to the present century?

No doubt the debate was destined to remain a permanent one, since it is basically the classic debate between the right and the left. The most we can do here – needless to say – is to follow its developments during the particular period we are studying. But these years of 1849, 1850 and 1851 are not only characterised by ways of perceiving and expressing the problems that are certainly dated, but are also remarkable for the exceptional acuteness of the discussions that took place. The moral crisis of these years was just as intense as those of the later periods of 1871, 1898 or 1936.

There are a number of ideological reasons to account for this and we shall try to indicate them in a moment. But the situation was perhaps aggravated by another factor, namely that the country appeared to be caught in a perpetual economic and social crisis.

Economic conditions in 1849–50

A limited improvement

The commercial and industrial crisis could certainly be said to be contained. Both home and foreign markets had picked up. This had the effect of reanimating the manufacture of consumer goods, that is to say the sector of artisan and small- and medium-scale industry. But no progress was made in creating new industries or stimulating new investment. Now, we know from the opposite experience of the early years of the Second Empire how decisive a role in the 'promotion' of metallurgy, heavy industry and consequently the whole economic machine can be played by the relaunching of large public works projects, in particular involving the construction of railways. The question that remains is precisely why such projects were not relaunched in 1849, and it is not a simple one to answer. One is tempted to produce yet another negative explanation and point out that the conditions of 1849 were not those of 1852: the system of credit 'needed' to be rejuvenated, modernised or – to be more accurate – simply created, and for that to happen a new generation of capitalists had to arrive on the scene; to wit, broadly speaking, the Saint-Simonians. And more generally, capitalists as a whole needed to be induced to take risks on the basis of their confidence in the political and social future. In the economic sphere, these precisely were the two 'benefits' that derived from the *coup d'Etat* on 2 December 1851.

A capitalism without leaders and without confidence

Now, where were the Saint-Simonians in 1849, 1850 and 1851? The Péreire brothers who had been the most successful socially, still held subordinate positions in the Rothschild enterprises and the head of the firm, baron James, was still too involved in his Orleanist past to feel at all attracted to the Elysée. In contrast, Enfantin, the spiritual head of the Saint-Simonian 'family' was still a republican and continued to make his voice heard through the press, advocating the organisation of a system of credit, just as others had in times past pressed for the organisation of labour – and with equally little practical effect. Some Saint-Simonians,

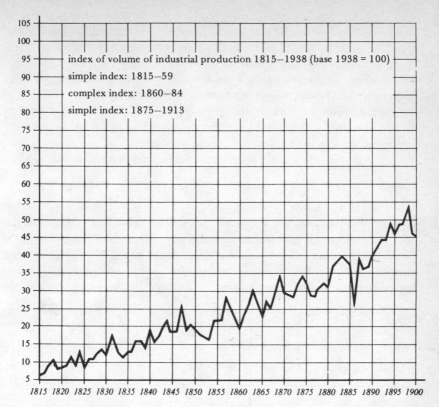

1 Industrial production

Note: There is, in the long-term, a striking coincidence between the four years of the
Republic and the long depression (both material and psychological) of the mid-century
years, sandwiched between the two spurts of the Industrial Revolution presided over
by Louis-Philippe and Napoleon III.

Fragment of graph based on T.J. Markovitch, 'Les Cycles industriels en France', in *Le
Mouvement social*, no. 63, April–June 1968, p. 32.

following the humanitarian aims of the doctrine to their extreme conclusion, had gone so far as to embrace socialism. One of the most representative of this leftist group of Saint-Simonians, Fulcran Suchet, who had been
Mayor of Toulon in 1848 and was the representative of the Var in the
Legislative Assembly, was even now in prison for having taken part in the
episode of 13 June 1849. We should, above all, not forget that a critical
attitude towards Christianity had been one absolutely essential element of
the doctrine. All the Saint-Simonians had remained profoundly anti-
clerical and it was therefore inconceivable that they should feel at ease in
the France of 1850 where the 'order' that was in power appeared to
conform increasingly closely with the desires of the Catholic Church. Any

idea that they might slip into power (given a political change of direction in which President Bonaparte might dissociate his personal political game from the party of order) was therefore an extremely remote one.

As for capitalists in general, they did not envisage any such development either. Sceptical as they were about the survival of the Republic in its present form, and poised between the hope of a 'good' *coup d'Etat* and an apprehension inspired by the inroads that the Mountain was making on public opinion, they were sure of only one thing: more upheavals were in the offing. We shall return to this subject later.

So it was that the second spurt of the industrial revolution was slow to come about.

The agricultural depression

But that was not the whole story. The crisis was growing in the country regions on account of the enduring depression of agricultural prices for produce. Perhaps a specialist could assess the weight of the various possible reasons: contagion from the overall economic stagnation; the effects of reduced consumption occasioned by the psychological cli-

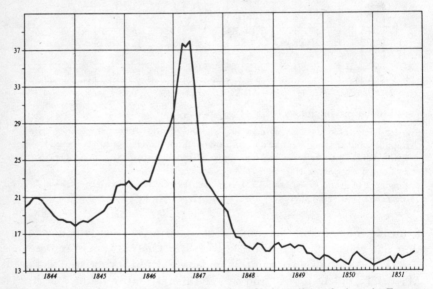

2 The price of wheat (average monthly price of a hectolitre of wheat in France between January 1844 and December 1851)

Note: This graph shows the two impacts made on the history of the Second Republic by the predicament of the wheat harvests: first an increase in prices and in penury which tended to crack open social antagonisms; then good harvests and a depression which, together, had the effect of introducing into the country regions a sense of insecurity which lasted for three years.

(From Labrousse (ed.), 'Panorama du crise' in *Etudes* XIX (Biblio. no. 3), pp. viii–ix)

mate we have described above; a consequence of the run of good harvests since 1848; or of a sense of unease stemming from further afield than the national situation? At all events, the fact is that agricultural produce was not selling well, the income of the peasants was diminishing and they were falling so much into debt both through their mortgages and through usury that the very ownership of their land was threatened.

The peasantry that universal suffrage had thus recently projected to the forefront of the political stage was one that was suffering and, graver still, one which, now that industry had partially picked up, was close to being the element in French society that was most under threat.

The presence of the peasant problem was reflected in the attention paid to agricultural education by all the successive governments of the Second Republic. A decree of 30 October 1848 set up an original three-tiered system comprising a farm school for each department, a number of regional schools of both a theoretical and a practical nature and, at the summit, a national Institute of Agriculture. The departmental farm school, a skilful and subtle conception, was simply a farm that belonged to a rich landowner who was an enthusiast for agronomy, and it served as a centre of apprenticeship where the State met the costs of fees and maintenance for the apprentices. It is true that the sums involved in the public financing of the system were minimal, but there was nothing comparable in the case of the workers.

During these years of 1849, 1850 and 1851, the peasant problem was thus a crucial one and Philippe Vigier,[1] who drew that conclusion from his own studies as well as from a whole series of other theses produced by the Ernest Labrousse school, has quite correctly emphasised the point, regarding it as one of the foremost subjects with which the historiography of the period should be concerned. In the towns the score was by now already known, but outside them it was this disturbed rural populace that the political parties were now in competition to win over.

The 'Mountain'

Its strategy

The Mountain entered upon this peaceful campaign with high hopes. As we have mentioned above, from its point of view the most important thing was that the minority of votes and seats won on 13 May 1849 was greater than those secured in 1848; and furthermore that the welcome extended to its propagandists gave grounds for hope of even greater success in 1852. This is one of the reasons that accounts for what could be called the 'legalism' of the red party. Respect for the law was, to be sure, inherent in their political philosophy (a point to which we shall return). But they were, furthermore, conscious that time was on their side

and that the very circumstances of this period – liberty frequently punctu-
ated by administrative and police harassment – in no way prevented
their propaganda from being successful and there were therefore good
reasons for tolerating the situation for as long as possible. It had very soon
become clear that the prefects of Bonaparte and Léon Faucher were
counting on disorder, driving the democrats into a state of exasperation
with an assault of pinpricks that were likely to provoke angry reactions,
which in themselves would foment further discontent. In the country
regions, where ill-educated peasants had thrown themselves into the
Mountain camp with the enthusiasm of neophytes that still combined
extremely 'primitive' aggressive impulses, it was all too easy for those in
power to provoke the masses into compromising themselves. So the militant democrats tried hard to keep their troops calm; or, to be more precise,
in their role as 'educators of the masses', they had two aims or were
attempting to purvey two lessons: one was to detach them from their old
conformist attitudes and teach them that it was necessary to enter into the
fight; the other was to detach them from their natural patterns of behaviour and teach them the way to fight. Now, the way that was both most
justifiable in itself and at the same time most likely to be successful was, in
their case, to make use of the ballot-box. That is the inescapable impression that must be formed by anybody studying the regional politics of this
period in detail without getting bogged down in the village incidents
which form a closely woven and highly coloured backcloth to the events.
But it is also the conclusion that could be drawn from the democratic
iconography of the time where voting ceremonies, processions to the
polling stations (often situated at the foot of the tree of liberty, under the
gaze of the great, exiled Ledru-Rollin) and the slogan of 'universal suffrage' all figure prominently.

The Mountain's newspapers and men

But who were the reds? So far as their organisation went they
differed hardly at all from those who had constituted the republican
'party' before 1848. In the first place they had their own press, either
newspapers from before 1848 (*La Réforme*, *La Démocratie pacifique*, *Le Populaire*) or survivors from the great expansion of March 1848 that had
suffered such a shake-up the following June (*La République*, *L'Evénement* –
produced by men close to Victor Hugo – *Le Peuple* – produced by
Proudhon, although, to put it mildly, he was something of a sharpshooter
among the democrats – and a number of others). There were also two or
three dozen provincial news-sheets.

Then there was the group of elected *montagnard* representatives, who
were in the habit of acting in a concerted fashion in debates, with each
man taking his turn to intervene from the rostrum, studying what posi-

tions they should adopt (we shall be coming across some examples presently), and, inevitably, at the same time analysing policies in general as a group. It was a large group and an aggressive and committed one, but its spokesmen had changed. We have seen how many of the great democratic leaders of 1848 had, as a result of proscription, ended up either as exiles in London (more and more the sole capital of European liberty) or else in prison. New leaders now emerged on the Mountain benches. Understandably enough, lawyers were the most prominent among them. It is well known that taking up the defence of militants or newspapers prosecuted for their views was, at the time, often the principal path to acquiring political fame and thereafter becoming a representative; and furthermore that a good leader of the rank and file in the elected Assembly had to be an orator. Thus the lawyers Michel (of Bourges) and Madier de Montjau, among others, were claimants for the leading role that Ledru-Rollin had vacated. Workers, such as Martin Nadaud, a mason from the Creuse, and Agricol Perdiguier, a carpenter from Avignon, were less prominent. More in the public eye were Lagrange, a veteran from the barricades, Miot, now a celebrity on account of his clashes with the all-powerful Dupin family in the Nièvre, or newspaper publishers with such famous names as Lamennais or Pierre Leroux. Finally, there were two other elected representatives who were more recent recruits to the social democratic cause, but they carried considerable weight. One was Victor Schoelcher, the other Victor Hugo. Schoelcher, an important bourgeois of great wealth and a liberal philanthropist, had as we know been a republican pure and simple in 1848, when he had been a specialist on the colonial problem and the anti-slavery campaign. Following the logic of his humanitarian philosophy and disturbed now by the threats hanging over the achievements and spirit of 1848, and conscious too that the social question presented many injustices that had to be remedied, he took his seat on the Mountain benches and became one of its best spokesmen. As for Victor Hugo, even as late as the end of 1848, he had believed a Bonaparte who was presumed to be popular to be preferable to the inflexibility of a Cavaignac. But, unable to tolerate the fact that the first action of the new president had been to help the Pope defeat the Italian patriots, he too came forward to take his seat on the extreme left. This great poet, sometimes accused even today of political opportunism, thus held ministerial rank for only one term of the four-year period of this Republic. Frequently thereafter, he took his stand at the rostrum, but his successes there were stormy ones. The conservative majority either detested him for having deserted their camp or could not stand his type of eloquence, as original, unusual, even as bizarre as his literary style. So it took delight in drowning his pronouncements with catcalls and jeers. Hugo's speeches were splendid targets for the ribaldries of the right in much the same way as was Pierre Leroux's wild hairstyle – said to be as disorganised and entangled as his ideas, or vice versa.

As is often the case, most of these 'stars' were representatives for the department of the Seine. It may be that, in reality, they made a less profound impact on the sequence of events than the obscure representatives from more distant departments where the red party had become implanted and who thus, naturally enough, provided the necessary liaison between Paris and the provinces.

Means of action and organisation

The basis of the party was obviously composed of those who read the newspapers and elected the representatives, and who were, as you might say, their clientèle, at least in the cases where the *montagnard* in question had brought the party his own personal popularity as a doctor to the poor or a philanthropic lawyer. Such cases were in fact quite frequent. The Mountain certainly numbered fewer and less wealthy notables than the party of order, but it was still very far from having replaced representatives of the 'notable' type – chemists, notaries or even men of private means – by ones of a militant character (workers, agricultural workers or school teachers). Nevertheless, it was quite remarkable that such a trend was already becoming detectable.

From a historical point of view, however, the principal problem is to define the means by which all these people were connected, from the parliamentary leaders down to the grass-roots supporters. One should not rule out the use, here or there, of groups that were already traditional, such as freemasons, or societies of a *carbonari* type or something similar. But these did not constitute the principal means of communication; towards the middle of 1850 and in 1851 secret societies made a reappearance, especially after the amputation of universal suffrage; we will say more about them when we examine that period. During the typically optimistic period of the rise of the Mountain, from the end of 1848 to the summer of 1850, our *démoc-soc* men wanted electoral success and therefore needed extensive means of propaganda and massive recruitment. Certainly, the law more or less ruled out the clubs by imposing so many restrictions upon them, but there were other forms that meetings could take.

We should not forget that the mid-nineteenth century was the heyday of the *cercles* among the bourgeoisie and the middle classes, and in some regions there were imitations of *cercles* that went by various names, even in popular milieux.

The *raison d'être* of a *cercle* was to bring together men with similar tastes so that they could enjoy leisure activities in one another's company. The friendly nature of these gatherings naturally predisposed them towards a certain political homogeneity. Another of their *raisons d'être* was to have a shared subscription to certain newspapers, for these were costly, and to allow a collective reading of them (aloud, in the case of popular groups which would include a number of illiterates). That was another reason why the *cercle*, in principle a 'recreational society', also spilled over into politics, for during this period politics were everyone's concern.

In our rapid survey of the situation, we are using the word *cercle* to cover not only those duly equipped with statutes and their own premises that were registered and authorised, but also groups of friends who were accustomed to meeting regularly and quite informally in the same café.

We do not intend to suggest that the *montagnards* ever deliberately chose to exploit the networks that we have sometimes described under the heading of 'habitual sociability', to transform them into organs of the party machine. But in regions where, under the influence of a worker or peasant movement during an electoral campaign of one kind or another, public opinion had been massively swayed in their direction, the existing associations had quite naturally become 'politicised' and political action was therefore no longer to consist merely in establishing communications between one *cercle* and another, either by correspondence or by paying personal visits. As we shall see presently, this was to prove an inexhaustible source of misunderstanding and harassment.

These *cercles*, societies and groupings of every kind were subscribers to Parisian or regional newspapers and were sometimes visited by their representatives who came to collect subscriptions or contributions to help defray the costs of some lawsuit or other. Thus one gains the impression that in many departments the nerve-centre of the 'party' was not so much the elected parliamentary representative, but rather the editor-in-chief of the red newspaper.[2] It is an impression that is confirmed when we find newspapers taking on as distributors representatives or salesmen militant workers who, sacked from their factory, were thus enabled to earn their living while at the same time working for the cause.

Political and daily life in red territories

Thus, in the red departments, we find the beginnings of organisations which may seem very rudimentary today compared with our present parties, but which were quite new for the times. It all seemed diabolically clever to people of conservative opinion and to the prefects, who formed a very exaggerated idea of the perfection of the system. All it amounted to, really, was a spontaneous encounter between a new point of view suddenly discovered by a whole section of the people and certain traditional structures of social life that were by nature incapable of rapid adaptation.

This process of reciprocal interpenetration between the new political ideals and traditional social practice was at work everywhere, promoted – as we have seen – by the political militant who turned his *cercle* into a kind of club, by the democrat publisher who entrusted his pamphlets to the carrier's bag or his political song-sheets to the barrow of an ambulant singer and by the peasants themselves as, with lawful political gatherings denied to them, they turned their folkloric festivals into red demonstrations. The fact is that folklore was perhaps more alive in the mid-nineteenth century than ever before in French history. The lives of the peasants were still half engaged in a world of tradition and oral culture. When, through the part of their life that already belonged to the world of education and politics, they discovered faith in democracy, it was clearly not to be expected that they should suddenly become 'defolklo-rised'. The only possibility was for the new political beliefs to become incorporated within a spontaneous folkloric syncretism; and that is indeed what happened, although there was no deliberate 'decision' that it should be so. Thus, the end of a carnival with its parody of a trial with judgement passed on an evil spirit would become an opportunity to express their dislike of a white mayor who was unpopular; in the *farandole* danced on the way back from the country chapel where the festival of the local patron saint had been held, all the dancers would sport a seditious poppy in their caps; on the wall of the local bar an effigy of the red Republic, wearing a Phrygian cap, might take the place of the image of Sainte Anne while, elsewhere, pictures of those exiled in London, grouped around Ledru-Rollin, would take the place of the old relics of the Napoleonic cult.

In these marriages between politics and folklore, songs were very important. In the files of the repression this traditional practice of singing popular, topical songs, often dialectical, full of dissatisfaction, plaintive or aggressive as the case might be, is recorded alongside the distinguished national repertory of songs where Pierre Dupont figured as a leading light. Béranger was, of course, still alive at this date but he was a very old man and no longer writing. His true successor was this Lyonnais poet, Pierre Dupont. He had written his best-known song in 1846; 'Les Boeufs', a song still marked by a rather naive sentimentality. But in 1848 he wrote the 'Chant des ouvriers', the 'Chant des paysans' and the 'Chant des soldats', and thereafter village demonstrators were prosecuted by the score for singing:

> To Arms! Forward to the fortress,
> Let the targets for our guns
> Be oppressors everywhere,
> The breasts of those Radetzkis!
> All Peoples are our brothers,
> All tyrants enemies.

(Aux armes! Courons aux frontières,
Qu'on mette au bout de nos fusils
les oppresseurs de tous pays,
les poitrines des Radetzkis!
Les Peuples sont pour nous des frères,
Et les tyrans des ennemis).

Often enough, so that there could be no mistake about the universal nature of tyrants, the line 'the breasts of those Radetzkis!' would cheerfully be changed to 'those Changarniers and Radetzkis!'.

This politicisation of popular folklore lends a special piquancy to the period for the historian who is able to relive it through the contemporary texts and documents. It is in itself testimony to the social depths to which the roots of democracy had penetrated in certain regions.

Eventually, it created conditions that made for even greater political penetration. As soon as folklore became slightly tainted with politics, as soon as there was a seditious flavour to it, it was attacked by the authorities. But by closing down a *cercle*, subjecting a singer to harassment, prosecuting a carnival, recording the words sung during a *farandole*, the agents of the authorities made the bemused (and – from a subjective point of view – quite innocent) villagers feel that their entire customary way of life was under criticism. Bonaparte's *gendarme* must thus often have made the same impression upon the villagers of Berry and Provence as the missionaries of 1820, who used to ban all dancing for the neighbours of Paul-Louis Courier*; they must, in short, have been seen as stupid and hostile oppressors. The red party did not fail to make the most of the situation.

The association as both a practical vehicle and a moral ideal

But apart from the successes won by defensive propaganda of this kind, what did the red party really want? One of the most deep-seated reasons for its success among the working class and in rural societies with strong communal structures was its approval of the association. It was prone to pronouncements that drew heavily upon the official slogan: Liberty, Equality and Fraternity, and the word 'Progress' would also often appear. To these words it might well have already added another: Solidarity, as the radicals of the end of the century were later to do. 'The workers' association' that would today more accurately be described as a 'production cooperative' remained their ideal, and many *montagnards* were staunch cooperative supporters to the bitter end, despite the exile of Louis Blanc, the dissolution of the Luxembourg Commission and – needless to say – the suppression of all official encouragement. Traces of Fourier's

*1772–1825. Man of letters and liberal newspaper publisher under the Restoration. Author of a famous pamphlet on the subject of villagers whose priests forbade dancing to them.

influence also inclined many of them towards consumer cooperatives: bakeries, butchers' or restaurants 'for society members'. Democrat doctors, often men of progressive spirit and pioneers in the field of homoeopathy played a distinguished role during the cholera epidemic of 1849 when, with the aid of party militants, they ran an ambulance service. Of course the *montagnards* were in favour of mutual aid and were committed trade-unionists. Anything that smacked of a workers' organisation new or old was considered 'red' and as such was subject to harassment. So even if not red initially it certainly soon became so ... Militant school teachers such as Arsène Meunier, Gustave Lefrançais and Pauline Roland now found themselves at the hub of democratic propaganda, fighting for secular primary school teaching and for the establishment of syndicalist instruction. It should be added that for Pauline Roland, who came from a Saint-Simonian background and who was to die during the events of 2 December, there was even a third battlefield: the struggle for womens' rights.

Even in rural areas the reds strove to instil or cultivate a collectivist mentality by encouraging mutual aid. Here the party had its own veritable rural specialist in the person of Joigneaux, the representative for the Yonne and publisher of *La Feuille du village*. The paper gave every kind of encouragement to associationism – for example by urging that when a peasant fell ill all the others should go in a group on a Sunday morning to do, in a few moments, the several days' work on his plot of land that their bedridden brother had been too ill to complete. So it was far from the case that the sole concerns of the reds were either propaganda pure and simple or strictly electoral activities. They were to a large extent engaged with immediate and practical aspects of reformism, and the hopes they placed in these were ambitious enough to remind us that utopianism was still, after all, not far from peoples' minds. We should, however, point out that this reformism was not, as is often the case nowadays, viewed with a measure of indulgence by the right, which regards it as a lesser evil than revolution. On the contrary, it was then considered by conservatives to *be* revolution, merely by reason of the fact that it stemmed from a socialist ethic. So it would be quite mistaken to underestimate its impact.

A combination of democracy and socialism

Meanwhile the *démoc-socs* placed all their hopes for the definitive accomplishment of socialism – that is the eviction from power of the forces of injustice – upon the lawful means that they (justifiably) considered that the Constitution had made available to them. Universal suffrage now existed and electors who were poor and hardworking far outnumbered the parasites. All that needed to be done was to make all of them conscious of where their own interests lay, and this aim seemed well on the way to being achieved. How could they fail to believe that at the double turning-point of 1852 (when the three-year mandate of the Assembly ran out as well as the four-year-term of the non-re-electable president), the partisans of the democratic and social Republic would at last come to power? All that would be necessary would be to pass some good laws and see that they were respected.

> In two years, two years – not long,
> The Gallic cock will crow.
> Strain to catch his country song.
> What will he say, do you know?
> He says to the earth's progeny
> With loads that weigh like lead:
> Here is the end of poverty,
> You who drink water and eat black bread.

> (*C'est dans deux ans, deux ans à peine*
> *Que le coq gaulois chantera!*
> *Tendez l'oreille vers la plaine,*
> *Entendez vous ce qu'il dira?*
> *Il dit aux enfants de la terre*
> *Qui sont courbés sous leur fardeau:*
> *Voici la fin de la misère,*
> *Mangeurs de pain noir, buveurs d'eau.*)   P. Dupont

The strength of the emotive, popular and socialist charge of this hope in victory is obvious. But one also senses that the victory was revered both for the effect that it would bring: happiness, and also for the manner in which it would be achieved: through the popular vote, a just and lawful system. The reverence the *montagnards* showed for the Constitution and the law, a reverence they strove to inculcate in the minds of the masses, in no way fell short of the respect felt for the Charter by the liberals of 1820 or that felt by the best of the Third Republic's parliamentarians for 'republican legality'. It was, furthermore, almost certainly this profound liberalism of the red party, together with its humanitarian inspiration, that increased its attractiveness to the elite of the blue republicans.

The *montagnard* ideology of 1850 can definitely be said to have been characterised by a combination of liberalism pure and simple, democratic ideals and a practical socialism derived from the utopians. So, notwithstanding the name 'The Mountain', adopted on the grounds of the universal prestige of the first Revolution, the party was in reality quite far removed from a spirit of neo-Robespierreism. This group of men has been the object of much derision since Karl Marx and Proudhon who, for once in agreement, considered it to be no more than a derisory imitation, almost a parody, of Robespierreism. But the truth is that these men were very much more the forerunners of Jaurès. So we should perhaps now grant them some of the respect which is rather easily given to the diatribes of Marx, whose taste for sarcasm was not, in our opinion, the most admirable of his gifts to history.

The unfortunate thing was that our *démoc-socs* were without a Jaurès* and their eloquence seldom matched the richness of their ideas and the magnanimity of their sentiments. The best of them expressed these things in a romantic grandiloquent style which provincial bourgeois and intellectuals from the ranks of the populace were just beginning to appreciate at the very moment that it was becoming unfashionable in cultivated circles of the elite. Thus Flaubert and his hero Frédéric, in *L'Education sentimentale*, are alternately attracted and disgusted by 'forty-eightish' emotion. In his case, a personal distaste for 'stupidity' almost smothered the natural impulses of his heart. But not altogether. All in all, the Arnoux and the Dussardiers come out of *L'Education sentimentale* slightly better than the Deslauriers and the Dambreuses. And, in *Bouvard et Pécuchet*, the two heroes may be more grotesque than their persecutors but they are, at any rate, less detestable. If we may be forgiven a gross over-simplification, we would suggest that for Flaubert the *démoc-socs* were merely stupid, but the bourgeois were both stupid and evil.

The 'party of order'

There can be very little doubt that if the *montagnards* often betrayed a certain leniency associated with optimism, the reason why the party of order was the party of hatred was that it was also the party of fear.

The age-old vigour of the anti-republican polemic

From the legitimists and from even further back, the ultra-royalists and counter-revolutionaries, the anti-republican polemic had inherited a long-standing tradition of sweeping, often slanderous attacks which the first Napoleon, and subsequently the detested usurper, 'Philippe', had encouraged. During the provisional government, the new masters of the hour had, in their turn, been heaped with abuse. Ledru-Rollin, a large man with an open countenance and a statuesque figure, and Marrast, an old bachelor of no fixed address and a bohemian way of life, whose lunch was brought to him in the Hôtel de Ville by an eating-house keeper, were reputed to indulge in Roman orgies. 'Little' Louis Blanc did not escape opprobrium either and was described (perhaps because his seat was in the Palais de Luxembourg) as a new Barras.† Their campaigns were not too

Jean Jaurès 1859–1914. The best-known French socialist under the Third Republic. His efforts went a considerable way towards synthesising the republican and the socialist ideals. In this respect the position that he represented is usually opposed to that of Jules Guesde (see p. 70, note).
†(1755–1829). One of the principal leaders of the Republic between Year III and Year VIII, that is during the last years of the Revolution. A lover of luxury, pleasure and wealth.

strong on logic. Although Flocon was so obviously austere that such calumnies could find no purchase, even he did not escape unscathed, but was made out to be a puppet or a fool. But these onslaughts were not so much reminiscent of the past as harbingers of the future. What we find at work here is a kind of law of conservative propaganda according to which, no sooner did a member of an extreme-left government become truly popular and alarming to the bourgeoisie than his private life became the object of a campaign of slander concerning wealth and 'robbery' which emphasised the presumed comforts and delights of power and (along with *La Fille de madame Angot**) forced the conclusion that 'there had certainly been no point in changing governments'. So it was that, each in turn, Gambetta, Emile Combes, Léon Blum and Maurice Thorez were presented as Luculluses or Sardanapalluses on the basis of either pure invention or inordinate exaggeration. In 1848, when illiteracy was still widespread and communications in some isolated regions were most precarious, naive country folk were on the receiving end of the most crudely slanderous concoctions. It is said that in deepest Auvergne there were peasants who believed that there reigned in Paris some kind of perverted dictator known as 'le dru Rollin' (the hard guy, Rollin), who had two mistresses, 'La Martine' and 'La Marie'. If that seems too good to be true, it was perhaps in reality simply a journalist quip for punning, today considered in rather bad taste, that was in those days much appreciated even by minds of distinction.

The horror story of social fear

To be sure, after that summer of 1848 the leading figures again became respectable to orthodox thinkers (*les bien-pensants*). But the escalation of the social peril had revealed another feature of the bourgeois mentality at work in the counter-revolution: a fascination with horror and excess. As is well known, during the June days, the most appalling rumours were rife in bourgeois Paris: the insurgents were said to be putting to death any mobile Guardsman who fell into their clutches by sawing him up alive, between two planks ... And it was put about that there had been discovered in the pocket of an insurgent prisoner a ticket 'for two ladies from the Faubourg Saint-Germain' (meaning: to be raped after the victory) ... etc.

All lies, of course. But it is hard to say how many of these cock-and-bull stories developed from the outrageous exaggeration of a tiny seed of truth, how many were deliberately put about by a coldly calculating, slanderous propaganda machine[3] and how many were spontaneous figments of the

---

*An operetta by Lecocq, performed in 1873, known today in particular by virtue of this phrase, which expresses the scepticism of the average Frenchman with regard to politics.

imagination. It would be more interesting to know what it was that encouraged such unbridled flights of invention and their uncritical acceptance. Was it the current high incidence of criminality to which the press under Louis-Philippe had devoted so much attention? (We are, perhaps, too prone to forget that just before the February days the banquet campaign met with strong competition for coverage from the 'number one' story of the newspapers: namely the trial of Frère Léotade, the murderer of a laundress by the name of Cécile Combettes.) Was it the effect of the *romans noirs* (horror stories) or of the serial stories? Or did it stem quite simply from the general background of poverty in the large cities, where almost as many people belonged to the underworld as to the regularly employed proletariat – and an underworld much less concentrated and localised than it is today, thanks to which it was easy to confuse what Louis Chevalier has defined as the labouring classes and the dangerous classes (*les classes laborieuses et les classes dangeureuses*). We have already acknowledged the bold innovativeness of Marx and Engels in distinguishing between the proletariat and the sub-proletariat. However, it is another historian from the intermediary period between Marx and our own contemporary Louis Chevalier who provides us with the following illuminating remark on the subject of the June days. Charles Seignobos writes:

> People were used to political insurrections in those days but they could not imagine the populace rising up without bourgeois leaders and without precise aims. Educated men had no idea about the workers' feelings, not even the superficial ideas that our own generation derives from literature. The only possible goal of men of the populace fighting on their own account must, it seemed to them, be looting or killing.[4]

A time of great misunderstandings

Of course, later, under the Third Republic, the political conflict managed to convey even to socialism's most adamant adversaries the idea that it was at least a doctrine and, even if one considered it a misguided one, it at any rate stemmed from mens' hearts and minds. But under the Second Republic the notion was still an unfamiliar one. For those who did not accept socialist ideals it was inconceivable that they should ever find acceptance in a normal world or normal minds. Socialism did not belong to the category of things that could be justifiable: it was perverse, pathological. Similarly, in our own times, most of our contemporaries who now agree to discuss socialism (that goes without saying), or even communism, still close their minds to the 'hippy' phenomenon which, quite simply, belongs to another world.

Thus the ideological battle between social democracy and conservatism fell into the category of the uncommunicable, and the polemical tirades that appeared in the press were a mass of generalisations and misunderstandings.

The party of order claimed to stand for a triad of principles: Religion, the Family and Property. With one addition and one omission (both of them significant), these were the very principles that the Constitution had declared to be the 'basis' of the Republic: 'The Family, Work, Property and Public Order'.

But at all events, the two parties were not in agreement about the meaning of any of these terms, or indeed about any of the key words used in the political jargon of the time.

Order
Order, which for the democrats could only be the order of law, for the conservatives meant the order of obedience and the absence of change. We mentioned earlier the groups of peasants who, full of socialist zeal, would go on Sundays to hoe the fields of some sick comrade. Now, these gatherings were invariably subjected to harassment, because the men would set off and return in a band, sometimes singing, sometimes following a banner and what this all boiled down to was a demonstration, with an exhibition of seditious symbols. Those in power read evil into what seemed to those involved the experience of a fine moment of moral behaviour.

Associations/conspiracies
Associations which, for the democrats, were close to embodying the most supreme virtues, since they represented fraternity in action and social progress at the lowest cost, were hounded by the authorities on the grounds that they were intrinsically perverse and opposed to individual enterprise and hence to liberty itself. Furthermore, any collectivity was *a priori* suspected of conspiracy. There was no common-law right to political association in those days and, since politics were banned in societies set up for leisure purposes, all concerted political discussion was necessarily illicit and was consequently either more or less disguised or denied. Now, the conservatives always refused to make any distinction between this enforced adoption of clandestine behaviour imposed by their own legislation and the deliberate type of clandestine action acknowledged by the 'secret societies' that involved a definite initiation. Despite all the pleas put forward by democrats acting as counsel for the defence, nothing made any impression, so deeply was this obsession with conspiracy ingrained in the bourgeois mentality. There it was lodged, in company with an obsession with crime, both possibly connected with a romantic or even sensationalised conception of history. Such attitudes certainly ran counter to the interests of the conservative bourgeois who might have done better to adopt the view – as some later did – that workers who were engaged on setting up a mutual insurance company or a cooperative would not be

interested in preparing for the barricades. Such, indeed, was the conscious intention of some of the socialist republicans, deeply committed as they were to policies of 'non-violence'. But these ideas were totally foreign to the right: around 1850 no cooperative could escape the accusation of being the pretext or cover for a 'secret society'.

Charles Seignobos, who was quite the reverse of a Bolshevik, but whose father had handed on to him a number of precise recollections about attitudes during the 1848 period, passed a bold if severe judgement upon the weaknesses of the bourgeois mentality that prevailed at that time: 'Just like the judges presiding over witchcraft trials, these magistrates, obsessed with their *idées fixes*, interpreted the facts laid before them by their agents through the bias of a set of systematic preconceptions'.[5]

Property

There were also misunderstandings about property. Whoever argued against the principle, suggesting that perhaps one day fields or workshops might become common property, were condemned for opening the floodgates to the most brutal type of rejection of the principle of property: which finds expression in theft. Thus, a conservative provincial newspaper for a time considered it amusing to introduce its accounts of violence or larceny with headlines such as 'Monsieur Proudhon's lessons do not fall upon deaf ears' or 'Another Proudhonian highwayman!'[6]

The family

Here too there were misunderstandings. There were those who criticised some of its usual forms, pointing out that an egalitarian conjugal union based upon love was much more moral – even in the Christian and customarily accepted sense of the word – than the bourgeois marriage that was based upon convention and business interests, often alleviated by adultery and completed by recourse to prostitution. Such critics were all condemned for preaching licence and vice. Whoever spoke of educating women, of organising them into trade unions, of informing them about political matters, was accused of favouring debauchery. Even the pure and chaste Emile Ollivier came under attacks of this kind. Perhaps it was because, even if unconsciously, many bourgeois in those days considered women to be mere chattels. At any rate, anyone advocating economic collectivism was automatically judged likely to encourage sexual promiscuity. But possibly this kind of interpretation is, after all, too rational. Perhaps sexual attitudes stem from fantasies that are not so easily explained.

Violence, the guillotine and the slaughterhouse

But the major misunderstanding was on the subject of violence and the party of order's greatest obsession was bloodshed. The houses of many militant republicans were subjected to police searches, prompted by false information that they were secretly preparing a guillotine 'that would set the heads of the rich rolling' in 1852.

It was, indeed, a complex matter. Conservative bourgeois remained convinced that the Second Republic would be a repetition of the First. They had not been convinced by the reassurances of 1848; on the contrary: the spectre of the Terror had been reawakened by the readoption of the name of the 'Mountain'.

In reality, the Mountain was deeply humanitarian. Victor Schoelcher, acting as its spokesman, was still trying to get the death penalty abolished even for offences of common law. A majority vote rejected the proposal. It was noticeable, on the other hand, that two June insurgents were executed by the guillotine, convicted of the assassination of General Bréa – an affair which was, to say the least, on the borderline between common law and politics. The truth was clear. It was the party of order that was the party of bloodshed. It had no horror of the blood it shed with legal sanctions, fearing only the illegal shedding of blood in the course of rebellions, and it did not believe that men like Hugo and Schoelcher could really temper the habitual behaviour of their electors. It was in fact haunted more by the idea of *jacquerie* than by that of the Terror. For a conservative bourgeois *jacquerie* meant the alarming prospect of *spontaneous* popular violence. This was because he attributed to the 'populace' (easily confused with the 'people') bloodthirsty instincts that were easily aroused. Nothing bears more convincing testimony to this than the anxious interest shown at this time in the question of slaughterhouses. In those days the public thoroughfares still tended to be treated as an extension of their working premises by many artisans, among others the butchers, who would sometimes slaughter beasts out there; and conscientious municipal authorities, as good town planners, were urging the construction of more slaughterhouses. Public thoroughfares would thereby become less congested, hygiene would be improved and 'the people would lose their familiarity with spectacles of bloodshed'. In point of fact, the improvement of the morals of the masses by dint of restricting butchery to within closed premises was considered desirable not only by this or that legitimist municipal council in Provence but also by a 'communist', such as Cabet, who makes an explicit reference to the matter in his *Icarie*.[7] Both the right and the left had misgivings about the violence still present in everyday life, the difference being that while the right feared that the left would use it, the left was concerned to exonerate itself from such suspicions. There can be no doubt that this concern to temper the behaviour of the people and those brought up on the streets contributed, with other factors, towards the adoption in 1850, at the height of the political battle, of the famous Gramont law which made it a crime to treat domestic animals with cruelty in public. Gramont was a conservative of some independence and originality; the Mountain, with Schoelcher as its spokesman, supported his proposal. There were only a few dissenting right-wing voices, a number of purists claiming, in the name of Holy Property, that it could be argued that the public powers had no right to intervene in the manner in which a carter whipped his own horse. However, they gained no support and a majority vote decided that animals should receive kind treatment, or rather that the street should be rid of spectacles of cruelty. The Gramont law may not have been a political event of great moment but it reflected a number of attitudes of the time.

Red phobia

It might be suggested that this phobia of bloodshed, which for the conservatives was aggravated by the idea that they had formed of the Revolution and socialism, served to reinforce their dominant obsession – namely their horror of the colour red. But perhaps that would be an over-simplification. The colour red was not attacked except as a 'rallying symbol', but as such it was the focus of severe attention. Countless charges were brought against the more or less deliberate exhibition of the socialist colour, whether flags or posies of wild flowers; even ties and headscarves were involved. This was no doubt just skirmishing, but the skirmishes were indicative of the constant hostilities taking place between the different parties or, rather, as we shall be showing, between the *montagnard* party and the government.

Religion

But before discussing that, we must mention the last of the great misunderstandings, namely, religion.

The *démoc-socs* were, with very few exceptions, quite prepared to call themselves 'religious' and to invoke God's name or even that of Jesus Christ. But what they meant by religion was a humanitarian type of syncretism that embraced every kind of Church and laid the greatest emphasis upon the voice of the conscience of the individual. For the party of order, in contrast, 'religion' was simply a way of referring to the Catholic Church, in the strictest sense, and in the most authoritarian interpretation of its doctrines. The party of order regarded the Catholic religion as a political source of support for the State and its institutions and as a moral inspiration for its propaganda, which thus took on the appearance of a crusade. Consider, for example, the way in which President Bonaparte stigmatised the democrat agitators, following the events of June 1849: 'The time has come for the Good to find reassurance and the Wicked to tremble.' The style is reminiscent of a preacher of 1820.

Given that the 1849 repression was referred to as 'the Rome expedition

into the interior', the tone was not hard to identify even at the time.
Besides, seen from a distance, the intuitive feeling of the conservatives was
quite correct: the red party *was* always strongest in areas where the way
had been prepared for it by anti-Catholic dissidence of one kind or
another, for instance in the zones of 'blue' bourgeois influence, where
attitudes had been stiffened by the anti-*chouan* campaigns (the eastern part
of the Sarthe department was a typical example); or regions with a
Protestant population (parts of the Gard, the Drôme, the Tarn, the
Deux-Sèvres and many others). In those days it was considered quite
normal that blues and Protestants should be devoted to liberal Orleanism
or to a moderate version of the Republic. But, faced with an official
Republic apparently determined to restore the clerical party to power,
even Protestant and free-thinking bourgeois were tending to rally to, or
now ally themselves with, the only opposition party of any strength, the
reds. Now, this process enabled the Catholics, in their turn, to claim that
heresy and free-thinking were sowing the seeds of socialism (which was, in
fact, another very real aspect of the problem) and as a result they were all
the more determined to preach their own 'wholesome' doctrine.

'Preach' really is the word, for the Church was turning out to be one of
the foremost agents of order. But what, in the last analysis, was the party
of order?

Means of action. Propaganda

It was certainly even vaguer in outline and structure than the
'party' of the democratic and social Republic. At the top were the newspapers (*L'Assemblée nationale*, *Le Constitutionnel*, *L'Union*, *L'Univers*, *La Patrie*,
Le Pays and many others besides, a plethora of them, all with varying
nuances of opinion); and the representatives, hundreds of them, whom it
became increasingly difficult to persuade to act in concert. Certainly,
though, there was one committee of influential leaders who continued to
act as a group. This was the old 'rue de Poitiers' band, which had now
regrouped to include men who ranged from Thiers to Berryer, in particular Molé, Guizot and Falloux – all old royalists of diverse inclinations. It
was considered amusing to refer to them, in current slang, as '*les burgraves*',
in memory of the solemn ancients of Victor Hugo's drama of the same
name, which had enjoyed a considerable success as a farce in 1844.
However, *burgraves* are a very different matter from the manipulators of
organisations, and that is a point of essential importance.

The truth was that the conservatives and the *démoc-socs* stood in contrast
to one another as much by reason of their behaviour as by that of their
doctrines and aims. Although the fact was not spotted or a theory
explicitly constructed from it until André Seigfried came along, that
phenomenon underlies the remarks of all the observers of the time: the

democrats were men of Organisation (a strictly egalitarian and, so to speak, horizontal structure) while the conservatives were men of Influence (a structure of vertical relations). From the reactionary prefects and public prosecutors of 1850 to the republican historians of the early twentieth century (Tchernoff and Seignobos, for example), there is not a single description of the red party that is not first and foremost a description of groups within a structure formed from a network of associations, *cercles*, societies, '*chambrées*', lodges, *cabarets*, 'salons' and *brasseries* – the list is interminable. It was a type of sociability based on habit and custom that stemmed from the age-old forms of collective life, and it caused all the large provincial towns of France from Flanders (Lille) and Alsace (Strasbourg) to the south (Toulouse, Marseilles, Toulon) to be viewed with suspicion (a suspicion that was expressed in remarkably similar terms), wherever they happened to be located. In contrast, references to any forms of independent, popular organisations in the conservative camp are most unusual. It has sometimes been suggested that 'white Mountains' in fact existed, but if they did they were extremely rare; or perhaps what was meant by the phrase was the network of good works organised by the Church, but that is rather a different matter. The right-wing press in the provinces, mainly legitimist in attitude, was no less abundant than the democratic press, but it does not appear to have attempted to enlist popular distributors or to penetrate popular *milieux* in the same fashion.

Pamphlets

It will perhaps be objected that, on the contrary, the party of order was extremely concerned to spread popular propaganda, since it published a large number of low-priced pamphlets attacking socialism. These are certainly renowned. But in those days selling such literature or even distributing it to readers or seeing that it was read was not enough to win converts. There is no indication that the notables of the right made anything like the efforts of the militants of the left to master the difficult art of communicating with humble folk; organising little groups, working their way through one village after another. And peasant conservatism must have stemmed more frequently from individual prejudices than from the effect of doctrinal propaganda. On the other hand, it seems highly likely that these pamphlets, together with the other newspapers, did serve to reinforce the convictions of city-dwellers and bourgeois in general. Today, it is these pamphlets more than anything that provide us with a picture of those beliefs. It is in them that we find the red 'party' depicted as something morally and intellectually – indeed almost physically – monstrous. Socialism is represented as 'theft on the largest scale', communism as a summary 'redistribution' which will pitch civilisation right back into a state of primitive savagery, and, above all, the impending electoral outcome of 1852 is seen as an occasion for '*jacquerie*', that is to say an apocalypse of greed and bloodshed.

Some authors proposed remedies for the situation. Most stemmed from a conservatism that was in no way exceptional, but some had the ring of counter-revolution pure and simple, and even went so far as to reject legal values of a quintessentially bourgeois kind. Thus Romieu's *Le Spectre rouge* produced an ordered defence of 'feudalism' in the past and military force in the present. The force that was thus expected to save the situation might have been that of Tsar Nicholas I, who was the primary 'bogey-man' to the 'reds' of Europe and who, it is interesting to note, was at the time enjoying a strange surge of prestige. On the other hand, salvation might equally well come from a national military intervention.

Thus, in some of its exaggerated flights of anti-democratic hatred, the propaganda of the bourgeois order almost went so far as to advocate military dictatorship, despite the professed liberalism, or at least legalism, of its parliamentary founders. We shall return to this contradiction in a later chapter.

Containment, above all

There was a real danger that impassioned conservatism of this kind would one day become as authoritarian in its doctrines as it already was in its practice.

At this period more than any other, past or future, conservatism was firmly tied to the secular tradition of influential leadership of the people in the provinces within a moral framework provided either by the rich notables or by the Church or – in many cases – by both at once. As a white vote was considered to be the 'natural' outcome of these relations of force and daily influence, the party of order deliberately strove not so much to promote political action that would justify its position, as to prevent any political action that would upset it. This accounts for its horror of mass propaganda and organisation and its phobia where societies and teachers were concerned.

> Some were for the Empire, others for the Orléans, others for the comte de Chambord; but they were all agreed upon the need for decentralisation and a number of ways of achieving it were suggested, such as: breaking Paris up into a large number of main thoroughfares so as to establish villages around them, transferring the seat of government to Versailles, concentrating schools at Bourges, doing away with libraries, putting everything into the hands of divisional commanders; and the countryside was lauded to the skies, illiterate man possessed far greater natural commonsense than the rest; and hatred was seething: hatred of primary school teachers and wine merchants, hatred of classes of philosophy, history lectures, novels, red waistcoats, long beards, hatred of all independence, all demonstrations of individualism. For what was necessary was to 'resurrect the principle of authority'. It did not matter in whose

name it was exercised or where it came from so long as it was 'Force, Authority'!

(*L'Education sentimentale*).

Any ethico-social structure on the defensive produces policies that are necessarily repressive. The party of order was not only *in* power, it was also very much the party *of* power. Its rank-and-file leaders, its elected representatives and, more generally, the beneficiaries of its actions may have been notables, but its militants were first and foremost the civil servants and the clergy. It is a point worth stressing, for this connivance between conservatives of all allegiances and the governmental agents, more and more of whom were to become specifically Bonapartist, continued to be the general rule in most departments and communes even after the disagreements that broke out in high places between the men of the Elysée and the *burgraves**.

The country was covered by three networks of civil servants. Each communicated its findings to the various ministers whose desks, like those of the historians who made use of the relevant archives, thus accumulated a mass of information, the richness of which can seldom have been rivalled. Information would pass from the *gendarmerie* squads to their lieutenants and captains etc. and eventually to the Ministry of War; from the police superintendents and mayors to the sub-prefects to the prefects and thence to the Ministry of the Interior; from the justices of the peace to the prosecutors for the Republic to the public prosecutors to the Ministry of Justice. All these officials combined to keep the process moving, each keeping to his own specific role, although things did not always run quite smoothly. In particular, Haussmann, prefect for the Var in 1849–50, and Maupas, prefect for the Haute-Garonne in 1851, both on occasion caused considerable alarm to the leaders of the general departments of public prosecution of Aix or Toulouse by reason of their cavalier attitude to formal legal procedures.

As for the clergy, it needed no encouragement to identify the reds (admittedly with good reason in some cases) as its old opponents from classes and regions with unorthodox attitudes (*mal-pensants*), and it embarked upon its crusade against them with a greater alacrity given that, for the first time in twenty years, it now found itself in close collusion with the authorities. Missions began again, processions to ancient sanctuaries were resuscitated, religious committees were reinstalled in a number of deserted monasteries. It was even dared to hold regional synods and soon, as we shall see, the clergy were to address themselves to the problem of schools.

Les Burgraves (see p. 9, note) had a cast of noblemen who were very old, very proud and very solemn. Any success the play enjoyed was mainly due to its nature as farce.

Regional variations

However, before resuming our general political account, we must linger for a moment over this picture of France around the years 1849–50 and try to rectify its excessively general character and dispel its geographical anonymity. How were the political parties and forces distributed over the various regions of France?

Charles Seignobos sketched in the picture more than half a century ago (in volume VI of Lavisse, which we have already cited several times) on the basis of two sources of evidence: the results of the 13 May 1849 elections to the Legislative Assembly and the reports on the mood of the public compiled and synthesised by the public prosecutors, to which we have referred above. It was an all-too-hastily constructed geography and often a superficial one. Nevertheless it had the rare merit of homogeneity which stemmed from that of its sources. Since those days our knowledge has increased, but not uniformly. We are admirably informed on the subject of public opinion (regarding social and other conditions) in the Gard or the Côte d'Or or in the alpine region, to name but a few. And these profound local or regional analyses have revealed links and processes at work on the basis of which it has been possible to make a number of general extrapolations. Some of the 'generalisations' we have ourselves suggested may well owe much to these studies.

But the fact remains that the bright light thus shed upon one particular region or another understandably plunges neighbouring regions, by contrast, into a relative shadow, so that the overall picture resembles a veritable chequerboard with alternate black and white squares and is, in the end, less easy to decipher. Modern historiography replaces Seignobos' familiar but blurred image with a picture that resembles a cracked mirror.

The 'montagnard' provinces

From Seignobos the reader derives the impression that the Mountain was above all the party of the working class – a widely spread working class, extending from the industrial workers to the artisans in the towns and *bourgs*. We certainly cannot suspect the old republican professor of any sympathy for historical materialism; but all the same he reflected his sources – the reports emanating from the public prosecutors' departments. Now, the fact is that, like their contemporary Marx –although their sympathies lay in different quarters – public prosecutors were obsessed with the class struggle.

But, as we have said, the Mountain's real strength lay in its partial penetration of the rural world. The penetration was not uniform. A straight line running from La Rochelle to Metz could be seen as roughly separating the two zones. To the north and west lay a collection of regions where democracy could claim practically no peasant support, while to the south and east of that line there were strong rural pockets of sympathy which, in conjunction with the urban strongholds, made it possible for the democrats to pick up a large number of votes, and in some places an absolute majority.

A particularly impressive and continuous zone of democratic strength was formed by the departments of the Cher, the Nièvre, and Allier, the Saône-et-Loire, the Jura, the Ain and the Rhône – that is, approximately the centre and eastern centre of France, speaking in geometrical terms, for the area cannot be reduced to the geography of natural regions nor to that of historical provinces.

To the south it bordered on another zone of strength, the Alps (this comprised the Isère and the Drôme) and, although its intensity petered out a bit, it extended right across the Basses-Alpes as far as Mediterranean Provence.

The central zone stretched out through the Haute-Sâone towards Alsace. On the west it continued, skirting the Massif Central, to the west of which there was a further bastion comprising the Haute-Vienne, the Corrèze and the Dordogne. There was, finally, one more area that belonged to the democrats between the Massif Central and the Pyrenees: it stretched from the Tarn to the Pyrénées-Orientales and included the Aude and the Ariège. But we should stress that, quite apart from these strong pockets of democratic support, the party had some representation everywhere in the south. Even in the departments in between those we have mentioned the percentages of support were quite respectable.[8] The only parts of southern and eastern France that really do appear to have been unreceptive to the Mountain were, precisely, the mountain areas, namely the departments of the Doubs, the Hautes-Alpes, the heartlands of the Massif Central, Corsica and the western, Atlantic, side of the Pyrenees.

Following other observers of the period, Seignobos believed he could discern two explanations for this contrasting behaviour on the part of two sections of the French peasantry. The first was purely material: in areas of tenant farming and share-cropping men voted conservative, not because they had no complaints, but because they were 'in the grip of' the local noble or bourgeois landowner; while in areas where a peasant owned the holdings he farmed it was possible to become a red because he was independent. The other factor was a spiritual one, namely the influence of the Catholic clergy which, according to whether or not it had maintained its hold over the minds of the rural electorate, either counteracted the inducements of social origin or, on the contrary, allowed them free rein.

The conservative provinces

In northern and western France, which socialism had still not succeeded in penetrating (except, as we have noted, in the towns and a few *bourgs*) there were also plenty of variations between one region and another.

It was the same party of order, but neither the same type of conservatism nor the same type of notables that reigned on the one hand in the west of the Brittany peninsula, which was often both 'feudal' and clerical, and on the other in the well-to-do bourgeois provinces surrounding Paris, stretching from lower Normandy to Picardy and Champagne. Finally, the regions of the Charente, the Loire valley and the southern part of the Parisian basin, which were hesitantly Orleanist or timidly republican, represent a sort of transition between conservative and radical France.

It would be possible to introduce innumerable modifications and nuances into these descriptions and attempted explanations. But we must repeat that, although each new attempt made since Seignobos has been tested in one or another particular field of application, no incontestable general conclusion has emerged, neither has one been attempted.

Any observer alert, as were those of the time, to factors such as inter-social influences and relations and the facilities offered by various types of sociability, even rural ones, to the circulation of propaganda might feel tempted to describe the opposition between a potentially democratic France and a conservative one as an opposition between the France of the 'villages' and the France of the 'countryside'. It is not a suggestion Seignobos himself takes up, but one that had already appeared in Vidal de la Blache. However, the minority of exceptions to this possible correlation is too strong to allow it to stand.

Separate provincial moods or a unified national one?

Contemporary historians would be more inclined to wonder whether the differences in the political temperaments of the various regions of France did not stem rather from profound cultural differences, that is, in the last analysis, from the residual traces of different nationalities.

Perhaps the confrontation between the *montagnard* south and the France of the party of order was occasioned by an *Occitanie* seeking its identity. However, the answer must be: not at this date, at any rate. Such an explanation is contradicted by the existence of impressive democratic strongholds in central France, in Burgundy, the Nivernais and Berre, all areas directly bordering upon the *langue d'oc* regions, but which do not belong within the same zone.

It is true that, although Seignobos did not pose the question of the '*Midi*' (the south) – of which he was himself a native – he did note in passing that in Alsace the democrats were stronger in German-speaking cantons, while the conservatives were stronger in the French-speaking parts. Similarly, in Brittany the 'French' regions were the most strongly legitimist, while areas where the Breton language prevailed were, relatively, the least inaccessible to republicanism.

Perhaps the democrats, for the very reason that they *were* democrats, were at this period more successful than the conservatives in adapting themselves and their propaganda to popular customs and speech. But there is nothing to prove that they did so deliberately. The fact is that, from a bird's eye view, no correlation of that kind emerges.

The vast and varied area known as '*Occitanie*' includes quite a range of different situations. As for the other regions with strong individual cultures, they do not present a common aspect either. In the Basque country, the Flemish districts and by and large in Brittany, the overall individuality of each of these areas operates in favour of order, because it is intimately linked with a Catholic traditionalism. In contrast, the Catalan area was ultra-red and in Alsace the population was divided up, in a regular fashion, into conservatives, moderate republicans and democrats in accordance with social criteria influenced by their various religious loyalties. Alsace followed the struggles of the democrats of the Rhineland with interest (it was no mere chance that, out of all the French democrats, it was Ferdinand Flocon to whom Marx and Engels were closest at this time), but that was on account not so much of German sympathies on the part of the Alsatians, but rather more of French sympathies and francophilia on the part of the German left. The situation on the Rhine under the Second Republic reflects that of 1789–92 more than it looks forward to the situation of the beginning of the twentieth century.

But that being said, it must be admitted that an analysis of the regional problem from the point of view of the political propaganda of the Second Republic is a task that still remains to be tackled. We have only odd scraps of information at our disposal. Nevertheless, we do believe it significant that the Provençal *félibrige* movement* was not founded until 1854. At the time of the Second Republic its two founding fathers had not yet come together. Joseph Roumanille was an Avignonais kind of emulator of Louis Veuillot, and Frédéric Mistral a distant disciple of Lamartine. So, although the men were friends, they did not agree about politics and, anyway, they both identified and classified themselves in terms of the national parties. It was not until after the catastrophe of 1851 that Mistral

---

*A literary (and at times vaguely political) movement, the aim of which was to preserve and enrich the Provençal language and culture (today known more generally as the Occitan culture).

– by now a disappointed and disenchanted republican – and Roumanille – a clerical conservative liberated by the very victory of his cause – both found themselves ready to turn their backs upon day-to-day politics. At that date, on the basis of the love they shared for the local language, they constructed a whole doctrine of Provençal civilisation that was much more remote from the contemporary scene and perhaps more farsighted. But it remained for a long time too ambitious to have any popular appeal and inspired no politics other than those of an idealistic kind. Perhaps it would be possible to extend this analysis of Provence to other peripheral areas?

To the extent that one might hazard the interpretation that the surge of regionalism in our own day is a substitute for the democracy and socialism that have disappointed the hopes placed in them, one must conclude that at the time of the Second Republic, by contrast, very little thought was devoted to the cultivation of local nationalities for the very reason that much greater hope was placed in the young French Republic.

In fact, everybody wanted to be French: those members of the people who had not reached a stage of thinking for themselves politically voted as Frenchmen, following the lead of the notables and priests who did their thinking for them. And those who were becoming alive to social democracy were fervently expecting an improvement in their lot through the offices of the existing Republic, which would make the France of 1789 accessible to the people as a whole. In 1849–50 the simple people were at last travelling the same path as the bourgeois elite groups of the first Revolution. Like those groups, they were now 'patriots' because they imagined the French regime to be an absolute in terms of political desirability. From that position they slipped without realising it into the belief that France itself held an absolute value.

Algerian 'France'

It was a France that was hoping to expand by incorporating Algeria. As we know, the influence of the army chiefs in the councils of the government was every bit as strong as it had been before 1848. Cavaignac had been summoned to Paris to become Minister for War. He had been replaced in the general government of Algeria by another soldier, Changarnier. Changarnier was to be followed by three other generals, Charon, Hautpoul (another future minister) and Randon. By now the occupation had become definitive. It was thus decided, but by pretermission, to pursue the same policies as before 1848 towards the native population. On the other hand, the Republic introduced new measures with respect to the colonials. In March the provisional government decided to grant them the right to vote, and decided also that the administrative organisation would be remodelled, in progressive stages, upon that of metropolitan France, with departments, prefects and so on. Both these measures appeared to be in tune with the mood of the moment and nobody at the time foresaw how great an obstacle this democratisation of the colonialist micro-society would be when it came to extending justice more generally. Thus, as early as the elections to the Constituent Assembly, an intense political life came into being in Algeria in which most of the *colons* (colonialists) closely combined an attachment to the Republic and freedom of speech with an inveterate hostility towards the natives. As one *démoc-soc* candidate to the Legislative Assembly, dragged from obscurity by A. Julien[9], noted, the programme of the Mountain alternated with declarations of a colonialism of the most inveterate kind. That the historical aftermath of the tradition was to stem from such attitudes is now well known.

Even as early as the Second Republic there were two other circumstances which reinforced this Algerian radicalism. In the first place, at a time when France was thought to be over-populated, with too many urban unemployed and landless peasants, North Africa, about which in truth very little was known, was considered to be inexhaustible, more or less a *res nullius* (property that belonged to nobody). After June therefore, the repressive government fell into the habit of despatching to it crowds of rebel workers considered undesirable in metropolitan France, and any colonialists with socialist theories to try out. Colonial democracy was inevitably reinforced. It was the democracy of people of small resources, in competition with the natives in material living and too under-privileged not to adopt spontaneous attitudes of racial prejudice. Secondly, the slide of the presidential Republic to the right reinforced authoritarian tendencies in Algeria just as it did elsewhere. Now, in Algeria, the power of the general government was power for the military, and the military were particularly disinclined to tolerate electoral success and freedom of the press for republican *colons*. Hence, political life there became a series of polemical debates, incidents, minor provocations and even 'plots' and trials, many aspects of which made Algeria resemble some red department in metropolitan France.

But although the *colons* and the military may have been in disagreement over their politics, they were at one when it came to maintaining and extending their conquest. In the autumn of 1849 a native revolt in the south Constantine area, provoked by excessive taxation, was crushed with a degree of brutality that rivalled anything that had taken place during the Bugeaud period.

As for extending French dominion (the Kabilia expedition of 1851), this was prompted solely by President Bonaparte's need for a campaign to justify the promotion of General de Saint-Arnaud so that he could plausibly be recalled to France and appointed minister with an eye to the *coup d'Etat*. Thus, Algeria in the short term at least, brings us back to our general history. But from a long-term point of view we should not forget the place that it was assuming in the geography of French opinion.

The Antilles

There is not much to say about the other colonies except for the Antilles. Here the problem of slavery was posed in its strongest terms and, for a brief moment, the Second Republic consequently acted decisively. The abolition of slavery was a logical step for the Republic to take and had been one of the legacies from the Convention, before the Consulate had dared to regress. So the spokesmen for the *colons* of the 'old colonies' had been in the habit of following debates concerning their own economic interests in the Chamber of Representatives and ministerial offices. As early as 25 February 1848 those who were in Paris began to besiege Arago. But Victor Schoelcher, who had returned from Senegal a few days after the Revolution, now eloquently reminded the provisional government of its principles. He persuaded it to introduce an under-secretary's office at the Ministry of Marine Affairs (it was, in effect, a Ministry for Colonies, although it was not known by that name). He also obtained a decree abolishing slavery and powers to set up a working party which prepared seriously for the application of the reform, not neglecting to provide for compensation for the *colons* who were being dispossessed of what had hitherto been their 'property'. The April decrees were implemented in a calm atmosphere and it was possible for voting to take place as early as August 1848. Universal suffrage operated, quite normally, in favour of those who had been oppressed, and Victor Schoelcher found himself at the head of two lists of representatives triumphantly elected in Martinique and Guadeloupe. He was allowed to retain his seat for Guadeloupe, where he was re-elected for the Legislative Assembly, at the same time as being a representative for the Seine. In 1850 Schoelcher had to divide his attentions between national politics (where we have already seen the role he played) and defending his work in the Antilles, where reaction set in just as it did everywhere else. The governors were now playing the white planters' game, and there were instances of harassment of the left-wing press, while fiscal policies as a whole were aimed, for example, at making it difficult for black workers to acquire property and forcing them to become wage-earners. All the regime's administrative measures and regulations thus once more operated against the new citizens, who remained proletarians and 'niggers'. This was the source of a whole series of political incidents and episodes in the courts of law.

However, the essential point had been gained. The abolition of slavery, only a marginal issue in Algeria, was a decisive transformation here, and the extension of universal suffrage, only a partial measure in Algeria, here made its effects felt much more deeply: at every popular level of society it brought home the possibilities of both radicalisation and integration. The result was not – to be sure – the end of the colonial system, but a very different type of evolution from that in Africa.

Paris, the centre of fashionable society. The Elysée

Let us return to metropolitan France, where we must now describe the situation in Paris. Paris defies general classification and, as we have several times pointed out, it cannot be considered typical of the country in general. In one sense the capital could be said to be the place where the class struggle was most keenly felt and fought, since it was the great city of workers, the stage for the June days. But while it was certainly the capital of the bourgeoisie it was even more the centre of intellectual life, the headquarters for the leaders of political groups and for the newspapers, the place where doctrines were invented, and where every nuance and complexity was to be found. So it is no paradox to say that in a sense it was also the place that most escaped the class struggle. At a time when most towns in the provinces now recognised only whites and reds, every shade of political opinion, from grey through blue to pink, naturally came to see the light of day in this central cradle of thought and politics.

At all events, within the framework of daily life the atmosphere of revolution gradually faded away. The repaving of the streets and the rebuilding of houses were simply repairing the June days, but then came the moment when the *préfet de police*, Carlier, also set about 'repairing' February: the trees of liberty were uprooted.

Social life resumed, with receptions in high society and an animated life in the big boulevard cafés. There was animated life, too, though of a more discreet kind, in the *cercles* where gentlemen of the aristocracy or the upper bourgeoisie would congregate according to their affinities; and, if Flaubert is to be believed, there were other gatherings in Paris, gatherings which looked forward to the *fête impériale**: 'Some wanted the Empire, others the Orléans and others the comte de Chambord ... The salons of the courte-sans [whose importance dates from this period] were neutral territory where reactionaries of various persuasions would come together ...'

And during the season the whole of Parisian society gathered at the races. The horse was king.

Along the paths of the Bois de Boulogne (which had not yet been taken over, improved and arranged by Haussmann, but were nevertheless already much frequented), the president could be seen almost every day galloping along at the side of Miss Howard, a beautiful English girl who was virtually his official mistress.

Louis-Napoleon, a 40-year-old bachelor, was a man of pleasure by natural inclination, but it was also by deliberate policy that he went in for a certain amount of display and sought to make the Elysée a centre of

---

*For many years this was the classic phrase used to refer to both the general prosperity and also the sparkling social life under the Second Empire. The republicans, however, who tended to take a puritanical attitude, gave Napoleon III's *fête* a rather more pejorative meaning: the phrase '*faire la fête*' for them meant 'pleasure, licence, waste'.

fashionable life. His politics would profit thereby. He was intelligent, not particularly cultivated in a strict sense, but clever and highly experienced, and he was well equipped to exploit private conversation to seduce the hesitant and win them over. Meanwhile, where the more distant spectator was concerned, for example the Parisian 'man about town' with an eye for smart carriages and bright lights, he was keen to create for himself the image of a monarch, one who might – alas – not last for long but who was nevertheless worthy of the tradition. There was no question of a court, but all the same the family was to some extent beginning to rally round. Although one cousin, Napoleon, who was a representative of the people, had taken his seat amid the ranks of the Mountain, Uncle Jérôme lent the president his prestige as a former king and the last surviving brother of the emperor.

The president's half-brother, the duc de Morny, who under Louis-Philippe had pursued his career as a businessman and deputy who had nothing to do with the Bonapartes, now remembered his relationship to the family and also came to join the president's *entourage*, where he was said to shine by reason of his witty sayings and gradually became discreetly useful by dispensing his advice.

Paris, the intellectual centre. Political circles

The Elysée however, did not hold a universal attraction. Among the educated Parisian bourgeoisie it was distasteful both to those who still hankered after a more spartan republic and to those who yearned to re-establish a different kind of court, that is a genuine one, in the Tuileries. There were many such at the *Institut* which was dominated by an intelligentsia that was Orleanist, both because Louis-Philippe had pampered it and also, at a deeper level, because 1830 had been *its* own revolution. The year 1848 had considerably disorientated these academic circles of liberal royalism. It is true that their own great man, Guizot, had at that time taken refuge in London. But Guizot had been back since early 1849 (a sign of the times indeed) and the upper bourgeoisie was now reassembled in full force and – as we shall see – in all its diversity.

There were not many Bonapartists in university circles either. There, the regime was chiefly criticised for the way in which it and the Church supported one another. A new journal was being produced on that basis with the telling name of *La Liberté de penser* (Freedom of Thought). It could not really be called political, but it was indirectly influential and carried articles signed by many prestigious names that were identified with the opposition: Daniel Stern and Eugène Sue, Michelet and Henri Martin, Ernest Renan and Jules Simon, Ernest Bersot and Emile Deschanel.[10] Michelet went even further. He had been won over to the idea of the Republic shortly before 1848. At first he had been explicitly anti-socialist and at that date the materialist view of the French Revolution that Louis Blanc presented had shocked him. Since then, however, as he persevered with the task of editing his works on 1790, 1791, 1792 and 1793, his faith in democracy had grown increasingly profound; and although he did not become actively involved in political life (his private life being now much fuller than it had been before 1848), his thought and feeling inclined towards the Mountain, as did those of his friends Béranger and Lammenais and, above all, his beloved Quinet.*

In the offices of the newspaper editors there was equally active and independent thinking. We should recall that in Paris the press was too diverse and subtle in character to be divided neatly into newspapers on the side of the party of order and socialist newspapers; neither is it possible to give a uniform description of either group. Among those that could not or would not define themselves within the framework of that crude alternative were – to name but three – *Le National, Le Siècle* and *La Presse*.

Emile de Girardin, the publisher of *La Presse*, was something of an original political force on his own account. He was a man with many means at his disposal: intelligent and energetic, with a wealth of journalistic experience as well as a large fortune, and the added advantage of a brilliant position in both fashionable and literary society. His feud with Armand Carrel† in 1836 had cut him off from his natural allies, the men of *Le National*, as was clearly seen in the summer of 1848, when Girardin was one of the few bourgeois to denounce Cavaignac's authoritarian measures. Now, in 1849–50, carried along by the same logic and also attracted by the views of that other sharpshooter, Proudhon, Girardin was evolving towards socialism and even called himself a *montagnard*. Nevertheless, he kept himself somewhat aloof from the Mountain and, through Jérôme-Napoleon, also kept a foot in the door at the Elysée. He is not a figure of the first importance, but can be seen as a convenient symbol of that political life of Paris and 'society' which eluded the simple definitions that could be applied to the battle in the provinces and the strong passions of the city *faubourgs*.

Paris, the people's centre. The workers' movement still active

In the working-class districts of Paris and its suburbs, life went on. It was a depressing life, in its cramped, over-crowded and unhealthy

---

*Béranger, 1780–1857. *Chansonnier*, writer of patriotic, liberal and Voltairian songs which played an important role in the struggle against the Restoration. Lammenais, 1782–1854. A former priest who, having tried to enlist the Church's support for liberalism after 1830, was censured by the Pope and thereafter pursued his own solitary evolution towards the democratic republic. E. Quinet, 1803–75. Professor of literature, historian, philosopher, strongly committed to first the liberal and subsequently the republican movement.

†1800–36. Journalist, first a liberal, then a republican, killed in a duel by Emile de Girardin.

urban setting – the pre-Haussmann setting, in a word – where cholera struck cruelly once again during the course of 1849.[11] So much for daily life. As for politics, there were certainly thousands of families lamenting the deaths and 'deportations' of June; the repression had either imprisoned or exiled the best known of the leaders; and above all it had effectively paralysed all attempts to open clubs or demonstrate in the streets. To that extent, but only to that extent, Paris could be said to have been laid low by the drama of the summer of 1848. Nevertheless, at the same time, hundreds upon hundreds of workers and artisans who were both educated and devoted to the cause had by now had time to be won over to socialism by the Luxembourg Commission as also by the clubs and the press; they were not all in prison and enough socialist publications remained to continue to diffuse the idea and, while their propaganda could not be directly revolutionary, it could still promote socialist ethics and economics.

As we have mentioned, this kind of socialism, which remained more or less lawful, was the socialism of the associations. Gustave Lefrançais was well aware of the situation when he declared: 'Direct revolutionary action, which is now impossible on account of the blood-letting of June, has taken a new form which, while inevitably slower, will be no less fruitful'.[12]

In short, the repression had not halted the action of the workers' movement; it had simply denied it the possibility of expressing itself by erecting barricades, and this had the effect of steering it all the more firmly towards expression through the associations. Of course it is impossible to tell how many of the militants who joined the associations placed full confidence in them, and how many regarded them as no more than a secondary activity, paving the way for the eventual revolution. But what is certain is that many workers' associations, whether of 'communist' or *démoc-soc* inspiration, of a type we would today describe as mutual assistance companies or cooperatives, did exist in large numbers and that in 1850 they were just as common in Paris as they were in towns in the red provinces. They were economic experiments, declared as commercial enterprises and so, although the government kept a close watch on them, it had no grounds for objection. The movement had its ups and downs: it was more flourishing in 1849, when the unemployed flocked to it, and rather less so in 1850, when the economic recovery sent many of the more skilled workers back to private workshops,[13] but it remained strong, imbued with what was at the time known as 'a desire for emancipation' (*un désir d'affranchissement*) and founded upon a combination of class consciousness and a desire for liberty. In October 1851 there were no fewer than 190 socialist-inspired workers' associations in Paris. Militants and publishers of left-wing newspapers took an interest in them. The socialist press encouraged the associations and they, in their turn, discreetly served to maintain some kind of organisation and system of contacts without which it would, for example, be difficult to account for the strength of the mobilisation of Parisian workers on the occasion of the by-elections of the spring of 1850. (That is a subject to which we will return.) Efforts were made to launch newspapers which would express the associations' point of view, and there were even attempts to unite the various associations and establish connections between them. The best known is the *Union des associations des travailleurs* (the Union of Workers' Associations), chiefly organised by Jeanne Deroin (towards the end of 1849). Proudhon's *Banque du peuple* (People's Bank) could itself only have meaning if it was the economic crown to a labour organisation of this kind. Needless to say, both endeavours were prosecuted but, while such prosecutions regularly removed the leaders of all attempts to provide the workers with a central organisation, they did not strike at the roots of the vitality of the cooperative movement.

Towards the end of 1851 the potential dignity and power of the Parisian working class seemed such that Girardin's *Presse* launched the idea of choosing a democrat candidate for the presidential election of 1852 from within its ranks. The man he had in mind was Martin Nadaud, a mason who had migrated to Paris from the Creuse and was the representative for that region. He would have been a good symbol of the alliance between the urban proletariat and the poor province from which he came and which he was radicalising. The *coup d'Etat* was soon to put paid to this initiative, which no doubt would have incorporated every ambivalence inherent in Proudhon's theories on working-class power. The important thing was that around 1850, in a Paris that was in fact more animated than is usually suggested, indications of the coming seething passions of the sixties were beginning to be visible. It was the authoritarian Empire, not the reactionary Cavaignac period, that brought about a veritable split in the hitherto shared history of the workers' movement and what remained of Republican structures.

During 1849 and 1850 political and social life in France was still very much alive, and unless we remember this it is not easy to understand the chain of events that were to lead from the Rome expedition to the 'Coup of 2 December'.

5

Between the conservative order and the Bonapartist order (June 1849–November 1851)

During the autumn of 1848 Louis-Napoleon Bonaparte and the group of *burgraves* of the rue de Poitiers had mutually adopted one another, but the relationship was not a warm one. Victories of their alliance had fallen on 10 December 1848 and 13 May 1849 and they had set about governing together. But the solidarity of interests between them did nothing to attenuate their differences which, on the contrary, became increasingly glaring as they were forced to coexist.

Bonaparte and the bourgeois. 1: an antithesis

The bourgeois leaders of the party of order were solemn, dignified gentlemen, at least so far as their social façade went – 'notables' in all the accepted meaning of the term – and they regarded Bonaparte as some kind of an adventurer. His princely birth impressed them very little, since they were quite convinced, as were all 'well-informed' people at the time, that the son of Queen Hortense was the fruit of an adulterous liaison with Admiral Verhuell.[1] That he had subsequently been a student in Switzerland, a rebel *carbonaro** in Italy, a conspirator and State prisoner in France and a 'special constable'† in England were considered as so many points against him rather than in his favour by these people for whom romantic adventure outside the covers of a novel was considered to be in rather bad taste.

These bourgeois were quite satisfied with the existing social order. They were definitely unwilling to endanger free enterprise in any way to help those who had lost their livings, displaying a measure of hesitation only over the alternatives of dispensing charity, philanthropy or dogmatic encouragement to resignation. Bonaparte in contrast had in the past entertained grandiose projects for ways to 'eliminate pauperism'.

*See p. 50, note. The Charbonnerie also existed in Italy among conspirators and in the prisons.
†Voluntary citizen police force formed in London to put down Chartist subversion, if necessary.

These bourgeois were statesmen, indeed men of the State, for whom politics were a matter of relations between monarchs, chambers and councils. Their perception of problems concerning the masses, the country as a whole or nationality was much less clear. Bonaparte, in contrast, was more sensitive not only to social problems but also to the people and the nation.

Perhaps one could sum up by saying that the culture of the gentlemen from the upper bourgeoisie was cold, rationalistic and classical, whereas Bonaparte had romantic affinities and sensibilities. It is true that they could quote Greek and Latin a thousand times better than he, but then his grasp of foreign languages and the practical sciences was better than most of theirs.

Finally, the notables of the party of order were jurists and parliamentarians. It was doctrinal conviction in some cases, necessity and habit in others, that had made them liberals, men of the rostrum, men of discussion and legality. Bonaparte, on the other hand, was no orator and had he been one would still have remained faithful to his own family myth, his personal destiny committed to undivided command and disdainful of all forms of collegial power.

It is difficult to see how Guizot's successors at the head of the French ruling class found it possible to adopt as their leader a man who was the living antithesis of Guizot himself. The only possible explanation must be the common danger they faced: the democratic upsurge that made itself felt at the end of 1848.

Bonaparte and the bourgeois. 2: equivocations

The situation has been described already: the rue de Poitiers' committee had not been able to come to an understanding with Cavaignac and there was no single individual among its members who was sufficiently well known to take on the challenge of universal suffrage. They – quite correctly – considered Bonaparte to be alien to their own particular world, but they believed him to be a mediocre individual who would be easily led: here they were quite wrong. But, from the opposite point of view, we must ask ourselves what can have been Bonaparte's reasons for accepting the pact. The answer must be that he wanted power and he knew that, once the notables had helped him to secure it, he would be able to retain it even against their opposition. In the light of similar relationships entered into at other periods of French history – between Louis-Philippe and the revolutionaries of July 1830, Adolphe Thiers and the monarchists of the 1871 Assembly or Charles de Gaulle and the partisans of French Algeria in 1958 – the presidential rise of Louis Bonaparte seems but one of a series of historical instances of one party in the compact taking the other for a ride.

Another point is that the compact only made sense so long as the party of order felt threatened by democracy. This is one of the keys to an understanding of the period.

Bonaparte and the *burgraves* were alternately in alliance or in opposition, depending on whether the red peril, their common adversary, appeared imminent or distant.

As for whether Bonaparte wanted power in order to follow his personal star, or whether the fulfilment of his destiny answered a more rational and more collective need – and if so, what? – is a question that we have to defer discussing for the moment.

The effects of joint repression

For nine months (June 1849–March 1850), uncertainty continued to reign.

Repression

The president and the party of order (represented by the strong conservative majority that dominated the Legislative Assembly and also by the ministers of Odilon Barrot's cabinet, which had been slightly re-shuffled in June), were in agreement on the essential issue: the repression of democratic propaganda.

A state of siege was declared in departments where disturbances had taken place on 13 June. Those representatives who had taken part in demonstrations on the boulevards were stripped of their mandate and transferred to the High Court of Justice. A new law on clubs was passed, to remain in effect for a year (but with the possibility of prolongation; and it was indeed renewed in 1850). It gave the government the right to prohibit any club or public meeting. (The rest of the laws that had been passed in July 1848 remained unchanged.) Finally, on 27 July, a law concerning the press established a number of new criteria for political offences – for instance, insulting the President of the Republic – while another on distribution by carriers made this subject to prefectorial authorisation.

The first signs of disagreement

But it was not long before discordant notes were sounded. On 18 August 1849, the president wrote to his personal friend, Edgar Ney, who was also an heir to the Empire, and who was in command in Rome. In this letter he declared that the French presence in the Papal states should not be understood as providing support for total reaction. It was published on 7 September and it created a sensation among the public, as it had done earlier when it burst upon the council of ministers. It proved, at one stroke, that the president had ideas of his own, that where foreign policies were concerned his were more to the left than those of the Catholic notables and, finally, that Bonaparte was not going to be a puppet Head of State. The prudent liberalism of this French diplomacy was revealed by a number of other indications too. Tocqueville, who was in charge of it at the time, was trying to check Austro-Russian reaction, following the defeat of the Hungarian patriots and, with England's support, was at least successful in winning the concession that Kossuth, who had fled to Turkey, should be allowed to transfer to London rather than to the prisons of Vienna or St Petersburg.

But the essential point was the crack that had appeared in the French constitutional system. After this warning it was not hard to guess that the parliamentary regime which had been established in the spring of 1849 (with its ministry composed in accordance with the majority, following the tradition established the previous year by the Constituent Assembly) would now depend upon the consent of the president much more than upon the letter of the Constitution, even though the latter was clearly based on the presidential system. This became quite clear when, on 31 October, Louis Bonaparte sent a message to the Assembly announcing that he was forming a ministry in accordance with his own views and which would be accountable to himself alone; and that henceforth the Assembly would be required to limit itself to its essentially legislative responsibilities.

Odilon Barrot's ministry (containing most notably Falloux, Tocqueville, Dufaure and Faucher) was replaced by a team deliberately picked for its less brilliant qualities which would guarantee its greater dependence upon the president. The (nominal) head of this 31 October ministry was General Hautpoul. Ferdinand Barrot (thereafter known as 'Cain' for having played a rotten trick on his brother) was entrusted with the Interior, Rayneval with Foreign Affairs, Baroche with Justice, Fould with Finances, de Parieu with Education and Religion, and J.–B. Dumas with Commerce. The last four named were believed to be very close to the president and even to constitute the nucleus of an 'Elysée party'. The majority in the Assembly was shocked and for a few weeks tension followed. But, after all, the party of order was still represented in the Council by a number of royalists of varying nuances and there was still no prospect of these burying their differences so as to mount a united opposition to the president. Such a protest would have had no legal footing, and anyway it was not believed that there would be any change in Bonaparte's politics.

So the majority reconciled itself to the ministry of 31 October and pressed on with its chief concern, which was the law on education.

The Falloux law

A law was needed to resolve the confusion surrounding policies towards the universities, since none of the post-Napoleonic monarchies had managed to do so. Two conflicts in fact overlapped, one between freedom for teaching and the university monopoly, the other between the spirit of freedom of thought and Catholic-inspired dogmatism. However, these conflicts were not logically congruent, as freedom of thought was considered to be better – or less inadequately – assured in the universities than in the religious colleges. Hence, the true liberals (that is, those who were for freedom of thought) favoured the university monopoly while the clerical party raised the banner of freedom for teaching. It will be remembered that, despite passionate conflict, this state of affairs had persisted under Louis-Philippe. At the very end of the reign Guizot had definitely inclined towards the 'Jesuits'; one of his last mistakes had been the banning of Michelet's lectures at the Collège de France. The Revolution of February 1848 had produced a movement of secular revenge: Michelet was restored to his chair and Carnot was installed at the Ministry of Public Instruction. We have already noted how Carnot's eviction from that ministry in August 1848 had been one of the earliest clear indications of the beginning of the reaction – a conservative reaction with a strong clerical element.

But the teaching problem was not simply a conflict that had been flaring up periodically in a series of episodes ever since 1808. There were now new and specific aspects to it, connected with the progress that had been made in primary schooling. It will be remembered that this owed much to Guizot – the Guizot of 1833 – for he had made it obligatory for each commune to run its own primary school, leaving it free to entrust it, as it so wished, either to secular or to religious teachers. During the 1830s it was deemed important to inculcate the people with some elementary ideas of culture and morality, but they were still considered to be quite beyond the sphere of politics. Indeed, the census-based system of suffrage did bar that sphere to them, and so the implicit philosophy of their teachers had very little impact upon the progress of public affairs. The whole situation clearly changed in 1848 with the advent of universal suffrage. If the peasant was an elector, the teacher who helped to shape his mind inevitably found himself promoted to a level of responsibility analogous to that of the priest or the doctor, the *cabaret* proprietor or the notary: he became a guide to opinion, a man who controlled many votes, a small-scale notable. Thus, the almost 50-year-old quarrel over the *lycées* (secondary schools) was now extended to a similar argument over the commune schools.

It is well known on what basis the solution was found. Secular conservatives, for the most part traditionally Orleanist, and clerical conservatives, mostly legitimist, suspended their quarrels in the face of the 'social peril'.

Indeed, they went further: they agreed upon a diagnosis of the situation. They held it to be a proven fact that a spirit of free examination, especially among the poor, was an encouragement to socialism and that only teaching on a religious basis could inculcate a solid respect for order and property in minds that were without it. Montalembert devoted to these themes an eloquence which at least had the merit of being founded upon an ancient and sincere religious faith. But Thiers and his friends had undergone a rationalist training and were themselves not believers, so for them it was a veritable conversion. As René Remond has noted, this was the first example of a group of men and a trend of opinion that were initially leftist passing over to the right. It was a process that was to recur several times in the later course of French history. Their conversion was a confession of impotence. But was it really not possible to found a system of instruction promoting social order upon rationalist principles? Jules Ferry later attempted to do so, with some success. But Thiers was not a man of powerful intellect and this year of 1848 had most certainly filled him with panic. 'Let us hasten to cast ourselves into the arms of the bishops, they alone can save us ...' The bishops had opened their arms wide and had insisted that Falloux should enter the ministry of January 1849, where he represented not so much the legitimist group as the Church.

In this way social fear robbed the secular camp of a number of conservative bourgeois and altered the previous relations of power. This made it possible for the Church to enjoy a success that they had long been seeking in vain.

Their success was scored particularly at the expense of the school teachers. The thousands of 'appalling little orators' were considered largely responsible for the red peasant vote. In our opinion, this was a very exaggerated view of the situation at the time: in the regions where we have undertaken a close examination of the process of the radicalisation of the rural masses through the influence of the notables, we have come across far fewer school teachers than true bourgeois – doctors, notaries, even the scions of leading families. But the phenomenon of the socialist school teacher was widely believed and, besides, the law could only get grips upon the school teacher; it could not touch the independent notable.

In short, following their negative success with the dismissal of Carnot and the abandonment of his project for the development of primary teaching (by making the teaching programmes obligatory, free and secular), the party of order set about their own task at the beginning of 1849. Falloux set up an extra-parliamentary study committee presided over by Thiers, in which Victor Cousin and Mgr Dupanloup were the foremost participants. Their prolonged efforts, which lasted for the whole of 1849 and were from time to time interrupted by the political crises that we have described, now at the beginning of 1850 resulted in two laws. The first and more simple of the two, known as 'the little law' or the Parieu law, was passed on 11 January 1850 and settled the fate of primary teaching. It was made as easy as possible for *congréganistes** to become teachers (the certificate of competence could be replaced by the *baccalauréat* or waived in virtue of being a minister of religion, or by a *certificat de stage†* or even, in the case of nuns, by no more than a letter of obedience). Above all the administrative authorities were entrusted with surveillance of the teachers. The prefects were thus enabled to revoke wrong-thinking (*malpensants*) teachers in their hundreds.

As for the matter of the university, that was more complex and the 'Falloux law' (which for historical purposes kept the name of its initiator even though he was no longer minister by the time the vote was taken) was not adopted until 15 March 1850. President Bonaparte did not want the institution established in Napoleon's time to be totally abandoned, while the Catholics for their part were not convinced that complete liberty would operate in their favour. Thanks to these feelings of reticence and doubt, the existence of the university was saved, although it became a university fragmented into a number of departmental academies on the councils of which a bishop would sit *ex officio*. But although the university continued to exist, freedom for teaching was also introduced, since anybody with an ordinary Bachelor's degree could open a school and no special qualifications were necessary for those who taught in it. The university retained authority over the marking of examinations. The system was thus a complex one but its trend was obvious: the law 'favoured the Church both outside the university, with a liberty that was granted to the Church alone, and also within the university itself, since the practical privileges granted to it enabled it to oppose the university' (A. Prost).[2]

But the law's complicated nature, which was the result of a compromise, was inevitable, since it emanated from a party of order that was itself composite, given that it was the product of a recent coalition.

The effects of the Falloux law

The important point was that by making clericalism one of the master elements in the conservative system the Falloux law had the counter-effect of solidly uniting those who defended secularity for the schools and a democratic programme for the State.

From this point of view the law was an important event. While its aggressive measures were – as is well known – to be moderated thirty years later, the moral situation that it created in French politics was to last for

*Members of a religious congregation, or order, devoted to teaching.
†A document vouching for a measure of teaching experience, even if very brief. Easier to obtain than a diploma.

more than a century. However, we should at this point modify our analysis: the immediate result of the law was a plethora of new church schools and colleges which contributed not a little towards the impression France gave in 1850 and 1851 of a Catholic renaissance. The impression was to some extent paradoxical, since the clerics 'thus busied themselves with developing a free teaching system in competition with the public system at the very moment when they no longer had any cause to complain of the latter'.[3]

All the same, the communal *lycées* and colleges did manage to preserve an atmosphere somewhat different from that of the Catholic establishments and thus to offer a safeguard to those who were resisting the Church. In this way, as was pointed out many years ago, the Falloux law truly did inaugurate the era of 'two categories of youth' (two categories of French students brought up separately within the rival systems of the university and the Church). Now, this was a deep division between two philosophies. The Catholic crusade had now become something quite different from the fight against socialism, which is how it had begun. For militant Catholics of the time, such as Louis Veuillot, a Voltairian, Protestant or Jewish bourgeois was an enemy to be fought or a soul to be won just as much as a socialist was. Favoured as it was initially by the climate of social fear and a desire to defend conservatism, at first the Falloux law seemed to offer the Church the chance of a much more profound victory: its revenge upon the Enlightenment. This was a theme that Victor Hugo developed, with more grandiloquence than success, in the famous speech he delivered to the Legislative Assembly. He was, fundamentally, quite right: it was no longer just a matter of economics, order and property. The Falloux law had moved from the terrain of the class struggle into that of the wars of religion. It had been promoted so as to wipe out 1848, but had now reached the point of contesting 1789.[4]

All this may seem exaggerated. We would simply like to suggest that in this year of 1850, at the very moment when it seemed quite clear (to Karl Marx, for example) that French society was going to divide along clear social lines (the people against the bourgeois and socialism against liberalism), traditional politics had brought another split to the surface: for or against the spirit of 1789. The fact that these two types of division do not coincide was to prove a decisive factor in the complexity of French politics, both at this period and, even more, in the future.

The political turning-point of the year 1850

The passing of the Falloux law marked the climax of the movement of conservative reaction begun in June 1849 and continued on the part of majority and president alike (despite a number of differences between them). However, at this very point a series of changes began that was to transform the immediate political situation yet again.

The by-elections and the law of 31 May
The period of March to September 1850 thus represents a turning-point in the history of the conservative Republic.

On 10 March elections were held to fill the seats of the *montagnard* representatives who had been stripped of their mandate after the 13 June affair. Twenty-one of the red seats were at stake. Eleven *montagnards* and ten conservatives were elected. Nowadays such a result would certainly be regarded as no more than satisfactory by the party in power, since it deprived the opposition of ten seats. But we have now for a long time been accustomed to universal suffrage and its role as a political thermometer. In 1850 things were different. The only thing that seemed clear at that time was that, despite a year of political containment, *montagnard* opinion had not totally collapsed; so it was not simply a passing aberration but a tenacious evil that had taken root. Furthermore, for reasons that are obvious, the Parisian vote was considered more important than that of the provinces. Now, in Paris the reds had held on particularly successfully, managing to retain all three seats in question there. A list of three candidates skilfully composed and supported from all sides (which – horror of horrors – implied a certain degree of concerted action) consisted of Carnot, the erstwhile minister, a vaguely socialist but principally secular republican and a fervent opponent to the Falloux law; F. Vidal, a former secretary to the Luxembourg Commission and a journalist who was in favour of Fourier; and P. Deflotte, another socialist journalist. It was Deflotte, above all, who caused alarm. He had been a prominent figure in the insurrection of June 1848, where he had simply been trying to evaluate the situation and if possible to intervene to avoid a massacre; his only reward was to be placed under arrest and then to spend several months in the process of being 'deported'. So the man for whom the capital was voting was not, strictly speaking, a 'June insurgent' but simply a socialist militant and a man of deep convictions. But the bourgeois, in their state of panic, made no such fine distinctions. There was worse to come: Vidal was also elected in the Bas-Rhin and decided to take up this seat so there had to be yet another election for a seat in the Seine department, on 28 April. It was now the party of order's turn to exploit a symbolic figure and the candidate they put forward was a shopkeeper by the name of Leclerc, a National Guardsman who had fought for order in June 1848 and whose two sons had followed him into battle and there been killed. The left put up Eugène Suë to oppose him. He was the son of a rich family and a successful novelist, but he was a sincere convert to socialism and was the author of effective propaganda for the cause. The combination of his personal and political fame won him an overwhelming victory and bourgeois opinion was even more appalled than it had been on 10 March: the herald of socialism had defeated the hero of order.

The conservatives concluded that containment was still not sufficiently strong and that universal suffrage was incorrigible. The result of their conclusion took the form of two new laws. It was the poorer sector of the press that was the target. The law of 8 June made it impossible for it to survive by increasing the stamp tax and increasing the compulsory deposit it had to pay (to mention only the principal measures). Meanwhile, the section of the electorate that was affected was also the poor: to be included on the electoral lists it was necessary to be paying personal tax (this excluded all those who were indigent), never to have been convicted for however trivial an offence (which excluded all the ordinary people who were constantly in conflict with the *garde champêtre* as well as a large number of militants harrassed by the authorities) and to have been domiciled in a single place for three uninterrupted years (which excluded all those who had been uprooted, all migrants and all those who were unemployed and were seeking work by moving from one town to the next). The left was scandalised by the hypocrisy of the law (in effect it re-established the principle of census-based voting but did so by imposing 'technical' conditions without the right to vote ceasing to be reputed to be universal). It was also shocked by the provocative terms used to justify the law (Thiers' insulting references to 'the multitude, the vile multitude'). The Mountain embarked upon a fine oratorical campaign against the law and the republican newspapers and *cercles* launched a massive petition which within a few days obtained about 500,000 signatures.[5] When the law came up to be passed, the opposition managed to collect 241 votes (it had only managed 223 against the Falloux law and 183 against the state of siege in 1849), but the party of order bloc remained far stronger with 400 votes.

The application of the law of 31 May reduced the electoral body by almost one-third. The number of electors fell from roughly 9,600,000 to 6,800,000.

Were the two and a half million members of the proletariat who were eliminated all reds? That is by no means certain. But the important point to note is that they were believed to be. Whether this was considered a cause for rejoicing or for lamentation, it was generally taken for granted that the Mountain would now be unable to win the 1852 elections.

From this point onwards the whole political game was changed.

The left is driven back to conspiracy

For the opposition it was a blow struck against the optimism and legality that, in the previous chapter, we have noted as being characteris-

tic both of essential *démoc-soc* ideology and of the prevailing circumstances
of 1849–50. It was certainly by no mere chance that, after 31 May
especially, there was once again much talk of secret societies. Was it all a
myth or were they real? It was to some extent a myth in the sense that,
faced with twice as much administrative harassment, societies, *cercles*,
clubs, *chambrées* and other meeting-places where politics were discussed
now concealed this fact. They were therefore called 'secret' but it was not
really a fair application of the term. On the other hand there was also
some truth in it: there can be no doubt that some republicans (although
fewer than was claimed at the time) certainly did return to their old
conspiratorial ways, that is to the 'secret societies', although these should
really be described as 'initiatory' societies. Members would be recruited
with great circumspection, the information passed on concerning the ends
and means of the society would be partial and graduated, a solemn oath of
loyalty and obedience would be sworn, pass-words circulated and arms
collected. It thus transpires that, even in the most remote depths of the
countryside, peasants would be taken on a moonless night, blindfolded, to
some isolated sheep-fold where, with a hand placed on two pistols
arranged in the form of a cross, they would swear loyalty to the New
Mountain.

In October 1850 in Lyons the police arrested Adolph Gent, the former
democrat representative for the Vaucluse, who was establishing liaisons
between the societies in the south-east and Switzerland. All the essential
information regarding the networks in the Rhône valley, the Alps, Provence and southern Languedoc was in this way discovered. It became
known as the 'Lyons' or 'south-eastern' plot and it occasioned many
arrests which were followed, in the spring of 1851, by a large trial. The
sentences passed were heavy, despite the fact that no concrete evidence of
preparations for an offensive rebellion was found, only a network of
liaisons. Gent and two other leaders were condemned to deportation to
Nuka-hiva, a small island belonging to the Marquesas archipelago – in
other words the antipodes – an isolation of fabulous proportions for that
time and which made a profound impression upon the public.

With the efficiency of its police, the severity of its justice and its
legislation well and truly amended, the party of order could rest easy.
That is why, with their rear protected, the president and the *burgraves* were
once again in a position to indulge in their games of rivalry. In fact, it is
this which makes the new situation quite different.

The Elysée embarks upon its campaign

The initiative came from Bonaparte whose ambitions now began
to be revealed. He was entertaining more and more at the Elysée and
army leaders were received with particular attention. He also played up to

the ordinary soldiers, paying visits to barracks, reviewing the troops and bringing such glorious days to an end with lavish distributions of red wine and sausages. The bourgeois journalists might well jeer at these clumsy tricks, but the common trooper who was used to sadder duties was immensely grateful.

The president also made appearances in the provinces: in July 1850 he made a grand tour of the east, from Alsace to Burgundy, taking in the Franche-Comté and Lyons. In September there was a tour of Normandy. He knew how to linger in the fields to the acclaim of the peasants and also how to cope with demonstrations in the towns when hostile democrats shouted 'Long live the Republic!' and in some places (Strasbourg, and Besançon, for instance) came close to jostling him. And he knew how to say the right things in the right places: in the republican east he would pose as guarantor of the constitution (which could be interpreted as an indirect criticism of the law of 31 May, passed by the Assembly); in conservative Normandy, meanwhile, he would express his hopes for the continuity that was so necessary (which suggested how advantageous it would be to re-establish a monarchical system that revolved around his own person).

However, the most important thing was to meet the immediate problem: in order to become Emperor eventually, it was necessary to make sure that he would not cease to be president in 1852. Now, the Constitution prohibited re-election. So the Constitution had to be changed: the order of the day for Bonapartism was its revision. The president tried this method out. The prefects, who were becoming increasingly devoted to him, were given the task of inciting the general councils in their summer session (August 1850) to vote in favour of proposals for revision. This plebiscite of notables produced gratifying but insufficiently complete results. From eighty-three departments fifty-two revisionist proposals were forthcoming. The majority was good enough for the purposes of government but not for a plebiscite (even an official one) to authorise a total upheaval.

The president did not rule out methods of a less dignified nature. His movements around Paris were increasingly accompanied by a train of followers acclaiming him and capable of coming to blows with (or even bludgeoning) any passers-by who produced hostile (that is say republican) cries. This unofficial police force was an organised one: it was known as the '10 December Society' (so called to exalt the memory of the great 1848 election). Marx later diagnosed its appearance as another emanation of the sub-class of the underworld and Daumier immortalised its repellent character with the figures of Ratapoil and Cazemajou*.

The conservative notables were not at all pleased with all this; as

*Caricatures, created by Daumier, of Bonapartist thugs.

royalists, they recognised a competitor on the horizon; as liberals (where these rare cases existed), they feared a dictator.

So now parliamentary skirmishes started up again and they were considerably more lively and more frequent than they had been in the summer and autumn of 1849. At first they were concentrated upon the allowance granted to the Head of State. He was spending a great deal, both on himself and on his propaganda. He had returned to France at the end of 1848 without any great personal wealth and had lived on the credit afforded him by a number of financiers, one of whom was Fould, who had been dazzled by his name and political hopes. In short, he had fallen into debt and was known to be vulnerable on that score. In the Assembly, there were demands for increases which were either refused or eventually granted unwillingly, with delays and compromises. There were unpleasant tensions between the friends of the *burgraves* and the group of Bonapartist conservatives, which was growing as it kept pace with the mounting activism of the president. This group was now known as the 'Elysée party'. The tensions soon became centred on the question of the army – its discipline and its loyalties.

The failure of dynastic fusion and the conservative split

The Changarnier affair was to be, in a sense, 'the beginning of the end'. But before that point was reached, a new factor emerged to further complicate the fluid circumstances of the summer of 1850. On 26 August, Louis-Philippe died at his residence in exile in England. Would this prove the opportunity to reconcile the elder branch of the Bourbons with the Orléans? Louis-Philippe had a fine line of descendants whereas the comte de Chambord had none. It was conceivable that, in the event of a restoration, the comte de Chambord might rule France and subsequently name as his successor as head of the house of France his distant cousin, the comte de Paris who was the grandson of Louis-Philippe. This possibility would in itself increase the 'credibility' and the chances of a restoration. In short, the project of fusion between the royalists would have raised the existing alliance between legitimists and Orleanists, now known as the 'party of order', to a dynastic level; its success would have been a severe blow both to the Republic and to Bonaparte. The moderates in the two royalist camps, Guizot on the one hand, Berryer and Falloux on the other, worked hard to bring the fusion about. But there were difficulties: Chambord and a whole intransigent wing of the white party refused, as they later also did in 1870, to make the concessions that were vitally necessary: the acceptance of a tricolour flag and of a liberal constitution. There was also reticence on the part of the Orleanists, although for different reasons. Thiers had revised his opinion on the presidential election. He now maintained, with a measure of reason, that in 1852 an Orléans prince – either Aumale or Joinville*, both men in the prime of life, intelligent and with the advantage of their military prestige of fairly recent date – could do very well and even, without too many clashes, win a throne for their nephew (as well as a ministry for Thiers himself). Thus, most of the Orleanists who surrounded Thiers were less keen to revise the Constitution than to fight for the abrogation of the law that exiled the princes and thereby prevented them from presenting themselves to the people of France.

What with one thing and another, the fusion was a failure. It is fair to say that, towards the end of 1850, this renewed dynastic conflict, by creating a breach at the very heart of the royalist camp, accentuated the decomposition of the party of order and thereby increased the chances of the Elysée.

The rise of Bonapartism

The autumn of 1850 marked the real beginning of the political period dominated by the prospect of a *coup d'Etat*.

The army and the Changarnier affair

A *coup d'Etat* implies the use of force, and the most obvious force is that of the army. From this point onwards quarrels surrounding the generals were just as important as the constitutional struggles. It was a sign of the times.

There were hardly any Bonapartists in the high command. The active generals were too young to have served under Napoleon I. Those who, through personal inclination or family traditions, held definite political views were either republican (Cavaignac) or legitimist (Changarnier). But most were simply patriots without any other particular loyalties and they had grown accustomed to the Orléans. It is true that in the lower ranks the Elysée propaganda had made a few conquests. However, the key figure was clearly the commander-in-chief of the army in Paris. Reactionary policies had raised General Changarnier to this post. He was a conservative of legitimist inclinations, a man of ambition with dreams of becoming the sword and buckler of the Legislative Assembly in the same way as Cavaignac had filled that role for the Constituent Assembly.

If anybody had the means to oppose a *coup d'Etat*, it was Changarnier.

*The duc d'Aumale and the prince de Joinville: the younger sons of Louis-Philippe, brothers to the duc d'Orléans, the heir to the throne who died in 1842; they were thus the uncles of the comte de Paris (born in 1838), the duc d'Orléans' son, and in his turn heir to the monarchical aspirations of the Orléans family.

However, hardly anyone in the Assembly could see him as a champion of the Constitution. From the democratic point of view, which paid less attention to the subtleties of Parisian distinctions, Changarnier was seen as a military man of the right with very little sympathy for the people. As we have seen, his name was bracketed in popular songs with that of Radezki.

A review of troops at the military camp of Sabory was the occasion on which battle was joined. The date was 10 October 1850. During the file-past a number of regiments raised the cry of 'Long live the Emperor!' Others remained silent. General Neumayer, who had been responsible for making sure that the latter respected the regulations, was thereupon relieved of his command by order of the president. Great excitement followed. On 2 November Changarnier decided to come to Neumayer's defence by issuing, in the form of an order of the day, a public reminder that it was forbidden to shout slogans when carrying arms. It was a direct reproach to the unofficial propaganda of Bonapartism. At first the president's response seemed to be to draw back; he even changed his Minister for War. Changarnier enjoyed, indeed gloried in his triumph. In the salons and corridors of power his mocking references to the president, that 'melancholy parrot' were much bandied about, as were his boastful declarations as a guardian of the Law ('The president? I will have him taken to Vincennes ...').

The counter-attack came on 3 January 1851: now it was Changarnier who was relieved of his command. There was an outcry of indignation from the majority. The *burgraves* laid siege to Bonaparte with their complaints; even the ministers were alarmed and tendered their resignations. A long-drawn-out crisis ensued from which the president, who held on tenaciously, emerged victorious. On 24 January, he installed a ministry made up of figures even more obscure and more devoted to him than their predecessors. It was known as the 'little ministry'. The new team certainly came up against the distrust of the Assembly, where a majority was found to vote against it. (Most of the conservatives voted with the left, against the current power; only a minority of the old party of order, together with the friends of the Elysée, voted in favour.) But, as we know, there was nothing to compel the president to pay any attention.

The Changarnier affair was more important than it might appear. Not only had Bonaparte demonstrated his determination, not only had the obstacle that Changarnier represented been swept aside, but the party of order had been split.

Disarray in the Assembly

The Assembly, which two years earlier had consisted of two opposed blocs, about 200 democrats against more than 500 sympathetic to the party of order, was now divided roughly into four: republicans, Orleanists (who inclined more towards the left), legitimists (who were more or less hostile to the existing power) and the Elysée party. These were unstable groups: there were many different nuances and many comings and goings. Political life consequently now became much more complicated and esoteric. It was a period of contradictory majorities formed from alliances which were made, unmade and made again depending on the particular issues at stake. One result of this fluidity was the reintroduction of the republicans into the political game, since, in combination with other groups of one kind or another, they sometimes found themselves on the side of the winning vote. But this also proved a divisive factor for them for while a number of republicans – a minority, it would seem – continued to rest all their hopes in the popular struggle (to resist any *coup d'Etat* that might be attempted and at all events to demand and win the universal right to vote in 1852), others were placing increasing trust in the parliamentary fight where the friends of Thiers were adding their votes to those of the republicans more often than in the past.

The effects of such contradictory majorities were clear as early as February 1851. Within the space of a few days, three successive majorities, each differently composed, rejected 1. the president's claim for entertainment expenses; 2. the republicans' proposal for an amnesty and 3. the Orleanists' request for the exile of the princes to be revoked.

Failure for revision

However, the *coup d'Etat* did not take place immediately. In fairness to Bonaparte it should be recognised that he did make one more attempt to accomplish his ends by using a regular procedure. But the regular procedure in question was doomed to equally regular failure.

The spring of 1851 saw the relaunching of the revisionist campaign. This time the prefects did not work through general councils but circulated petitions among citizens.

These met with varying success in the different provinces, depending on the influence of the various parties there. The party of order was hesitating between three alternatives: (1) rejection of revision of any kind (which was, needless to say, also the line taken by the republicans); (2) acceptance of a partial revision limited to the clause whereby the president was at present ineligible for re-election (which was enough to satisfy Bonaparte at this point); (3) total revision (which was supported by the intransigent legitimists). There were rather less than one and a half million signatures for revision, mostly from the regions of Champagne, Lorraine, Normandy and the Aquitaine basin.

Bonapartism had little popular success in the south, where its campaign succeeded only in provoking a counter-campaign on the part of the republicans, who relaunched their petition for the abrogation of the law of 31 May. Although here and there, in the Gard for example, it won over a number of legitimists who were in favour of 'appealing to the people', this second circulation of the republican petition was not as successful as that of May 1850. Repression and discouragement had taken their toll over the past year.

Whatever the successes of these popular reactions however, the decision fell to the Assembly which, according to the terms of the Constitution, could embark upon the procedure of revision only with a three-quarters majority.

Since the republicans themselves made up more than a quarter of the voters, revision was most unlikely to win, and Bonaparte can hardly have believed that it would. That is why, at the very moment when the Assembly was beginning to debate the issue, he made a disturbing speech at Dijon in which he set all the public good that he was anxious to do against the obstacles that the Assembly presented. It could be seen as an omen of the impending *coup d'Etat*.

The vote was taken at the end of July, and 446 votes were cast in favour of revision; they came from those faithful to the Elysée and from most of the conservatives, legitimists as well as Orleanists. Against revision there were 278 votes, cast by republicans, liberal Orleanists (following Thiers' line) and a handful of legitimists who were holding out for all or nothing. These 278 votes represented overall an expanded republican left, while the 446 represented a weakened party of order. As the constitutional threshold of three-quarters was not reached, revision was rejected and the only alternatives now were a *coup d'Etat* or Bonaparte constitutionally relinquishing office in a year's time.

The latter was out of the question and we now come to the phase of direct preparation for the counter-revolution.

Important political manoeuvres

A number of technical preparations were made: Saint-Arnaud won the rank of *général de division* in Kabylia, so that he could be recalled to Paris for promotion. It was now that the president's unofficial staff officers, Morny his half-brother, Persigny, his old companion in exile and adventure and Fleury, his aide-de-camp, assessed what changes in personnel would be most opportune.

Meanwhile, there were political preparations too. At the end of September, the president declared himself in favour of abrogating the law of 31 May. With this prodigiously Machiavellian (and altogether typical) move, the president introduced the thin end of the wedge into the recent coalition between the republicans and Thiers' friends, since the former had been the principal victims and the latter the principal authors of the law in question. The conservatives, hostile to popular suffrage and now repudiated by the Elysée, suddenly found themselves isolated and out of favour. As for the republicans, the abrogation would bring fulfilment to all their hopes and they suddenly found themselves projected into the Elysée camp, that is into an extremely embarrassing situation and also – in all probability – into dissension and impotence. In the immediate term, the presidential proposal simply provoked a ministerial crisis. Once again, one or two ministers, reactionaries rather than Elysée supporters, tendered their resignations. One of them was Léon Faucher, who had returned to the Ministry of the Interior in the course of the reshuffles of the beginning of the year. The crisis was an opportunity to replace him with a docile Bonapartist, Thorigny. Simultaneously Carlier, the prefect of police, another staunch conservative but probably with royalist leanings, also lost his position and was replaced by Maupas, who had previously been stationed in Toulouse where he had attracted a measure of attention. He had requested that charges should be preferred against a number of republicans in the town. Before making out the charges, the department of public prosecutions had wanted to know on what proof they were based, whereupon Maupas had replied that compromising documents could be produced where necessary when the need to do so arose. A prefect of police such as this was a symbol, a challenge and a threat.

Unrest was growing in the provinces both on account of the surprising news from Paris and also simply as a result of the chronic conflict caused by police opposition to democratic propaganda. Given the right social climate, active conflict seemed imminent. In October, following a number of rural incidents in the Loire valley, two departments (the Cher and the Nièvre) were declared to be in a state of siege. In the Var, there was seething excitement in the villages of the Maures as attempts were made to protect the prospering cork-workers' cooperative against the harassment of a police force in collusion with the employers.

With intrigues on all sides and rumours of conspiracy rife, even in Paris, at the level of political society, the situation seemed to warrant urgent action. Would it be taken immediately? Some of Bonaparte's advisers pointed out that at the moment the red representatives were dispersed in their provinces on account of the parliamentary recess whereas, with the Assembly in full session, it would be possible to round them all up in one fell swoop in Paris. So the *coup d'Etat* was put off until the end of the autumn.

On 4 November, a message from the president repeated his intention of abrogating the law of 31 May. In a vote in an emergency debate in the Assembly, his proposal was roundly defeated by 355 resolutely conservative votes against 348, clearly a combination of the republicans and the supporters of the Elysée. Was this a set-back for Bonaparte? Not necessarily, since at least one result had been achieved, perhaps the very one he wanted: hostility between the republican left and the Orleanist centre-left was building up again. The latter were all the more determined to oppose the president now that they realised he was capable of making a pact – a tacit one at any rate – with the 'reds'.

The questors'* proposition

As each day passed, the *coup d'Etat* became more imminent. While the Assembly was holding its emergency debate it became known that the new Minister for War, General de Saint-Arnaud, had sent out a circular to the generals of the army in Paris, reminding them of the absolute, imperious nature of military discipline and the urgent necessity of blindly carrying out all orders received, and of the complete responsibility that army leaders held for all their subordinates.

Needless to say, he omitted to mention the fact that the Constitution in all cases over-rode military regulations and that violation of that Constitution would, *ipso facto*, disqualify any leaders guilty of such action from any legitimate command.

The implications of the circular were clear. It was easy to forsee that those who wished to defend the Assembly and the Republic would attempt to undermine the soldiers, opposing regimental discipline to the Constitution; and such attempts might well succeed, for the liberal groups in the Assembly included plenty of generals. There were Cavaignac and Charras (the latter only a colonel, admittedly, but an erstwhile Under-Secretary of State at the Ministry of War) on the republican side; Lamoricière, Bedeau and Le Flo for the centre-left; and Changarnier himself. Bedeau was even vice-president and Le Flo was a questor. Moreover, the names of these men were considerably more prestigious than that of Saint-Arnaud, a soldier of faded reputation who had received over-rapid promotion. It is not hard to understand the interest the latter had in inculcating his troops in advance with the principles of obedience to their immediate superiors and rejection of all outside influences.

Precisely because the situation was quite clear-cut, the anti-Bonapartist royalists reacted immediately, on 6 November, by launching the *Proposition des questeurs*. According to this text, the President of the Assembly received (or rather, was reminded that he held, as in principle he had always done,) the right to call upon the armed forces to ensure the security and, if necessary, the defence of the Assembly of National Representatives. It was, or could be, a move to parry any gesture of force on the part of the Elysée.

*The questeurs were members of the Assembly's bureaucracy, themselves representatives of the people (or deputies) who were entrusted by their colleagues with running the practical side of parliamentary life (the upkeep of the palace, security, management of subsidiary services etc.).

But this show of liberal energy, this devotion to the Constitution and the Republic on the part of the habitual disciples of Thiers and Changarnier were of too recent date for the left not to regard them as peculiar, even suspect. The Mountain, which had been shaken by one surprise after another in the course of the last few weeks, now split. Should it vote for the *Proposition des questeurs*, which came to the same thing as forming an alliance with Thiers and others working at the eleventh hour to resist Bonapartism, or should it oppose the *Proposition des questeurs*, which would amount to suspecting Thiers and his men of meditating a *coup* on their own account? To put it another way, should the Mountain regard the principal danger to lie in the Elysée or among the Orleanist benches? The first view, held by a few obscure figures, Marc Dufraisse, Pascal Duprat, Jules Grévy and by all the military republicans led by Cavaignac and Charras, was the correct one, as events were soon to show, but it was not the one that prevailed. It was the second view that won the day: without realising it, three-quarters of the Mountain party were about to play into the Elysée's hands, their misgivings lulled by the argument which their leader Michel (of Bourges) put forward with his customary force: '... even if there were any danger, there is an invisible sentinel which watches over you. I need hardly name that sentinel: it is the people ...'

But in truth the underlying cause for the unfortunate vote cast by the *montagnard* majority was the insurmountable distrust they felt for certain figures among the conservatives. One of those who on this occasion voted with the majority (Victor Hugo, sad to say) made the following entry in his notebooks: 'I am not particularly alarmed by the Elysée but I am worried about the [conservative] majority. I see no Napoleon but I do see a Pichegru*.' He expressed a similar anxiety in verse:

> The Revolution displays some surprise
> To find Thiers as a friend who will fraternise ...
>
> (La Révolution montre quelque surprise
> Quand Thiers devient aimable et se familiarise ...)[6]

Thus it was that, on 17 November, the *Proposition des questeurs* was rejected, receiving only 300 votes. Votes numbering 403 were cast against it, representing a new alliance between *montagnards* and supporters of the Elysée, swelled on this occasion by a whole confused group of conservatives by now resigned to the situation. The increase in their numbers since the vote of 4 November is an indication of the power of attraction that Bonaparte was exerting upon this dislocated group. But the essential factor in the situation was really that the last, tardily constructed liberal defence was collapsing under the pressure of those who nursed their

---

*1761–1804. A French general during the revolutionary period who, having formerly been a republican, later conspired with the royalists against the Republic.

theories of an invisible sentry and who had, regrettably, now banded together with the manipulators of real flesh-and-blood soldiers. The division in the National Assembly was clearly a profound one and it gave the conspirators, who had followed the debate of 17 November with considerable excitement, time to put the finishing touches to their preparations and to act at just the moment when tension was generally believed to have abated.

6

Bonaparte's *coup d'Etat* and the republican resistance (2–10 December 1851)

In some respects the *coup d'Etat* perpetrated by President Bonaparte was a logical extension of the policies of the preceding months. As an independent force, Bonapartism aimed to oppose royalist bourgeois and republicans alike. It took over some of the demands of the democrats (the repeal of the law of 31 May, for example) on the one hand to isolate the bourgeois and outflank them on the left and, on the other, to win over the republicans' own popular clientèle. The man of 2 December had certainly emancipated himself from the party of order.

In other respects, however, the episode created a new twist to the situation, even a regression. On 2 December it may have looked as though Louis-Napoleon had detached himself from the old-style conservatives; but a week later he appeared, on the contrary, to have resumed his place at their head and to be acting on their behalf just as he had in December 1848 or in June 1849. Once again he sounded the clarion call of social defence. The fact of the matter was that, although the *coup d'Etat* was a technical success, it was a political failure. Far from being neutralised by the Bonapartist demagogy, the popular classes revealed themselves as the principal obstacle to his dictatorial ambitions. Faced with this unexpected situation, Bonaparte changed roles; he almost changed flags.

The important point to note is that the confluence of the political and social struggles – struggles claimed not to be associated – manifested itself more clearly in the provinces than it did in Paris. But that did at least tally with the logic of the 'Republic of the Peasants'.

The 'coup d'Etat' in Paris

The proclamations

As we have mentioned, the moment for the *coup d'Etat* had several times been deferred. However, the rejection of the *Proposition des questeurs* had afforded the president a period of respite and he profited from it to choose his day carefully. The anniversary of Napoleon I's coronation and also of the victory of the battle of Austerlitz fell on 2 December; this date

138

would thus set the enterprise under the sign of the 'Bonaparte destiny'. As he wrote 'Rubicon' on the cover of the secret file that contained the documents relating to the preparations for the *coup*, Louis-Napoleon was also laying claim to the patronage of Caesar – the Caesar of the civil war. All the same, his own task was easier than that of his predecessors, given that he had neither a Pompey nor a Barras* to contend with. His material power was already established, for he was in control of the executive and had had his own way when it came to the composition of the prefectorial body and the leadership of the police and the army.

So the *coup d'Etat* of 2 December did not involve winning power, but being in a position to counter the resistance that his unlawful constitutional changes would provoke. With the advantage of choosing its own moment, the conspiracy was able to benefit from the effect of surprise and mount no more than 'a rather cursory police action' at dawn, at the expense on the one hand of the legislators, who were soon to be abolished, and on the other of those political leaders who were most capable of organising active resistance. However, in the short term, with no terrorist measures of any kind envisaged, it was of capital importance to launch a vast propaganda operation to get the *coup d'Etat* accepted by the public. Nowadays, this would be achieved by the immediate occupation of radio and television stations. In 1851 the only means available were posters. That is why the *coup d'Etat* started, at midnight on the night of 1–2 December, with the occupation of the national printing works and – a point not hitherto sufficiently emphasised – this was an operation of the greatest delicacy. It had been necessary to ensure the complicity of the director, to find a pretext for summoning all the workers at such an unusual hour and to divide up the texts and proclamations to be composed and distribute the various passages between different teams of workers, so that no single typographer would be able to fathom the object of the enterprise by reading the pronouncements *in toto*; it had, naturally, also been necessary to surround the whole press building with armed troops. The operation was successful and on 2 December, at dawn, the billboarders employed by the *préfectures*, under police escort and surveillance, placarded every wall in Paris with proclamations addressed to the army on the one hand and the general population on the other. The latter, which were the more important, announced the dissolution of the Legislative Assembly, the preparation of a new Constitution and a plebiscite to ratify it. In justification of these measures the text developed the classic antithesis between the merits of the achievements of the Consulate as opposed to the lengthy delays involved in deliberating assemblies, and

*Pompey: legally held power in Rome when Caesar crossed the Rubicon to impose his dictatorship. Barras: legally held power in Paris when Bonaparte staged his *coup d'Etat* of 18 Brumaire (see p. 12, note).

above all it announced the re-establishment of universal suffrage through the abrogation of the law of 31 May 1850. In this way the men of the *coup d'Etat*, who in these early days set more store by demagogy than by violence, placed themselves more to the left than the now dissolved Assembly had been.

The arrests

That did not mean that they were expecting the approval of the republicans, as became evident from the list of arrests that were made.

During the last hours of the night when the proclamations were being posted, Morny installed himself at the Ministry of the Interior (which the spineless Thorigny had vacated without protest), the commander of the Parisian National Guard despatched trusted men to shatter the various legions' drums – to prevent any zealous officer from sounding a summons to recall the troops – and Saint-Arnaud flooded the capital with his regiments. And while all this was going on, dozens of teams of police, which Maupas had spent the night assembling, were fanning out through Paris equipped with minute instructions. The targets of these nocturnal bands included, in the first place, some eighty democrat militants known to be influential and active and regarded as possible 'barricade leaders' and, secondly, twenty or so representatives outstanding for their political opposition.

Significantly enough, among them were nearly all the military men in the Assembly, from Changarnier to Charras and including Bedeau, Lamoricière, Le Flo and Cavaignac as well as two non-commissioned officers who belonged to the Mountain. The authorities were aware of the hostility of these men and with good reason feared their energy and in particular the influence they could wield over the military agents of the *coup d'Etat*. They also arrested Thiers, who had revealed himself of late as a determined opponent and, in the past, as a statesman with considerable powers of initiative and pugnacity. They arrested half a dozen *montagnards*, those who were known to be closest to the people through their own origins, together with the most committed activists: Martin Nadaud, Greppo, Miot, Perdiguier, Lagrange.[1] Finally, they also arrested the two Orleanist quaestors, Baze and the already-mentioned General Le Flo, who had also played leading roles with their proposition for the defence of the Assembly. In order to lay hands on these two men, whose functions obliged them to lodge in the Palais-Bourbon, it had been necessary to have a squad force its way into the palace precincts and overcome the guards in a surprise attack. This was the first act of violence against the Assembly.

All these men were completely taken by surprise, in bed or even asleep. They protested vehemently, in some cases calling on the law, in others putting up a physical struggle or attempting to arouse their neighbours as the police dragged them off to the waiting carriages. But the streets were still deserted and it did not take long to reach the Mazas prison. From there, the military men, who were regarded with particular mistrust, were quickly transferred under escort to the Gare du Nord and thence to the prison of Ham.

As for the rest, from Dupin, the President of the Assembly, to the mass of remaining republicans and even the people of Paris, the conspirators were counting on their intimidation and disarray when they discovered themselves deprived of their customary leaders. But things were not as easy for them as they had expected.

The resistance of the Assembly

It was the representatives who remained at liberty who were the most directly concerned by the affair. Three attitudes predominated among them. The largest group was the one about which least has been said. About half the members of the Assembly, long since or recently won over to the Elysée, accepting the *fait accompli* for want of an alternative solution or simply through lack of courage, stayed at home and kept their heads down. The reaction of about two hundred others was to try to get together to study ways of mounting a lawful resistance. This group consisted essentially of the liberal bourgeois who had gathered around Thiers' Orleanist friends, together with a few legitimists and a few moderate republicans. Finally, a few dozen *montagnards* opted for a smaller and more clandestine meeting, the aim of which was to organise a people's uprising and armed resistance.

As we have mentioned, a regiment was in occupation of the Palais-Bourbon. The few representatives who went there to express their indignation did so in vain. They were again met by an iron wall of passive obedience[2] and opposed by well-schooled soldiers, who appeared totally incapable of understanding the accusation of complicity in the president's disqualification. It must at this point be stated once and for all that this dialogue of the deaf between citizens appealing to the Law and soldiers appealing to their Orders was to be a feature of every moment and every episode of these days of 2 and 3 December. Being driven away from the Chamber, all this handful of representatives could do was to move on to the home of their president. There, they awakened Dupin, who had not achieved the honour of being arrested. He stammeringly declared that although they, the representatives, clearly had right on their side, those other gentlemen certainly had force on theirs, so all they could do was go away. On hearing this evasive back-down the other representatives left him in disgust to seek out the main body of their colleagues. These, finding the Palais-Bourbon occupied and moving from one meeting place to another, had eventually, during the mid-morning of 2 December, managed to find a hall that they could use. It was in a public building, the town hall of the 10^e *arrondissement* (that is the 10^e *arrondissement* of those days, which was on the left bank and close by).

A lengthy, improvised meeting followed. It was conducted with scrupulous formality – a formality which some might regard as futile but which was, in reality, symbolic. After all, it was a matter of setting a reign of rules, of formality – in short, of Law – to oppose an enterprise which was a denial of all of these things. So a count of those present was taken, they were declared to 'constitute a sufficient number for deliberations to take place', a staff was set up around the Vice-Presidents Vitet and Benoist d'Azy. The charge was drawn up and the company deliberated upon it. After a few brief debates in which Berryer (one of the few legitimists who had chosen to take a liberal line) played a leading part, unanimous agreement was reached. A number of votes were taken: the president of the Republic was agreed to be disqualified by virtue of article 68 of the Constitution;[3] the 10th legion of the National Guard was to be requisitioned to defend the meeting hall; the army of Paris was to be ordered to put itself at the disposal of the Assembly with General Oudinot (one of the few representative generals who was still at liberty) at its head; and prison governors were to be given orders to release all arrested representatives. At this juncture the police arrived upon the scene, supported by a regiment of soldiers. There were solemn protests, and passages from the Constitution and decrees were declaimed, but, as we have said, the military remained unmoved. Their mission was to disperse the 'gathering', seizing only those who offered resistance. However, the representatives had the dignity to carry their symbolic defiance right through and insisted upon the arrest of one and all. A long column of prisoners flanked by two walls of soldiers thus set out for the Mazas prison. A roll-call made in the courtyard named two hundred and twenty representatives and included Berryer, Falloux, Odilon Barrot, Rémusat and Tocqueville. It was just after 3.0 p.m. Their incarceration was of short duration. Nevertheless, it left memories which were to continue to weigh heavily upon the relations between the liberal elite of the upper bourgeoisie and Bonapartism.

Popular resistance

Around midday the news in Paris was that the Assembly was putting up a resistance in the town hall of the 10^e *arrondissement* and that the army had had to use force to disperse a column of young people marching from the *quartier latin* to join it. The Assembly in question, which was a gathering of the liberal right for the most part, had refused to send out emissaries to call the people to arms, despite the fact that the idea had been floated by the few republicans who had taken part in it (Marc Dufraisse, Pascal Duprat). Was that because of a devotion to absolute legalism, or social fear? Both motivations may have been at work. What-ever the case, those six hours of symbolic resistance had usefully helped to create the impression that the *coup d'Etat* was in difficulties.

Most of the republicans, for their part, had immediately opted for an appeal to the people – a move that was also in conformity with the Constitution, namely with article 110. They spent the day of 2 December seeking one another out and coming to agreements in clandestine meet-ings and eluding the police – sometimes only narrowly. Some of them, with the aid of journalists from the republican press (which the army, with its occupation of the printing presses, was to prevent appearing) managed to reproduce and distribute the Assembly's decrees as well as other texts hostile to the *coup d'Etat*. Others set about haranguing passers-by in the groups that gathered on the boulevards. By the end of the day this group of representatives had managed to elect a small resistance committee,[4] composed of Victor Hugo, Victor Schoelcher, Carnot, Michel (of Bourges), Madier de Montjau, Jules Favre and Deflotte. This was the committee that decided that on the following morning, 3 December, the *montagnard* representatives would go out into the streets to summon the people to the barricades. It seemed as if this would be a difficult but not an impossible task.

The people had certainly not manned the barricades spontaneously. During the morning, in front of the posters, the news that universal suffrage was now restored and that the conservative notables had been dispersed had for a while produced some favourable reactions. The man in the street was on the whole neutralised or hesitant. However, by the end of the morning it was noticeable that when Bonaparte, accompanied by his entire staff, emerged from the Elysée on horseback for a brief inspection of the troops and the central quarters of the capital, he was acclaimed by the soldiers but hardly at all by the passers-by. During the afternoon, the crowds of bourgeois strollers on the boulevards were in a state of high excitement and animated by much discussion, most of it hostile to the deployment of police and military force. It looked as if the effects of the immediate neutralisation were now wearing off.

Early on the morning of 3 December, groups of well-wrapped-up repre-sentatives, led by Victor Schoelcher, began to move along the Faubourg Saint-Antoine, talking with the workers, explaining the situation, urging them to take action. They met with some reticence and there were some hostile remarks about representatives who received a daily allowance of 25 francs. The workers did not feel inclined to get themselves killed on their behalf. It was at this point that Baudin came out with the exclamation: 'You will soon see how one can die for 25 francs a day.'[5] Other workers objected that they had nothing to fight with. The *faubourg* had been without arms ever since June 1848. But perhaps weapons could be obtained. With the help of a few militants, the representatives invaded two isolated guard posts. They managed to disarm the soldiers whom they surprised there, seized a few rifles and distributed them. Finally, urged on by them and following their example, the workers set about moving a number of vehicles to block the *faubourg* – thus setting up the beginnings of barricades.

It was at this point that a large column of troops arrived from the place de la Bastille to clear the way. Most of the representatives, led by Schoelcher, approached them, empty-handed, exhorting the soldiers to respect the law. Baudin, for his part, remained on the barricade, still talking to the militants surrounding him. Schoelcher had no success with the soldiers who shoved him roughly aside. Believing him to be in danger, one of the militants on the barricade fired at the soldier who was pushing Schoelcher and killed him. The other soldiers responded by firing at the barricade and now it was Baudin who fell, fulfilling his earlier prophetic exclamation and gaining an immediate place in legend. It was, as can be seen, a somewhat over-simplified legend but not necessarily a false one. Victor Baudin, born from the provincial bourgeoisie, had sacrificed a fine medical career for the life of a militant and doctor to the poorer quarters of Paris and had earned the right to defend the honour of the representatives and to remind the workers that what was at stake, behind what appeared to be the unexacting mission of a few men, was the rights of everyone. But, as is well known, the repercussions of the Baudin episode were not felt until much later. In the immediate instance it did not galvanise the *faubourg* and Schoelcher's group continued to canvass it vain, eliciting no more than the acclamations due to him for his ill-fated courage. In other quarters, however, in less spectacular circumstances – on the Faubourg Saint-Marceau on the left bank – other representatives and militants had met with more success. A few barricades were erected and a few shots exchanged. The news of the death of a representative of the people spread and tension mounted. The crowd was by now more disposed to acclaim the harangues of the republicans.

Resistance is crushed

The atmosphere at the end of 3 December was so different from that of the preceding day that the resistance committee was in an optimistic mood. Meanwhile, in the *préfecture de police*, Maupas was panicking, and at the Ministry of War Saint-Arnaud was decreeing a state of siege and issuing terrible threats (whoever was caught constructing a barricade was to be shot on the spot). Only Morny, at the Ministry of the Interior, remained cool. It was he who judged that 4 December would prove the decisive day.

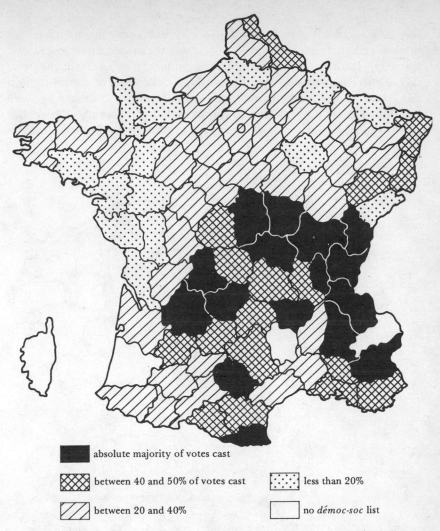

4 Votes obtained by the *démoc-socs* in the legislative elections of 13 May 1849

Note: For the commentary to accompany this map, see above, chapter 4.
(Based on J. Bouillon, Biblio. no. 43)

Legend:

- absolute majority of votes cast
- between 40 and 50% of votes cast
- less than 20%
- between 20 and 40%
- no *démoc-soc* list

It began as a day of fighting in the classic style of Parisian revolutions gathering momentum: following the first incidents of bloodshed on the previous day, barricades were appearing in increasing numbers with new waves of fighters flocking to man them (although the numbers remained nothing like so high as in July 1830 or February 1848). The fighters were determined and put up an energetic defence. History records the death of the young Denis Dussoubs, in the rue Montorgueil. Having borrowed the official sash of his brother, the representative for the Haute-Vienne, who was sick and unable to leave his bed, he had come there to take his brother's place. In the rue Saint-Denis, it took the cannon hours to dislodge a perfectly constructed barricade of paving stones. Was it a classic insurrection of the Parisian poor from the working-class alleys of the centre and the *faubourgs*? It was both more and less than that. The people were certainly fighting in much smaller numbers than in February or June, but those who were did so with infinitely more sympathy from the middle

principal insurgent rural zones

o principal *chefs-lieux* invaded or occupied for a while

x pitched battles

• other places where violent incidents of note took place

5 December 1851: insurrectional incidents
(Based on E. Ténot, Biblio. no. 48)

classes. There was, for Bonaparte, no repeat of the backing for Cavaignac
provided by the mobilisation of the Parisian bourgeois that had given the
latter such powerful support against the June insurgents. Along the boulevards of the more elegant quarters, within earshot of the cannon, the

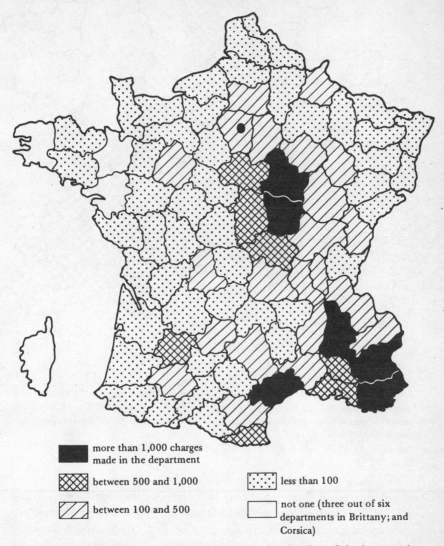

■ more than 1,000 charges
made in the department

▨ between 500 and 1,000   ⠂⠂⠂ less than 100

⧄ between 100 and 500   ☐ not one (three out of six
                                    departments in Brittany; and
                                    Corsica)

6 Number of individuals arrested or charged on the occasion of the insurrection
of December 1851

Note: The dark patches on the map of repression coincide with those of the insurrection,
but the former tend to be much larger.
(Based on Arch. nat. BB 30 424)

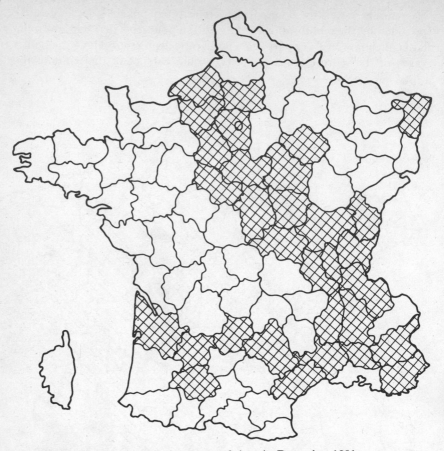

7 Departments declared to be in a state of siege in December 1851

Note: The state of siege adds a new nuance to the map of political mistrust. To be sure, it features, as expected, the important rebel zones of southern and central France. But it also shows industrial towns and regions which were to some extent suspect *a priori* (Bordeaux, Strasbourg, Normandy etc.).
(Based on G. Weill, Biblio. no. 34, p. 272, note)

'yellow gloves' (so called because those articles were typically worn by the bourgeoisie) were shouting 'Long live the Constitution!' and hurling insults at the passing troops. Would this moral support for the insurgents soon become practical aid? Would shots be fired at the troops from the windows of the boulevard des Italiens just as they were in the rue Beaubourg? The soldiers whom the generals, on Morny's orders, were now deploying in thick columns appear to have thought so. When a few isolated shots were fired in the boulevard Bonne-Nouvelle, the troops replied with an intense and general fusillade, moving from one boulevard to the next and shooting down hostile but unarmed onlookers crowding the balconies, just as if they had been enemy militants. After a few minutes of this murderous fire, the Parisian bourgeoisie was bleeding and terrorised and the political situation was, by the same token, reversed.

By the end of the evening, the troops, whose numbers and arms were far superior to those of the republican combatants, had flattened most of the barricades and, more importantly, what was left of their defenders knew that they could hope for no extension of the struggle. The 'boulevard fusillade', though of derisory tactical importance, had scored a decisive psychological success by revealing the determination of the Elysée men to stop at nothing when it came to violence.

But on the morning of 5 December, as that full realisation was sinking in throughout Paris, the villagers far away in the provinces were still quite oblivious of it. Their political chronology had by now only reached the point where that of Paris had been two days earlier.

Resistance in the provinces

The provincial resistance was the outstanding event of this month of December, indeed perhaps of the entire Second Republic. Although it was far from universal, the armed resistance of the departments against the *coup d'Etat* made the episode quite unique. It has by now become a commonplace to point out that, whereas in all the other changes of regime that took place in the capital throughout the nineteenth century, 'the provinces' merely passively registered and followed them, the one that took place on 2 December was exceptional in that they attempted to oppose it. Yet, had not the beginning of political awakening in the provinces been the most essential factor in the three preceding years?

What perhaps needs to be pointed out is that this important event is not so well remembered as it deserves to be. Between the '*chouanneries*' (in the widest sense of the term) of the First Republic, which were crushed by the Consulate, and the resistance put up by the *Maquis* in 1943 and 1944, there were hardly any other instances of armed rebellion of any size in France, apart from the insurrection of 1851. But the general historical memory of that insurrection suffers perhaps precisely because it took place in the provinces, especially in one particular part of them, namely the south. The preconception, admittedly founded upon the most general situation, is that the mid-nineteenth-century French 'peasant' was narrow-minded, conservative and Bonapartist. But the republican peasant of central and southern France represents an exceptional case which, in the simplifications of the general memory, is pushed aside and expunged. And yet, less than a quarter of a century later, this minority was to become a majority and, as such, was to consolidate a new French Republic, one which this time lasted for more than a century.[6]

Meanwhile, however, it was a matter of defending the existing Republic.

General causes

It was known in the provinces, as it was in Paris, that such a defence would be necessary. Wherever republican propaganda had penetrated, it had made articles 68 and 110 of the Constitution known even in the remotest villages. And by virtue of these articles the news of the *coup d'Etat* was *ipso facto* a signal of insurrection. It is true that the news of the violation of the Constitution arrived at the same time as that of the re-establishment of universal suffrage. But it would appear that the assuaging power of this piece of Bonapartist demagogy was less effective with the peasants than it had been with the Parisian workers.

For obvious reasons, anti-parliamentarianism is always less extensive in the provinces than among the people of Paris. Most importantly, perhaps, the red provinces were more exasperated by the regime in power than was the population of Paris. The prefects' tenacious war against the *cercles*, republican municipalities and republican newspapers was particularly keenly felt precisely because here, in the provinces, municipal life was more a part of the daily scene and newspapers were rarer and more vulnerable. In the departments, repression on the part of the police and the law had perpetrated dozens of little local *coups d'Etat* and the people were waiting for the signal to take their revenge. This is no abstract deduction: the detailed history of the insurrections makes it quite clear. Nowhere was the resistance to the *coup d'Etat* so strong as where it was a means of making local reparation for a recent injustice, such as the killing of an innocent female cooperative worker, the suppression of 'the' newspaper or the dissolution of a representative municipal council. One even senses that in some instances Bonapartist demagogy itself recoiled against those in power and that the declaration heard so often on 4 and 5 December in the insurgent villages: 'The people are coming into their rights again' stemmed from an amalgamation of the right to rise up in arms granted by article 68 and the right to vote granted by the abrogation of the law of 31 May.

The red provinces were not wanting in enthusiasm, then. But why did the insurrection there not 'take off' in one fell swoop on 3 December?

The factors of failure and success

In the first place, why 3 December in some places, 4 or 5 December in others? One primary obstacle to simultaneity was the length of time it took for news to circulate, ranging from a few hours to two days, for although nearly all the prefects could be reached by telegraph, the news then had to be relayed to the *sous-préfectures* by mounted couriers. Whether it was private correspondence, newspapers or simply travellers that brought the news, the maximum speed with which it could reach most private individuals was invariably that of a steady horse trot, as the railway was as yet only operational on certain discontinuous portions of the main routes of communication.

However, that was probably not the principal factor. Convinced though they were of their right, or even of their duty, to stage an insurrection many leaders, before giving their orders, took the time to make sure they would not be acting in isolation. It was not so much that they were waiting to know the outcome of the struggle in Paris, for on 4 December it still looked as though this would be successful. Rather, they were anxious to see what would happen in the nearest regional capital – Lyons, Marseilles or Toulouse – or even in some more modest *chef-lieu*. And it was here, in the decisive relaying of communications between these capital towns and the villages deep in the country that the insurrection was to be lost and the conflict won by those who held the power. The large towns were full of troops and resolute prefects were in command there, while the republican party was not as strong as in Paris and had fewer active leaders. This last aspect of the problem should not be under-estimated: the provinces were often short of leaders. Some were in prison, or had been sentenced to deportation to Nuka-hiva; others, who were representatives of the people and were consequently surprised by the event while in Paris, judged it more important to help to rouse the people in the rue Saint-Denis or the rue Montorgueil than to return to the distant provinces where their electors lived. Those who were on the spot in the provinces were in many cases replacements for earlier replacements and were neither the most capable of leaders nor the most popular. Some of them spent a great deal of time attempting to persuade 'their' prefect or 'their' prosecutor for the Republic or 'their' mayor that article 68 stipulated that they should resign their offices.

Finally, the insurrection was limited to localities where the people of the small towns and countryside, the – so to speak – 'second-degree provincials', had powerful local motivation (perhaps the zeal of an exceptional leader or some deeply-felt local contention) that encouraged them to adhere to the movement's general order of the day.

Where such motivation existed insurrection was possible, for although the large towns were held by the army and many small towns were also held by the combination of a garrison and a National Guard composed of armed conservative bourgeois, a red cantonal *chef-lieu* could quite easily overcome its *gendarmerie* squad just as a village could its *garde champêtre*. But even there local customs had to be taken into account. Whereas the peasants in the large *bourgs* of southern Provence, whose dwellings were densely concentrated, could be 'reached' each evening in their *chambrées* in the same way as urban workers could be in their *cabarets*, in a number of communes in central France[7] the insurrection only 'got going' on Sunday 7 December in the late morning, because, whether or not they attended mass, that was the only time during the week when the peasants met together.

After these general considerations, we may now take the principal events in the order in which they took place. First we will give an account of the places and dates in question and then move on to an analysis.

Chronology. The first days. Central and south-western France

On Tuesday 2 December, the prefects received the news by telegraph and marshalled their military and police forces. The republicans could do no more than begin to get together. But all this applied only to the large towns.

On Wednesday 3 December the news spread, now reaching all the towns of any importance throughout the country and, in the northern part, the entire territory. As we know, however, in that particular district most of the country was conservative.

Towards the end of the day, in most of the large towns there were gatherings of republicans in the street and in front of the town halls, and these sometimes developed spontaneously into demonstrations. Where these gatherings were large they were contained by the forces of order. Where the reaction was not so strong or non-existent, the prefects ordered the arrest of the militants. But in many cases (in Agen, Auch and Béziers, for instance) the republicans did not show themselves in the streets, but remained plotting in secret, sending emissaries out to warn their brothers in the countryside that the action was to take place on the following day, 4 December.

However, in a number of small towns or *bourgs*, such as Saint-Amand (Cher) and Le Donjon (Allier),[8] the first vigorous demonstrations were already taking place on Wednesday 3 December. In some cases they assumed the form of insurrection: the town hall was invaded and the municipal power changed hands (for instance, in La Suze (Sarthe), Poligny (Jura) and Orange (Vaucluse)).

By Thursday 4 December the news of both the *coup d'Etat* and the first instances of resistance was known everywhere. This day, which was the decisive one in Paris, was also the one when most of the provincial democrat localities engaged in combat.

By now most of the large towns were cowed and street demonstrations were again repressed in Toulouse, Marseilles, Limoges, Perpignan and Bayonne. Militants who wished to fight were left with no alternative but to move to small towns in the neighbourhood. Thus the Var insurrection started to form its army on the 5 December under the leadership of 'general' Duteil, a journalist from Marseilles whose articles in *Le Peuple* had made him a well-known figure. However, in Orléans, unlike most other places, representatives had that morning arrived from Paris, and throughout the day there was excited unrest in response to their appeals.

But above all, the first offensive moves were being made in the country regions. The villagers of Le Donjon went to invade the *chef-lieu* of their *arrondissement*, Lapalisse (Allier). The villagers of the Bitterois entered Béziers to come to the aid of the republicans in the town and some violent incidents ensued. The peasants of the Gers marched on Auch and were only stopped by the army at the gates of the town. The insurrection was declared in other small towns of the Gers too – in Fleurance and Mirande for example. In the Lot-et-Garonne several communes in the *arrondissement* of Nérac marched on Agen where they were halted by the garrison. Other attempts at invading *chefs-lieux* were less successful, as for example in the Gard where villagers (almost all Protestants) from communes in the Vaunage marched towards Nîmes.

Finally, on the evening of 4 December, the insurrection got under way in even the most remote places, for instance in the depths of the Hérault, in the little industrial town of Bédarieux, where there was also bloodshed; and in the Var, at Le Luc and La Garde-Freinet, both – for different reasons – ardently republican communes, and those which later furnished the principal contingents for the movement in this sector.

> *Chronology (continued). The movement faces set-backs in some places, gains ground in others. The south-east*

In the course of Friday 5, a number of events took place simultaneously by reason of the inevitable variations of timing and, needless to say, in total ignorance of what was happening elsewhere. In the regions that were late in being alerted to the news there were more uprisings, while in those which had got going first the movement suffered its first defeats. Thus, Le Donjon, to which the inhabitants had returned, having failed to win over Lapalisse, was occupied by a column of troops sent from the *chef-lieu* of the department; Poligny was also occupied that same evening.

In the Gers it was also a day of set-backs, despite the uprising in Condom and the formation in Mirande of a column to march to the *préfecture*. It is fair to say that in the south-west and the south the authorities were successful in defending the *chefs-lieux*. Only a handful of remote localities still held out and remained governed by republican commissions – for example; Bédarieux and Capestang (Hérault) and Marmande and Villeneuve-sur-Lot (Lot-et-Garonne).

But it was also the day when Clamecy (Niévre) rose up after two days of waiting and also Montargis (Loiret), where the news of the movement in Orléans, on the day before, acted as a signal.

Above all, 5 December was the day on which the departments in the south-east joined the insurrection, and here it took place on a larger scale than elsewhere and with more spectacular strategic movements than anywhere else. In the Var, the insurrection was rapidly suppressed in the neighbourhood of Toulon (and it was a failure – and a bloody one – at Cuers), but it spread throughout the central region. Columns of insurgents began to be organised from two bases: Brignoles, which Duteil had now reached, and the Maures *massif* (La Garde-Freinet). The *chef-lieu*, Draguignan, where the prefect was being protected by a small garrison, was cut off from the rest of France.

In the Basses-Alpes the signal for insurrection came from the Manosque region, the *sous-préfecture* of Forcalquier fell and the whole of the southern part of the department rose up in arms and gathered, here too threatening the *chef-lieu*, Digne.

Finally, in the Drôme, where the villages had been in a ferment of excitement for the past two days, the republicans of Valence decided to spread the order of the day for the expected insurrection. A few hours later they cancelled the order, the bad news from Paris having meanwhile reached them; but it was already too late: half the department, especially in the Protestant areas, were already in a state of insurrection.

On Saturday 6 December, the forces of order repressed the last, tardy street demonstrations in Bordeaux and Strasbourg and continued to regain control of the situation in the south-west and in central France (except at Clamecy), but in the south-east the government was still at the stage of organising repression in its urban bases. In the departments that had risen up, the insurrection was spreading and becoming organised. It even reached the *arrondissement* of Apt in the Vaucluse.

Sunday 7 December saw a few spasms in the Loire valley (to which we have referred above), the dispersal – after some fighting – of the people of Marmande and, above all, a kind of running battle starting in the south-east. The columns organised from the gathering of the various village contingents were shaken. The Drôme column, which was trying to reach Valence, was halted and overcome at Crest in a veritable pitched battle. The Var column, gathered at Vidauban, gave up the idea of attacking Draguignan and instead, moving northwards, embarked upon a 'long march' lasting three days, with the vague plan of meeting up with the men of the Basses-Alpes.

On the other hand, the latter, assembled in their thousands at Malijai, were successful in overwhelming Digne where the garrison capitulated. It was the first (and only) *préfecture* in France that fell to the republicans.

Far away at Clamecy, where the success of the *coup d'Etat* must by now have been known, discouragement reigned and the men began to disperse spontaneously.

On Monday 8 December the forces of order arrived at Clamecy. They were now beginning to appear systematically everywhere in the centre, in the southern regions of Languedoc and Aquitaine and also in the Drôme, re-establishing official powers in the now reoccupied communes.

In the south-east, the counter-offensive started in Marseilles and from there pressed forward towards the Var interior and the valley of the Durance. The forces of order moved through the red villages emptied of their fighting men and sought to come to grips with the two remaining columns that were still intact. But that same day also saw the formation of a third column in the Apt region, in an attempt to get the inhabitants of the Vaucluse to rise up and march on Avignon.

On Tuesday 9 December the Vaucluse revolt foundered before the closed gates of Cavaillon and the men dispersed. In the heart of the Basses-Alpes, at Les Mées, republicans who had entrenched themselves to bar the route to Digne fought a battle against troops who had marched from Marseilles; they were overcome after a lively exchange of shots, just as the republicans in the Drôme had been two days earlier.

Meanwhile, in the Var no contact had yet been made between the hostile forces, but news of their total isolation had by now reached this last group of insurgents and discouragement was gaining the upper hand.

On Wednesday 10 December, at Aups, they too were routed after a very brief battle. This was also the day when, many kilometres away, Capestang and Bédarieux were reoccupied without difficulty. It is fair to say that this date, exactly one week after the first insurrectional moves, marked the end of republican resistance in the provinces.

Now the army's movements were reduced to sweeping through the countryside, tracking down the insurgents who, for their part, were making for the Spanish or Piedmontese frontiers or – if they were just naive peasants – trying to get home to their own villages. There, however, they found themselves at the mercy of denunciators or police enquiries. Those captured by the army or the *gendarmerie* in these December searches were similarly thrown into prison, though there were also a number of summary executions. The dramas that marked the collapse of this adventure were therefore similar, whether they took place on the barricades of Paris or in the skirmishes in the Morvan or upper Provence.

What had the adventure really amounted to?

The insurrection, seen generally, as a political and military event
One point should be made quite clear: in the provinces and Paris alike, the insurrection was founded upon article 68 of the Constitution

which ran as follows: 'The president is disqualified ... it is the duty of all citizens to refuse to obey him.' The natural deduction was that any administrative authorities who continued to obey Louis-Napoleon Bonaparte after 2 December were accomplices in his breach of duty and therefore should also be regarded as disqualified and replaced by citizens resolved to respect the Constitution and the Republic. But how was this to be done? Article 68 went on as follows: 'The executive power passes by right to the National Assembly.' Now, the latter had not had the time to seize that power; the citizens were therefore reduced to improvising forms of expression for their loyalty to the spirit of the Constitution. They did this, at the first and most popular level of power, in the town halls. Everywhere the movement was in the first instance municipal and the most elementary form it took was a request to the municipal council to meet, to declare the disqualification of the Head of State and to proclaim themselves to be in a state of insurrection. In localities where the councils or mayors refused to comply with this request, insurrectional success consisted in ejecting them from their town halls and in proclaiming their replacement by a provisional municipal committee. There was no time to talk of elections, but the list of committee members was in many cases at least ratified by the acclamation of the assembled 'people'. What is more significant about this source of inspiration for the movement is the scrupulous legal formality with which, during the course of the meeting, this municipal change was in some cases entered into the councils' official minutes.

For the rest, as we have already indicated, this municipal action was nowhere so enthusiastically carried out as in those localities where its effect was to restore to the town hall a red mayor duly installed by the elections three years earlier, who had since been dismissed on some pretext or other by a repressive prefect. In such cases it could truly be said that 'the people were coming back into their rights'.

Once installed in the town halls, the popular insurgents, already aware or suspecting that their civil servant superiors would not go along with them, turned their attention first and foremost to the matter of arming themselves. It was a difficult business, but perhaps less so than might appear to us, the unarmed citizens of the twentieth century. The men of the nineteenth century lived at a time when there was a National Guard, when a rifle in the hands of a civilian was in no way regarded as anti-civic: on the contrary. Besides, the occupation of the town hall in many cases resulted in the acquisition of the official rifles of the National Guard as that is where they were kept. If this was not the case, hunting rifles could be used or those belonging to one's neighbours. For arming themselves meant disarming their potential adversaries. The aim of many of these invasions of the *gendarmeries*, considered 'legitimate' since the *gendarmerie* remained under Bonaparte's orders, was to neutralise the *gendarmes* by seizing their firearms and their swords.

In many cases these operations took an unfortunate turn as the *gendarmes* tried to defend themselves, and also because there were old scores to pay off between the *gendarmes* and the rural insurgents, a whole backlog of harassment over matters ranging from the political to the social and from the issue of a red tie sported by some political militant to that of the deplorable practices of the day-worker-cum-poacher. This is an aspect of the situation to which we shall return. Arming oneself in some cases also meant disarming those civilians in the party of order, many of whom the republicans – sometimes with justification –suspected of being capable of fighting for their own particular flag. There were, in effect, plenty of noble or 'bourgeois' landowners, manufacturers and notaries who possessed rifles. There was also a long tradition of an active National Guard, and sometimes there were even white *cercles* or 'societies' prepared to come to the aid of the authorities. In many insurgent communes this was why visits were made to various homes for the purpose of requisitioning arms, and even why certain energetic members of the white party were imprisoned.

The columns

The *sous-préfectures* represented the next level of the authorities to be won over if the *coup d'Etat* was to be blocked and the Republic to be re-established. This was a difficult task. Every *chef-lieu* always had its own small garrison, a number of determined civil servants (the sub-prefect, the prosecutor for the Republic, the police superintendent) and a group of bourgeois among the population. Even where they were in the majority, the democrats in the *sous-préfectures* did not feel that the material power was theirs and for them, as we have seen, the insurrection in many cases consisted in alerting the villages and calling on them to rise up. This is why the December republican movement so often took on the appearance of a campaign to rouse the country regions to march on the towns, and it was principally upon that impression that the theory of *jacquerie* was to rely.

This need to assemble all available forces from the depths of the countryside, so as to be a match against the garrisons in the towns, occasioned the formation of the famous columns whose varying fortunes we have already described. Zola was soon to create a place in literature for one of them in *La Fortune des Rougons*.

With his unerring historical intuition (or knowledge) and with his inimitable gift for breathing life into objects with a symbolic value, the author of the Rougon–Maquart cycle of novels organised the entire drama of the Var insurrection around two 'protagonists', the Ramparts and the

Column. The Ramparts of Plassans, the timid little town, shut in on itself as it had been for centuries, symbolised an archaic conservatism, while the Column of peasants, unrolling along the highways, was the symbol of the people's movement.

Zola well understood this Column,[9] with its vague attempts at military organisation, its heteroclite collection of weapons and, above all, its strongly village-based structure: the marching men remained in their native groups, the various companies or sections simply represented different villages and the lower-ranking officers were none other than the militants who had always been recognised as rank-and-file leaders in their own communes. Higher up the staff officer group was far more unstable, and it was not the case that it had emerged, ready-made, from the clandestine assemblies of the 'secret societies'. It was very much an improvised affair and there were many tensions. Once chosen, the principal leaders took to wearing a red scarf to distinguish them, and moved to and fro on horseback. They were accompanied by a doctor who took care of the sick, a law student who drew up the orders of the day and a notary's clerk who kept some kind of rough accounts. Above all, they included a woman who acted as standard-bearer. Zola, who paid less attention to some of the other details, certainly assigned her an important role. Today we may well wonder how we should regard it. Was it proof that democratic and social militancy was beginning to spread to women? Or did this woman, on the contrary, represent an already archaic memory, was she a kind of dummy chosen to play the role of 'goddess of liberty', as in the festivals of the First Republic? These are problems that we have discussed elsewhere, finding indications to support both interpretations, which may, indeed, be combined.

All of this – the seizure of power in the town halls, the taking up of arms, the organisation of fighting columns to seize power in the administrative *chefs-lieux* – constituted the series of operations logically determined by the movement's desire to defend the Republic. It is probably true to say that this is the form that an uprising would have taken all over France if it had not, in so many departments, sooner or later been checked before it could develop fully. The Var and the Basses-Alpes were virtually the only departments where the entire process took place, but it was a process that had at least begun everywhere else as well. So it is fair to say that these political – or perhaps legal-cum-military – aspects were general and typical of the democratic movement of December.

The insurrection: sporadic economic and social factors
However, there were many other aspects to the movement, and we must now consider it in greater detail.

There were a number of instances of bloodshed in the first stage of the uprising, but they were remarkably rare when one considers the large number of localities that were involved. In some cases (Cuers and Bédarieux), the bloodshed occurred in the course of the invasion of the town hall and *gendarmerie* and was simply the unfortunate, but, so to speak, normal consequence of episodes of that kind. In others (Clamecy and Béziers, for instance), a long way from the political action and incidents that were taking place, blood was shed in the course of more obscure clashes: these involved accidents and even private actions of revenge, the details of which are unclear even today.

A few instances of theft are recorded. Despite all the precautions and appeals of the leaders of the movement, these took place during some of the invasions of post offices and town halls or during the requisitioning in private houses.

Action was taken, or attempted, against a number of unpopular institutions that were in no way connected with the Constitution (but were, on the other hand, very much connected with the people's aspirations for a better life). There were thus many proclamations, in many different places, against indirect taxation. The departmental Commission in power in Digne from 7 to 9 December was forced to decree the total abolition of the tax on wines in the Basses-Alpes. On 5 December, in Cuers, the insurgents who emerged triumphantly from the invasion of the town hall and *gendarmerie* immediately went on to the receiver of indirect taxes to burn his registers.

Finally, there were some actions that were coloured by revenge or social rancour. The cork-workers of La Garde-Freinet made prisoners of two of the employers, along with other notables, and took them along, heavily guarded, with the marching column. The workers from the textile factories of Bédarieux, who were in control of the town on 6 December, made the most of their power by holding meetings to study how to improve wages and ordering the bakers to bake bread for the unemployed. The peasants of Saint-Etienne-les-Orgues (Basses-Alpes) went in all innocence to loot the mayor's house in order to recuperate the sums he had been extorting from them in his capacity as notary and moneylender. The peasants of Baudinard (Var) marched as one man, convinced that the true Republic would not fail to see that they won the lawsuit that the commune had for years been engaged in with the duc de Sabran (over users' rights in the forest).

However, there are two differences between this series of particular events (murders, thefts, attacks against institutions, individuals or property), and the general series of purely political actions. The first, as we have indicated above, is that the actions in the latter category were, precisely, general and universal, whereas those in the former category were sporadic. The second difference is that the actions of a political, legal or military nature were taken with the unanimous approval of the insurgents, whereas the other type were often the cause of tensions between them, within the insurrectional movement. The political leaders did what they could to prevent useless violence and theft, to ensure humane treatment for the few bourgeois and *gendarmes* they had taken prisoner, and to contain the exaltation of the people within the framework of a scrupulously lawful movement; but it cannot be denied that they were not always successful. The general anger of the rank-and-file insurgent was not always able to distinguish between the struggle against the perjured president and the struggle against a local village oppressor.

That is the main problem for the historian – as indeed it was in the immediate political context.

Interpretations and consequences

The local incidents of violence or social rebellion were neither the most numerous nor the most typical. But they were the most spectacular and, above all, they were the ones that it was most opportune to bring to general attention. The conservative press, the only sort to appear at this point, devoted exaggerated attention to them and deduced its theory of *jacquerie* from them.

'Jacquerie'

As we have already indicated in passing, this theory was based first of all upon an assumption of a geographical nature: here was an insurrection which did not come from the large towns but from country regions in the depths of the provinces (and *what* provinces! The old fanatical areas of Provence and Languedoc and the 'wild' mountains of the Alps and the Morvan). This simply had to be seen as a sign not of 'progress', even of a most misguided kind, but of regression! And then there were all those marches of peasants, woodcutters and raftsmen (from the valley of the Yonne), tramping through the bourgeois quarters (of Clamecy and other mini-capitals!). '*Jacquerie*', as diagnosed from the evidence available, became the key word for the press and for French politics generally during that winter 1851–2. It was claimed to be a premature explosion of the brutal subversion and basely economic rancour (the poor against the rich!) that the reds were purported to have in store for 1852. The party of order were determined to find confirmation here for the appalling image of socialism that they had created for themselves. The press weighed in for good measure to complete the demonstration. It ignored the principal 'facts', that is the truly political processes at work and, instead, singled out the few episodes involving bloodshed and larceny, presenting them quite misleadingly as if they had been generally typical rather than exceptional.

The thesis of *jacquerie* was furthermore embroidered with details that were pure and simple inventions, but which, now as after June 1848, revealed a singularly tenacious streak of sadism in the imaginations of the right-thinking (*bien-pensants*) journalists. There was not a single dead *gendarme* around whose corpse a kind of 'scalping' dance had not been performed; the red looters at Clamecy were said to have forced the wives and daughters of the principal notables to serve them at their banquet, and this was clearly designed to lead to an orgy and so on.

Other, more serious, authors meanwhile based their arguments upon less contestable facts, but slanted them with a tendentious interpretation. The most common of these travesties was to describe as 'looting' (that is to say 'theft', and that meant 'socialism') the requisitioning operations that had been carried out by the insurgents. Such operations had certainly taken place. It is not possible to move bands of several hundred men, far from home, for many hours or in some cases for three or four consecutive days at a stretch, without making some provision for the material essentials of life. The insurgents had certainly not been demanding when it came to quality. They were content enough with bread, wine and straw (to sleep on), but these commodities were required in large quantities. The leaders of the insurrection had thus done what all leaders of armies on the march did in those days: they issued formal requisitioning demands, scrupulously recorded and accounted, to all the mayors (even the conservative ones) of the communes selected as stopping-places. Most of the 'looting' incidents reported were in fact of this kind. Cumulatively, they added up to a very large factor in the chapter of misunderstandings that we have described above.

The importance of the thesis of 'jacquerie'. The immediate political consequences

The interpretation of the provincial insurrection as *jacquerie* immediately assumed great political importance. Bonapartist and liberal conservatives alike competed with one another in their zeal to denounce the insurrection in this way and, in so doing, found themselves in agreement once more. Not the least – albeit involuntary – achievement of the republican movement was in effect to have reconstituted the unity of the party of order. The red peril provided justification for the one group (the provincial royalists, who might otherwise have felt scruples about the dispersal of their elected representatives) for having allowed the *coup d'Etat* to take place and also for the other (the Bonapartists) for having staged it. For the *jacquerie* myth immediately made it possible for Louis-Napoleon and those who surrounded him to give their propaganda a clever new slant: now it was in order 'to save society' from the revolutionary peril that they had had to consolidate the State. In Paris on 2 December, the Bonapartist *coup d'Etat* had even had a vaguely leftist air (to such an extent, indeed, that it had at that juncture been viewed with a measure of indulgence by Proudhon). Now, however, by 10 December, it had become a radically conservative enterprise. This was a new turn in the oscillating history of the political relations between Bonaparte and the majority of the governing classes. One Bonaparte – the man with 'Napoleonic' ideas, the befriender of nationalistic groups, vaguely socially minded, at all events an innovator who was progressively disso-ciating himself from the *burgraves* and the priests – was laid aside, at least for a while. His place was taken once again by the Bonaparte of Decem-ber 1848, the standard-bearer of all traditional order. He made one significant move: it will be remembered that a few weeks earlier he had dismissed Carlier from the *préfecture de police*, regarding him as obstruc-tive by reason of his suspected sympathy for Changarnier. Now (on 8 December), this same Carlier was invested by Bonaparte as government commissioner on mission extraordinary to the departments of the Cher, the Allier and the Nièvre. The order that had to be restored there certainly did not recognise the sub-divisions that had earlier been so much debated by the Assembly.

This mission marks the beginning of the chapter of repression.

The theory of a struggle for right

However, before we embark upon that chapter, we should once and for all conclude that of the rural insurrection and the problems that it posed. In France, the republicans no longer had any means of expression. In exile, they did; and many of them immediately put pen to paper (Victor Hugo, Victor Schoelcher and Marc Dufraisse, among others) chiefly to denounce the *coup d'Etat* and give an account of the days in Paris. The days of the provincial insurrection had to wait more than ten years before they found their first historian in Eugène Ténot. His book which appeared in 1865 was the fruit of conscientious research and also of his undisguised republican sympathies. It gave an account of the principal features, presenting – in total opposition to the theory of *jac-querie* – the thesis of an insurrection in the name of what was right. It is not hard to guess the main points made: the reader was reminded of the Constitution, of the oath sworn, of the president's self-disqualification; the fundamentally lawful motivations of the insurgents were emphasised; the slanderous inventions put about by the white press were denounced; the truth of the matter in respect of the few crimes and infractions of the law committed by the insurgents was re-established together with a fair appraisal of the rarity of these occurrences; the leaders' respect for the law and their spirit of moderation was stressed; and finally a contrast was drawn between the small number of violent actions that could be ascribed to the insurgents and the many committed in the course of the disproportionate operation of repression that followed.

By the end of the Second Empire a work of historiography that was fundamental and unassailable thus existed, and by reason of those qualities it has ever since set the tone for the republican tradition as well as for academic works of history (it is well known that the two are often very close anyway as is shown, for example, by Charles Seignobos).[10]

Sociological considerations

But reactions often go too far and 'pink legends' can distort historical understanding just as much as 'black' ones can. We should point out, to simplify the matter, that behind the abominable exaggerations of the thesis of *jacquerie* lay the correct intuition that the movement was to some degree coloured by the class struggle. In contrast, the republican historians, motivated by their praiseworthy desire to denounce the slanderous accusations of *jacquerie* (looting, stealing, etc.) have tended to minimise or even to veil the part played by the class struggle.

They did so above all on the basis of the famous statistical records of 'arrested individuals' compiled by the Ministry of Justice, which indicated the professions of all those individuals. Seignobos notes that, out of a total of more than 26,000 people, there is only a minority of peasants (5,423 agricultural workers and 1,850 day-workers); the majority were artisans and workers in old-established crafts (foremost among them 1,607 cobblers) and furthermore the number of bourgeois is impressive (1,570 individuals with private means, 325 doctors, 225 lawyers). However, the argument is a fragile one.

The statistics were drawn up on a national basis and related to many quite different local situations. If we consider separately the regions where the insurrection had time to develop fully, we find that the proportions of peasants are already considerably higher: 48 per cent in the Basses-Alpes and 40 per cent in the Vaucluse, according to Philippe Vigier,[11] and 43 per cent in the Var, according to our own investigations.

And, above all, Seignobos failed to take into account the fact that these statistics relating to individuals *arrested* did not correspond absolutely with the statistics for *actual* insurgents. There can be no doubt that there were large numbers of known republican propagandists arrested who were considered by the authorities to have organised or connived at the uprising, despite the fact that they took no part in it or even advised against it. (In the Var, the statistics thus include thirteen doctors taken into custody, of whom only two marched in the column). But this is a subject to which we shall return. On the other hand, in particular forest villages where a hundred or so poor peasants are definitely known to have set out together to join the column, only a handful of individuals were arrested. The rest, the mass of simple and ignorant peasants, went home and lay low and were left alone.

There can therefore be almost no doubt that the famous statistics over-estimated the proportion of the political classes (the bourgeois, the intellectuals etc.) and under-estimated that of the peasants.

And then there remains the evidence of the facts revealed by studies of particular localities: to be sure, they were fighting for what was right and for the Constitution, but they fought for them twice as hard when injustice had the familiar face of a detested local squire, notary or employer, and when the abstract appeal to what was right could be backed up by a desire for concrete justice.

Any explanation of the provincial insurrection of December 1851 thus confronts the problem of the relation between the social and ideological motivations at work in the popular movements. It was the problem of the Republic itself that was at the core of this struggle.

Ideological considerations

The Republic ... In principal it was the Republic founded by the Constitution of November 1848, which had been functioning for the past three years. But there was little reason for that Republic to be truly popular and the insurgents were really fighting for a different one. They called it 'the Holy' or 'the Beautiful' or 'the Right' one (La Bonne) and by the last term what they meant was the authentic one, the true one, as opposed to the disappointing and falsified Republic that currently existed.

There was still an idea that, since the Republic established the law of the majority and since there were many more poor than rich, it must necessarily be democratic and social. If that was not the case, then the regime was still lacking in something essential, there was something anomalous that should be put right, the Republic had not completed its apprenticeship. The present Republic was conservative because it was imperfect; the 'true republic' would be social because it would be complete. It was this completion that the Mountain expected to take place in 1852 and that is, beyond doubt, also the hope that found expression in the insurrection. For the people, chasing out the president who had failed them and 'coming back into their rights' was making 1852 happen immediately, since the normal calendar had not been respected.

In this respect, there was no difference between the bourgeois leaders of the republican party and the masses. Victor Hugo, Ledru-Rollin and their emulators in the provinces all thought that the Republic had to be democratic and social.

The difference, when it existed, lay elsewhere. It was not a question of ends, but of timing. The most educated of the insurgents and therefore the most legalistic (that is to say often, but not always, the most bourgeois) believed that to re-establish the Constitution, with universal suffrage restored, would bring the situation back to the *status quo ante*, that is to the possibility of a free and massive vote which would, given normal circumstances, bring victory to the Mountain by means of the elections and that would result in laws that promoted social progress. In contrast, the more deprived sections of the population, who were less capable of thinking the process through in abstract terms, derived from certain formulae (for instance, 'the People restored to its rights') and perhaps also from the very atmosphere of the insurrectional process – a massive uprising, fighting and movement – the idea that this social democracy would begin without delay. For them, the burning of a few registers was not a guilty anticipation of the law that was to come, but an exuberant celebration of the end of the old regime.

But the general idea was common to everyone: it was that the form of the Republic and a content of social reform were indissociable. The *coup d'Etat* thus provided the occasion for the reappearance of a Republic with a vocabulary of legality and a socialist heart.

There were to be twenty more years of trials and tribulations before it once again saw the light of day. We shall presently give an account of the first of those years, from December 1851 to December 1852. But by even the first week after the *coup d'Etat*, the principal elements in the record of the historical period that opened in 1848 were indicated in this intimate coupling, within the name of the Republic, of the ideas of Right and Popular Aspirations.

7

From the *coup d'Etat* to the Empire (December 1851–December 1852)

The first Bonaparte took four years to move from the assumption of personal power to the Empire, so distasteful was the idea of monarchical restoration to the men who had toppled Louis XVI ten years earlier. Louis-Napoleon, in contrast, and by reason particularly of the precedent set by his uncle, found public opinion had been better prepared for such a transition. His 'Consulate' lasted for no more than one year – one year to the day, to be precise, for Napoleonic superstition induced him once again, in 1852, to choose 2 December as the date for the re-establishment of the Empire. On the other hand, his uncle's Consulate had still been republican by virtue of the very title of 'Consul' given to its leading magistrates. Then, it had simply been a matter of 'Rome replacing Sparta.' However, the Consulate of Napoleon the nephew was from the first a principate, since after the *coup d'Etat* Louis-Napoleon officially assumed the eminently hybrid title of 'prince-president'. Thereafter, it was not hard to foresee that 1852, the year begun in the Elysée, would end in the Tuileries Palace.

Nevertheless, the unexpected resistance met by the *coup d'Etat* did have the effect of somewhat complicating the programme. The new constitutional system had to be set up even while the repression of the insurrections was taking place. The two operations together took up the end of the year of 1851 and the early weeks of 1852. In the interests of clarity, however, we will give separate accounts of them. After that, with repression organised and the Constitution functioning once more, we shall be in a position to consider the important social and economic decisions which gave the new regime its meaning and, finally, the preparations for the advent of the Empire which gave it its ultimate form.

The anti-republican repression

The principles upon which the repression was based

We have seen how, in Paris, the repression began in the very heat of action, with Maupas' and Saint-Arnaud's formidable series of arrests

166

and proclamations prompted by the state of siege that had been declared. The state of siege had then been progressively extended to cover all provincial departments where disturbances were said to be taking place. There, the army took no less brutal action and moreover did so with the complete collaboration of the prefects. It was an early stage in the 'mixed' action taken by various authorities in collaboration that we shall be discussing presently.

The details show that the army (and in many cases in the provinces, the *gendarmerie* too) sometimes took summary action and the 'man-hunts' for the fleeing insurgents probably accounted for as many deaths among them as did the actual pitched battles.

The reason for the massive and iniquitous character of the repression was the official assimilation of the insurrection (as it effectively took place) to a republican plot said to have been long in preparation. Here, the idea of the secret society, with all its equivocal aspects (about which enough has been said already) played an essential part: all militant republicans were clearly organised; any type of organisation was reputed to be a secret society and any secret society a source of conspiracy. Thus any insurrection that occurred must surely be the visible manifestation of the universal plot. This meant that any republican could be arrested as having been a potential insurgent, an accomplice or source of inspiration for the insurgents; all that was necessary was for him to have associated with political groups which the administration could dub 'secret societies'.

As we have indicated in passing in the previous chapter, this was the line of reasoning that accounted for the fact that in the statistics relating to those taken into custody we find many militant republicans who never took up arms at all.

Above all, it was the line of reasoning that led the army, the *gendarmerie* and the police to engage, between mid-December and January, in huge round-ups of suspects which filled the prisons to overflowing.

The mixed commissions

There were so many prisoners that, to sift them out, a ministerial circular was sent round at the beginning of the month of February, organising the famous *mixed commissions*. In each department, the prefect and general in command of the military forces found themselves joined by a third civil servant: a magistrate representing the department of public prosecutions. The mix was now complete. Prefects and magistrates had often been associated, in the days before December, in the task of organising surveillance over the *montagnard* party. The prefects and the military had, for their parts, worked together during the direct repression of the days of December. Now the three hierarchies that guaranteed the existing order were brought into close collaboration. In terms of morale, the very

institution of the mixed commissions had an appalling effect upon the republicans. Far from regarding the presence of a magistrate as guaranteeing justice, all they could see in this collaboration was a prostitution of justice on the part of the magistracy. It gave them yet another grievance against Bonaparte: he had flouted the principle of the separation of powers.

The mixed commissions indeed proceeded in a most summary fashion. They reached their decisions without discussion after a rapid examination of the case, but never hearing any evidence for the defence and allowing no possibility of appeal. Furthermore, they remained absolutely faithful to the official line described above. For them, it was not a matter of deciding who had or had not committed any particular actions of an insurrectional, rebellious or predatory nature ... but simply who, in the overall subversive situation, had played a role of any importance.

All those arrested and examined were arbitrarily divided into eight categories according to the degree of danger that they represented. The categories were distinguished as follows: (1) those who were sent before a court martial: these were the presumed leaders and insurgents who had fired upon the troops; (2) those who were sent to detention in Cayenne (Guyana) without any form of trial: all armed insurgents who were arrested; (3) those sent to Algeria under enforced residence (indicated by the famous sign Algérie +) and those sent there under free residence (Algérie −): this was the fate reserved for 'demagogues' of notoriety, depending upon their presumed degree of harmfulness; (4) those expelled from France or (5) temporarily removed from their homes: these two categories applied to republicans whose presence was 'an element of disorder'. Those who had simply followed the leaders were (6) interned in a specified town or (7) placed under surveillance. Finally (8) those detained for infractions of common law were sent before a court of summary jurisdiction.

As can be seen, categories (1) and (8) allowed for the application of the classic forms of justice. On the other hand, the others offered a vast field open to arbitrary action. The fates of thousands of men were sealed in this way simply because their militant pasts, seen through out-dated reports or summary snatches of gossip, assigned them labels as vague as 'fanatical', 'very dangerous' or 'a danger to society'.

The legal repression

But the justice of the legal forms of repression, whether court martials or courts of assizes, were no more satisfactory. It was to these that the few cases of murder committed in the course of the insurrection were referred. In the Cuers (Var) affair, which involved the killing of a *gendarmerie* sergeant, the prosecution was determined to obtain the death

penalty not only for the young, illiterate peasant who had fired the shot, but also for the young, educated and politicised peasant who had led the insurrection and who was accused (although he spiritedly denied it) of having given the order to fire. Both the magistrates and the jury, not content to exact retribution for a partial act of *'jacquerie'* (which was, besides, probably accidental), proved themselves anxious at all costs to demonstrate that the manifestation of *jacquerie* had been encouraged by politically conscious republicans.[1] The singular iniquity of this local affair was, as can be seen, brought altogether in line with the more general iniquity of the conservative thesis, which was now the official view. The Cuers incident was far from an isolated case. At Clamecy, similarly, the young republican leader, Eugène Millelot, the son of an employer-printer and an active and pugnacious leader of the insurrection, who was nevertheless scrupulous in his observance of legality, was condemned not only as the effective organiser of the uprising but also for the murder of a bourgeois of which he was quite innocent. He was sent off to die in the Cayenne penitentiary.

This spate of military brutality and provincial vengeance assumed such proportions that it became a cause for concern to the prince-president, who had no personal malice and might even have feared that his long-term policies might be jeopardised. After all, had not the Restoration been permanently compromised by a handful of episodes that had marked its advent during the White Terror?

In March and April three State councillors were despatched with the mission extraordinary of examining the doings of the mixed commissions in central, south-western and south-eastern France respectively, and also to prepare the measures of clemency that should be recommended to the Head of State. A number of major sentences were, as a result, commuted and a number of minor ones revoked. However, this episode – a significant one from the point of view of Louis-Napoleon's future policies – did not succeed in wiping out the memory of what had gone before. In the first place, quantitively, the remissions affected only a small number of those 'sentenced' by the mixed commissions, and secondly, from a qualitative point of view, these hastily decided gestures of clemency, far from mitigating the general impression of arbitrariness, were bound to contribute further towards it.

The banishment of the representatives

While the fates of the republicans in the provinces were being settled in this fashion, those of the leaders who had organised resistance in Paris were also sealed.

In Paris, as in the provinces, there were too many prisoners, and too many famous names among them. They had to be sifted out. The repre-

sentatives from the right-wing opposition did not long remain in the prisons of Mazas and Vincennes. They were almost immediately released, with the exception of five prominent Orleanists (Rémusat, Duvergier de Hauranne and three others) who were sent to join their friends Thiers and Baze, and also the generals, in exile. Sentences of banishment for the parliamentary opposition of the left were far heavier: they fell upon seventy-odd republican representatives. Among them were Hugo and Schoelcher, Madier de Montjau and Raspail, Nadaud and Perdiguier, Pierre Leroux and Edgar Quinet – to mention only the most famous names. A special fate was reserved for the dozen or so republicans (two of them representatives) who had roused Orléans,[2] and above all for the five representatives whom the police considered to be the leaders of the organised movement: Marc Dufraisse, Miot, Greppo, Richardet and Mathé. They were sentenced to deportation to Cayenne, a grim prospect and one that in time often proved fatal. However, at the last moment, the sentence was commuted: Miot was sent to Algeria while the rest were simply exiled, like most of their Mountain colleagues.

Cases of conscience

George Sand was probably instrumental in obtaining this first instance of clemency. In 1848 she had been an ardent republican, but had subsequently been considerably disappointed by the bourgeois republic and so, like Lamartine, had withdrawn from active politics. It was her very remoteness from the political scene that now made it easier for her to intervene with greater effectiveness in favour of individuals whose ideals she shared, although she was not directly associated with them. Other influences, directed to the same ends, were also at work upon the prince. All those who could be described as left-wing Bonapartists, individuals of progressive yet authoritarian inclinations, who had in all seriousness believed the populist line professed by the *coup d'Etat*, could not but feel alarmed at the massively conservative repression so heavily suggestive of the rancours of the party of order. For example, Jérôme-Napoleon, the Emperor's *montagnard* cousin, thus persuaded the prince to commute Demosthène Ollivier's sentence of deportation to Guyana to one of simple exile. Saint-Simonians, such as Enfantin, who had quickly rallied to the enlightened despot they considered Bonaparte to be, were pressing for similar concessions. It was no doubt the combination of these various pressures that succeeded in obtaining the most spectacular of these gestures of clemency, the recall of Pauline Roland from Algeria. Her family situation made her particularly worthy of pity: she had, in accordance with her feminist principles, been bringing up her two children single-handed, while at the same time leading the full life of a militant which took her from schools to cooperatives and from cooperatives to the barri-

cades. Unfortunately, her detention at Lambessa, followed by the trying return sea voyage from Algiers to Marseilles during the winter, combined seriously to undermine her health, and soon after her return to France, at the age of forty-seven, she died.

Republican consciences were troubled. Should they feel grateful to Bonaparte for being neither truly cruel nor truly reactionary or should they curse him for having abolished the rule of law? Michelet's entry in his *Journal* for 7 March 1852 records a painful conversation that he had had upon this subject with his old friend George Sand:

> I found Mme Sand as impressive and unaffected as usual, as good as usual, and that makes me forgive her a great deal. All the same, one cannot approve of her goodness. Why? Because it stems in part from a kind of sceptical facility she possesses that enables her to accept and like everything. I myself am by nature so opposed to such a state of mind that my whole heart revolted and I had to state my own beliefs. She herself provided me with the opportunity and indeed invited me to do so. She did not conceal the fact that she found little to choose between the victors of the day and the vanquished, since all of them claimed that the ends justified the means.
> 'And, in between these two camps, what about justice, Madame?'
> I thus replaced the subject on the solid ground of Justice and Right.
> No, the ends do not justify the means. And only right has rights. Only right can legitimately employ forceful means and mete out the severities of justice.[3]

The secession of intelligence

There can be no doubt that the great majority of republican intellectuals thought, like Michelet, that justice in politics – in other words, the Republic – could not be defined simply in terms of the people, but must also stand by the reign of Right; and the impossibility of their becoming reconciled to the Empire depended in direct proportion on the degree of their legalism, in the fullest sense of the term. It was the spirit of legalism that had swelled the ranks of exiles with a whole flood of voluntary *émigrés* as soon as it had become clear that the new regime was reintroducing a compulsory oath of loyalty for those holding public office. It was the enforcement upon so many individuals of an oath of this type that had, in the past, discredited the monarchies. (One is put in mind of Chateaubriand's sarcastic comment upon the old notables, the success of whose careers could be measured by the number of oaths they had sworn, in the same way as the age of old stags can be measured by the proliferation of their antlers ...) That kind of oath had been abolished by the 1848 Revolution as being essentially monarchical and contrary to liberty. The only oath of loyalty left was the one imposed upon the Head of State, who had to swear loyalty to the Constitution. And now Bonaparte, having violated the promise that he himself had sworn in December 1848, was

imposing an oath in his favour upon the citizens who had become his subjects. The university was deserted by its republican professors. Those who had been banished as rebels went off to fill the schools and libraries of Switzerland, England and Belgium. That is how Paul Deschanel, a future president of the French Republic, came to be born in Brussels in 1855, in the home of an exiled university teacher. Others found asylum in the *quartier latin*'s few free, secular establishments such as Sainte-Barbe, or lived as best they could from various free professions, constituting as it were a new circle of *émigrés* within France itself. One of them was Michelet: already deprived of his chair at the Collège de France, he now, through his refusal to take the oath, lost his principal function as director of the National Archives and was forced to live entirely by his pen, the prolificness of which was fortunately in no way diminished by his indignation.

All in all, it is fair to say that the combination of the repression and this refusal to take the oath resulted in a large proportion of the intellectual elite turning their backs upon the regime.

The story of the refusal to take the oath now brings us to the subject of institutional history.

The institutions

The first plebiscite

The plebiscite was, right from the first, the major preoccupation of the authors of the *coup d'Etat*. On 2 December it had been announced that a Constitution in conformity with the example of Year VIII would be submitted to popular vote. Its principal provisions were for the appointment of a Head of State responsible for ten years, ministers who depended upon the executive power alone, a Council of State to prepare laws, an elected Legislative Body to pass them and a second Assembly 'composed of the country's most illustrious men' to serve as 'a deliberating power and guardian of the fundamental pact and of public liberties'.

The voting was openly rigged. First the army and the navy were requested to vote through open registers, in the barracks. This produced 300,000 votes in favour, 37,000 votes against and 3,000 abstentions. Then, on 20 December, it was the turn of the civilians, who voted by secret ballot in the town halls. The results were as could be expected for a country in total disarray, with one-third of its territory in a state of siege, where opposition newspapers could no longer appear and all the politically minded who were not either in exile or in prison were lying low. The votes in favour totalled seven and a half million, those against 640,000, with 36,000 spoilt ballot papers and about one and a half million abstentions. Naturally enough, the strongest minority pockets of opposition were to be

found in the large towns. (In Paris, where the votes against totalled 80,000 and there were 75,000 abstentions, the 132,000 votes in favour represented less than half the ballot.)

Only one canton, Vernoux (Ardèche), where the majority of the population was Protestant, returned a majority of votes against. Overall, these came principally from localities that were liberal, although too moderate to have taken part in the insurrection: for that very reason they had not been terrorised by the repression. In contrast, in the most radical localities, where armed uprisings had taken place and fear now reigned, nobody dared to displease the authorities. The red rural areas were as if erased from the electoral map, and opposition once more became an essentially city-based phenomenon.

The favourable result was proclaimed with much pomp on 31 December. In a speech that became famous, Bonaparte took the opportunity to profess some kind of a guilty conscience.

He maintained in particular that France had understood 'that I only departed from legality in order to return to the law'. It was an uneasy formula which in effect reversed the terms, for it was rather a matter of having departed from the law and being about to establish a new kind of legality. He went on to make an implicit admission of guilt when he declared: 'More than seven million votes have just *absolved* me.'

The prince-president lost no time in making use of the full powers he had been granted. On 14 January came the simultaneous appearance of the promulgated Constitution and also a long proclamation, in which he gave his comments upon the foundations of the Constitution and the provisions that it made.

The maintenance of universal suffrage

The chief provision was for universal suffrage, maintained in the form it had taken before the law of 31 May 1850.

The seven million votes of 20 December seemed – when the circumstances were not too closely examined – to justify the action which had restored a say to the 'vile multitude' that had been muzzled by Monsieur Thiers.

The gaining of 'absolution' through the assent of the majority was certainly the most durable principle of the new regime: the plebiscite allowed the master in power to appeal directly to the people over the heads of the political classes whenever he wanted to. In this way he turned universal suffrage against the republicans, even though two years earlier it had seemed their only absolute weapon.

In effect, Bonaparte simply provided proof, if proof indeed were necessary, that universal suffrage is not a panacea and that it only serves the cause of progress in clearly defined conditions: total liberty for politi-

cal expression, education for the peasant masses, no political influence exerted by the clergy. The entire programme of the future Republic was to define itself in these terms in direct and explicit reaction against the use of the plebiscite by this 'Empire of the rural areas'.

Reactionary constitutional moves

Apart from the right of universal suffrage, the other elements of the political system were mainly regressions to the state of affairs prior to February 1848. We have already made this point in respect of the oath (article 14).

It also applied to the executive which, since the name of its titular holder 'Prince Louis-Napoleon Bonaparte' was writ large into the Constitution itself (article 2), was already more than half way to being monarchical.

And it applied to the Legislative Assembly which, among other provisions, again found itself divided into two Chambers (article 4). So as to avoid the re-establishment of a Chamber of Peers, 'a pale reflection of the Chamber of Deputies', as it had been under Louis-Philippe, a Senate was established. It was to reflect above all the views of . . . the executive, for it was composed of '(1) cardinals, marshals and admirals; (2) those citizens whom the president of the Republic sees fit to elevate to the dignity of Senator' (article 20).

Again, there was regression in the electoral system for the Legislative Body, through universal suffrage: 'deputies will no longer be elected . . . by voting for several members from a list' (article 36) and the preamble specifically declared that that voting system 'falsified an election'. In order to elude the mainstream currents of opinion which found expression more readily through lists of candidates made up within a departmental framework, there was a reversion to voting for a single name, a parochial system that favoured the notables and that had flourished under Guizot. There was regression even with respect to the number of deputies, which in itself represented a significant trend. Under the Second Republic the Assemblies had been large (750 members), as they had during the Revolution. The Legislative Body of 1852 reverted to a limited membership (less than 300) of the Chambers, as during the period of suffrage based upon census qualifications.

All in all, these constitutional measures incorporated all the elements of a veritable autocracy – the autocracy that was to function, following a simple change in title, throughout the authoritarian Empire. All we need note at this point is the already noticeable trend. Despite the insistent efforts of an anti-Orleanist demagogy, the model handed on by the Consulate was in some respects being modified by a few touches borrowed from Guizot's administration, but without the liberalism of the latter.

There were two other immediate political developments which can be regarded as fairly typical that served to support this Constitution, already in itself authoritarian: the regime imposed upon the press and the introduction of official candidates.

Other methods employed by the dictatorship

By 17 February, the fate of the press had been decided in one of those decrees with the force of law that the prince-president had received the right to issue on his own, in accordance with the temporary provisions of the last article of the Constitution. Newspapers were subjected to a regime of preliminary authorisation; stamp duty and caution money remained of course and – most importantly – a system of 'warnings' was introduced. A 'warning' was issued by the authorities when an article was considered offensive; once a certain number of warnings had been issued, the newspaper was automatically suspended. So there was now no need for the unpopular censorship. The system imposed a circumspection on the journalists that operated as an effective self-censorship.

There is perhaps a temptation to describe all this as hypocrisy, but we should not over-generalise. In the matter of electoral procedure there was, on the contrary, more of a tendency toward a cynical frankness. Reacting against regimes that had offered covert encouragement to what were in effect official candidates – the subtle intrigues of Guizot's prefects for example – Morny made official candidacies standard practice. Public notice was now given of the government's candidate, the prefect or subprefect would campaign openly and issue direct propaganda on his behalf, public facilities would be provided for him, and his opponents – in the event of there being any – would be subject to harassment.

The 1852 elections

In the immediate event, this radical absence of liberties carried the vicious excesses of the system to the point of caricature on the first occasion of its application. The elections held for the Legislative Body in February–March 1852 produced only eight representatives for the opposition. Five came from the right, noted legitimists who had not rallied to Bonaparte but who were too deeply rooted in their rural fiefdoms in western France to be dislodged. The other three came from the left. In three constituencies, two in Paris and one in Lyons, the electors had managed – with no public electoral campaign at all – to return republicans: they were Carnot, Cavaignac and Doctor Hénon. However, in order not to have to swear the oath of allegiance to the dictator, they renounced their seats.

The three who were not accepting election wrote as follows:

> We thank [the electors] for having considered that our names were, in themselves, protests against the destruction of public liberties and the

severities of arbitrary authority, but they would not wish to send us to take our seats in a Legislative Body whose powers do not extend to making reparation for violations to the law. We reject the immoral theory of reticence and mental reservation.[4]

On the other side of the political spectrum, Berryer for his part had managed to dissuade his Marseilles electors from adopting him as their candidate and voting for him, expressing himself in practically similar terms: 'What should I be doing in that Legislative Body deprived of any kind of vitality and in which I should not even find the independence and liberty that the Revolutions of 1830 and 1848 did not remove from us?'[5]

The election of Hénon, in the working-class district of La Guillotière in Lyons, had been a small triumph of organised clandestine propaganda spread from one workshop to the next and from door to door, under cover of darkness. Natural networks of communication existed in proletarian circles, where men were not only working companions but neighbours too, and the police could do very little about them. Clearly, during this extreme phase of contraction, the most solid nucleus of the republican party was to be found in the working classes of the large towns. This was perhaps the popular milieu least open to the influence of the clergy, which the regime elsewhere exploited to an excessive extent, particularly in the country regions.

The role of the Church

As we have repeatedly noted, the Catholic Church had often used its voice and influence in support of the party of order; it now similarly came to the assistance of the *coup d'Etat*. The vast majority of the clergy were much more sensitive to the 'red spectre' emphasised by official propaganda than to the reservations expressed – ineffectually, alas – by the handful of conservatives who had remained liberal. In the world of the notables, Montalembert, for instance, faithful to the line he had been pursuing ever since the summer of 1848, was producing eloquent theoretical support and propaganda for the alliance between the Church and the authorities now in power. So much in favour of it was he that he even agreed to stand as an official candidate, and so became a member of the Legislative Body. Bonaparte gave up listening to any left-wing views expressed by his entourage on this decisive point and went all out to please the Church. It was noticeable that the Constitution gave the cardinals a place in the Senate, but excluded representatives from other cults that had accepted the Concordat of 1801. It was also noted that the Panthéon was now restored as a place of Catholic worship. In this highly symbolic matter, political regression reached even further back than the July Monarchy, in fact as far back as the Restoration period. Like Louis XVIII, a predecessor whom he forebore to mention, Louis-Napoleon,

although of a sceptical nature and not inherently vindictive, out of political interest did nothing to prevent a measure of White Terror and the establishment of strong bonds between the throne and the altar. Again like Louis XVIII, he admittedly sometimes knew how to salvage what was essential by making a great stir rather than being truly effective. For instance, at the Ministry of Public Instruction, the circular that the Minister Fortoul issued, forbidding professors to wear beards on the grounds that these were 'symbols of anarchy', did not pass unnoticed. What attracted much less attention was the fact that the university continued to exist with only a few slight changes, despite the fact that the most fanatical of the clergy would have happily seen it totally dismantled.

On the whole, however, the political situation was one of conservative and clerical reaction, the effects of which combined with those of the Constitution and cuts within the administration to produce support of an extremely docile nature for the authorities in power.

What were they going to do with it?

What kind of social support was considered desirable?
The directives regarding the choice of official candidates which Morny gave the prefects received considerable attention:

> Men surrounded by public esteem, concerned more with the country's interests than with struggles between the parties, men sympathetic to the sufferings of the labouring classes and who, through a philanthropic use of their fortunes, have acquired both influence and well-deserved respect,

and:

> When a man has made his fortune by his labour, in industry or in agriculture, has improved the lot of his workers and has made an honourable use of his wealth, he is to be preferred to what is nowadays known as *a man of politics*; for such a man will bring a sense of what is practical to the passing of laws and will support the government in its task of pacification and re-edification.[6]

A fair reflection of the trend would be: 'enough of little country squires and bourgeois of private means! Enough of lawyers and journalists! What we need are industrialists!'

It was a doubly and profoundly illuminating choice. In the first place, most obviously, the regime's preference was intimately tied in with the politically reactionary situation. What was being rejected explicitly was the *political* class (a relatively homogeneous class: it would be incorrect to make an absolute opposition between its lawyers on the one hand and its landowners of private means on the other, for most of the lawyers of the time owned some land and most landowners of private means had done their share of studying the humanities). The political class was, then, a

class of men educated in the humanities, legalistic men, men of principle (whether royalist or republican); it was therefore a class of people who made difficulties. Better by far the new men, straight from their factories (and in many cases still, at this date, quite close to the people), who were less educated, less dogmatic and who would allow 'politics' to be run by the ministers. That, at any rate, is certainly how it was during the first two sessions.

But there was also a sense in which Morny's preference was innovative. Implicit in it was the idea that the world of the notables, the world of intellectuals and landowners of private means had not made enough room for those who were creating new wealth, for men who were useful, for the 'industrialists' (as the Saint-Simonians called them), or the *entrepreneurs*, as we would describe them. In short, the country needed to be impelled more strongly in the direction of economic modernity, and in order to do so it was necessary to recompose its ruling class with a stronger element of men working, in a practical way, towards progress.

There was undeniably a certain coherence in the political and economic preferences adopted by the *coup d'Etat*. We have considered the former. Now we must examine the latter.

The great economic initiatives

In substance, what Morny was advocating was the encouragement of industrialists – but philanthropic ones (men who were 'sympathetic to the sufferings of the labouring classes' and who had 'improved the lot of [their] workers'). Did this perhaps limit the choice? It should in all fairness be pointed out that 1850 was still close to the time when society was still mostly agricultural, when the principal source of pauperism was rural under-employment and when, consequently, the principal form of philanthropy in a canton was indeed the creation of industry, because this transformed its semi-unemployed into full wage-earners.[7]

Admittedly, the situation was beginning to change. Over the past ten years it had become apparent that the installation of industry created a pauperism of its own, and that a system that depended on the '*patrons*' was not necessarily paternalistic. Let us put it this way: both views, the pessimistic and the optimistic, existed at the time and the regime naturally chose the optimistic, that is it favoured industrialism of an energetic and socially minded kind.

Social policy

In this respect, one of the most significant measures was the decree-cum-law of 26 March relating to mutual insurance companies. It came, to be sure, after a whole series of decisions – emergency decisions

but lasting ones for all that – through which, within this framework of repression, all *cercles*, societies, *chambrées* etc., where men of the people could meet together, were closed down. At the same time, the surveillance of cafés and *cabarets* was reinforced. This was the climax of the conservative phobia of the life of the civic or social (in the wide sense of the term) associations. On the other hand, however, the regime was anxious to systematise the professional associations on account of their virtues in respect of working-class education, and through this, it was hoped, their encouragement of moderation. Mutual insurance companies were thus granted legal advantages, provided they complied with two forms of guarantee: (1) the inclusion of a few honorary (non-working-class) members and (2) the acceptance of a president appointed by the authorities. The Bonapartist strategy of dissociating the political from the social could be detected here: while the republican movement was entirely banned, if possible completely destroyed, the workers' movement, although controlled and channelled, in contrast was allowed – even compelled – to exist.

The affair of the Orléans fortune

Ambivalence reigned, and often a single set of measures would aim simultaneously to further political repression on the one hand and social progress on the other. So it was with the great sensation of 23 January: the nationalisation of the property of the Orléans family (that is personal possessions which Louis-Philippe had given his sons on 7 August, rather than return them to the State). It was an act of political revenge (and possibly precaution) against the Orléans princes whom Bonaparte judged to be, or potentially to be, rivals even more dangerous than the republican party. But it also represented a major move in his campaign to win over popular support, for the decree announced that ten million francs of this inheritance would be passed on to mutual insurance companies, ten million to finance housing for the workers and ten million to land-banks etc.

Perhaps the prince-president did not realise that his action would stir up the first political storm of his reign as prince. It amounted, in effect, to nationalisation, encroachment upon private property. The wealthy bourgeois, still recovering from their alarms of 2 December, for which they had by now almost forgiven him, since 'communism' had, as a result, been crushed, were astounded to find the latter rearing its head again just where they did not expect it. In the Institute, in the *salons* of society, even in the Council of State and the corridors of the ministries, a wind of rebellion rose against the president who was reverting to 'socialism'. And since, for the conservatives, socialism meant robbery, the ex-president Dupin produced a pun which enjoyed a great success: 'C'est le premier vol de l'aigle ...' (It is the eagle's first flight/theft ...)

For Louis-Napoleon, the most serious consequence was the disapproval of four of his supporters, Morny, Fould, Rouher and Magne. They all resigned their ministries so as not to be associated with the despoiling of the Orléans princes whose intimates they used to be. Unmoved, the prince-president replaced those who had resigned with other, minor figures, and waited for the furore to abate. Abate it did and the malcontents returned when it was realised that no other properties were under threat and that, on the contrary, the economic climate that the authorities were seeking would be more liberal and expansionist than ever.

Industrial expansion

For here lay the essential point: namely, the promotion of what we would today call expansion, which the world economic situation had needed ever since 1850, but which had been frustrated by the particular French political situation, overshadowed as it was with the spectre of '1852'. By making it politically certain that capital and free enterprise ran no short-term risks, the *coup d'Etat* in itself represented – and strove consciously so to do – a chance for re-expansion.

Stimulated by a number of astute technical measures taken by the ministry (slight changes in the statutes of the Banque de France, conversions of government stock), business in effect picked up again very quickly and the climate of the Bourse (the Stock Exchange) was euphoric. But Louis-Napoleon was determined to do even more to boost the economy.

He saw quite clearly that a new industrial boom would be launched if the railway network could be completed (because this would prove a radical means of facilitating trade exchanges and stimulating the industries of iron, coal and mechanical construction). But the railway companies were powerless without the banking groups. Now, the banking world was dominated by the Rothschilds, and for the past twenty years the Rothschilds had been associated with the Orléans and were therefore inclined to favour a political opposition of the Thierist type. If necessary, Louis-Napoleon would have to do without them and he believed himself capable of doing so. He had other capitalists on his side, for instance, the Fould brothers (Achille the politician and Benoît, who had remained the head of the family bank). As we have seen already, the Bonaparte–Fould political association was already of two years' standing and in the event was not to be compromised by the 'flight/theft of the eagle'. Furthermore, even within the Rothschild business there were two ambitious young leaders, the Péreire brothers, who through their profound Saint-Simonian convictions were committed to supporting an enlightened despot rather than the parliamentary regime. They were thus disposed to collaborate with the government. All this explains how it was that things got off the ground so rapidly.

The new capitalism

Through the offices of the Péreire brothers, business negotiations that had been dragging on for some time were soon brought to a conclusion, even without supplanting the Rothschild family. One such business was the Paris–Lyons railway, which the State had been obliged to buy back from a bankrupt company in August 1848, and the construction of which it had since then been slowly continuing. It would willingly have returned it to some private group had not the Assembly (in part reflecting rival financial interests) contained pockets of resistance which were opposed to placing the whole concern in other hands.[8] With the Assembly out of the way, by 5 January 1852 the government conceded the Paris–Lyons line to a consortium of financiers composed of Rothschild, Péreire and others. It was at this point and in this connection that a new bond was launched upon the public: 'a 300-franc bond, an inexpensive security paying *fixed* interest which was to accumulate immense savings from the middle social levels and become the keystone for the financing of the great railway networks for decades to come'.[9]

Here was industrial expansion, and it was using relatively 'democratised' capital: both aspects of the innovation were viewed favourably by Bonaparte.

Thanks, once more, to the Péreire brothers, 19 February saw the completion of another deal with the State that up till now James Rothschild had been unable to clinch: the *Compagnie du Nord* had its concession increased to 99 years in return for undertaking a number of extensions to the railway network.

Encouraged by these successes, the Péreire brothers now embarked upon their own personal game, staking a great deal on the new regime just as the latter staked a great deal on them. In this new situation the Rothschilds were the losers. But that was probably also in part because the time had come for a new type of business banking. It is important that we should, at this point, indicate how early these banking concerns made their appearance – even before the establishment of the Empire in the strict sense of the term. Thus, historical chronology yet again helps us to understand the *coup d'Etat* of the man sometimes referred to as a 'Saint-Simonian Caesar' (Louis Girard).[10]

The decision to favour large-scale, powerful, concentrated companies was quite positive. During the spring of 1852 Talabot, with the support of Rothschild (and this time in competition with the Péreire brothers) arranged for a merger between the Lyons–Avignon and the Avignon–Marseilles lines. It was only later that the PLM (Paris–Lyons–Marseilles), one of the six great companies to emerge from definitive mergers of this kind, was established. Let us simply note that as early as June 1852, on the occasion of the Lyons–Avignon–Marseilles merger, Morny gave his

official blessing to the theory of 'powerful' companies, the only kind in a position to entertain expansive views and effect bold improvements, thereby serving the public interests.[11] As for the rupture that this particular deal caused between James Rothschild and the Péreire brothers, it prompted the latter to take the decisive step. In September, the *Crédit mobilier* was set up with the backing of the Péreire brothers, Benoît Fould, Mirès and the duc de Morny in person. The establishment that was quintessentially typical of imperial neo-capitalism was thus created. Bold, innovative and expansionist, its ambiguous aim was to democratise wealth, possibly with a tendency to monopolise the creations of that wealth. As an eminent specialist on the subject wrote:[12]

> [The *Crédit mobilier*] was set up first and foremost as a sleeping-bank for the development of the railways and metallurgy, but also as a financial establishment in a position to deal with all operations on a governmental level, with a special responsibility for maintaining or increasing the quotation price of the values in its own group.
> The originality of the new enterprise lay, in particular, in the methods projected to drain capital: in order to increase its own resources, it planned to borrow from the public, at high interests, by issuing bonds, some short-term, others repayable over longer periods. The Péreire brothers intended to reinject this borrowed money into industrial investment, State loans and Stock Exchange tactics, but their real aim was to gain a kind of monopoly over large industrial creations.
> No doubt they dreamed of gaining control over the large railway and metallurgical companies, absorbing their stocks and turning the *Crédit mobilier*'s own stocks and shares into some kind of 'universal security' which would represent the debts of all the large enterprises assembled through mergers under its aegis ...

It was a vast programme and one which, as is well known, eventually failed in its ultimate ambitions. But it is significant that it saw the light of day in 1852.

Agricultural policies

'Democratising' the diffusion of railway or metallurgical shares would assist industry. These same men thought they would also redress another weakness of previous regimes by 'democratising' another type of credit in order to assist agriculture, which was ailing. It was to this end, at any rate, that they founded the *Banque foncière de Paris* which, in December 1852, took the name *Crédit foncier de France*. These were extremely interesting aims, but, as may be seen from a study of the Second Empire, the undeniable improvement in agricultural production and in the condition of the peasants was in the end obtained by much less direct methods, almost through the force of circumstances.

So it would be quite false to represent the regime as interventionist. While capable of intervention to provide stimulus in certain decisive areas

(such as railway mergers), it remained in all other respects deeply attached to the free play of private interests and initiatives. Where agriculture was concerned, for example, the authorities adopted a position more or less directly opposed to the protective policies that the Assemblies before the *coup d'Etat* had been successful in promoting.[13] In the first place, as goes without saying, the members of the chambers of agriculture established in each *arrondissement* were now no longer elected, but were instead appointed by the sub-prefect. Furthermore, the *Conseil général de l'Agriculture* ceased to meet and fell into disuse. Above all, the farm schools were abandoned and finally, in September 1852, the Agronomic Institute of Versailles was closed down. The Ministry for Commerce and Agriculture once more became attached to the Ministry for the Interior. It was the end of the road for all the fine agronomic zeal so characteristic of both the July and the republican regimes. Louis-Napoleon desired progress in the countryside no less than his predecessors, but what he wanted was progress that would be spontaneously diffused as a consequence of the general economic impetus, without costing too much to the State, for which expenses of a more classic nature were already envisaged.

For monarchical pomp and military glory would cost a great deal. And the prospect of such things could be glimpsed on the horizon. Already the seat of President of the Senate was occupied by a former king, namely Jérôme, the last surviving brother of Emperor Napoleon.

The return to imperial monarchy

The first quarter of the year 1852 had been entirely taken up with the resolution of the aftermath of the uprisings, the establishment of new institutions, the launching of a new economic policy, the little 'affair' of the Orléans possessions and the legislative elections.

The session of the Legislative Body

By the end of March, it became possible to return officially to normal life. Pacification being now completed, the state of siege was lifted everywhere on 28 March. On the following day, the Legislative Body embarked upon a three-month session. Only one meeting was necessary for a block vote to approve a budget prepared by a series of decrees during the period of transition. For the remainder of the time there was well-behaved discussion of various laws of an extremely technical nature. No great orations, just serious work. 'In this Assembly of clients only M. de Montalambert* seemed to be perpetuating parliamentary memories'

---

*1810–70. He had held a seat in the Chambre de Pairs (the House of Lords) under Louis-Philippe. As an Orleanist, he should have been a liberal, that is he should not have compromised himself in a servile and ill-judged fashion in the legislative coup of 1852.

(Albert Thomas). He was later to admit that he had been misguided in doing so.

The tour of Provence

The prince-president wanted to renew his contacts with the country, as he had done in 1850, in order to prepare for the next stage in what he liked to call the construction of the 'edifice'. Boldly, he decided to visit the southern regions of France, where the recent insurrections had just provided a reminder that Bonapartism had never, even at the time of the Emperor, been very popular. He passed first through the departments of central France, which had also recently been involved in the insurrection. Police precautions were strict, but there was no marked hostility. Once beyond Bourges, it was noticeable that the local authorities, possibly obeying orders from Paris, began to get the troops to shout 'Long live the Emperor!' as the procession passed. The tendency became more marked as the progress continued. After descending the Rhône valley, the prince-president arrived in Marseilles on 25 September. This visit was particularly important and minute preparations were made for it. There were proclamations from the prefect and the mayor, old soldiers of the Empire were recalled and republicans reputed to be dangerous were preventatively detained. An agreement was even negotiated with Piedmont for the internment (in Nice) of any exiles who might have attempted to cross the Var in secret to make an attempt on the president's life.

And while on the topic of assassination attempts, preparations for some infernal device were indeed discovered in the Marseilles suburbs, but whether this was a real plot or a frame-up engineered by the police for the purposes of propaganda is a question that, even today, remains unresolved. Whatever the case may have been, Louis-Napoleon was received with much pomp, salvoes of artillery, peals of church bells, triumphal arches and all the rejoicing of a crowd showered with entertainment, festivals and ceremonial. In all the speeches, as on the pediments of the triumphal arches, there were allusions to the Empire. The imperial emblems left no doubt as to the political future.

But there were two powers that counted in Marseilles: commerce and the Church. The prince-president made the suitable gestures. On 26 September, after mass, 'His Imperial Highness' laid the first stone of the new cathedral and, in the afternoon of the same day, following the jollifications, he also laid the first stone of the new palace destined to house the Stock Exchange and the Chamber of Commerce.

On the following day Louis-Napoleon set sail for Toulon, where he astutely granted the town a satisfaction it had long been vainly demanding from all previous regimes, namely that the old military precinct should be dismantled, making it possible to proceed forthwith with the demoli-

tion of the ramparts and the construction of the new town that was considered indispensable.

The speech in Bordeaux

On 29 September, he left Provence for the Languedoc and Aquitaine, having already secured his essential objective. He had won a success of prestige with his ceremonious progress through a region of dubious sympathies and a political success with his symbolic gestures of renewed deference towards Catholicism and commerce. The remainder of the journey lived up to this promise.

The last stage in Bordeaux, from 8 to 10 October, was even more remarkable.[14] Haussmann, prefect for the Gironde, had put on a good show and, as is well known, reaped the benefit in the subsequent advancement of his brilliant career in Paris. The prince-president made his arrival by boat along the river. (As between Marseilles and Toulon, there were still no railway communications linking Toulouse and Bordeaux). He received a generous and dignified welcome from both banks. Nor was anything left to be desired in the town itself. There were reviews, receptions, visits, balls and also a *Te Deum*. On 9 October, at a banquet organised by the Chamber of Commerce on the occasion of the launching of the *Louis-Napoleon*, a fine ship with its prow 'decorated with a colossal figurehead of the prince', its happy sponsor produced his crucial speech:

> France today surrounds me with sympathy because I do not belong to the family of ideologues. To bring about the welfare of the country there is no need to introduce new systems, but rather to promote confidence in the present and security for the future. That is why France appears to wish to return to the Empire.
> However, there is one fear that I must answer. Some people say with misgiving: 'The Empire means war.' I say: 'The Empire means peace.' It means peace, because that is what France desires and when France is satisfied the world is calm.
> Nevertheless, I must admit that, like the Emperor, I have many conquests to make. I wish, as he did, to win dissident parties over to conciliation ... I wish to win over to religion, to morality and to prosperity that still numerous section of the population which ... is still barely aware of the precepts of Christ; and which ... has at its disposal hardly any of the primary material necessities of life.
> We have huge uncultivated territories to clear, roads to open, ports to dig, rivers to render navigable, canals to finish and our network of railways to complete ...
> That is what I shall understand the Empire to mean, if indeed the Empire is to be re-established ...

The following day, the whole of France learned of this declaration of intent; it was the signal for the process of restoration to get under way.

The restoration of the Empire

On his return to the capital, the Head of State was greeted with pressing speeches urging him, openly now, in the aftermath of all the acclamations and triumphal arches, to act upon his intentions.

In the terms of the Constitution, revision had to be proposed by the Senate. The opinion of this august body could not be in doubt, since it had been recruited by the prince himself. We should note, at this juncture, that it admittedly counted among its ranks the last survivor of the National Convention, the octogenarian Thibaudeau; however, this former regicide had also been a loyal servant to the first Emperor.

The Senate was duly convened and proposed modifications to the executive. The latter having ratified these, the next step was the establishment of the *senatus-consultum* of 7 November.

The title of Emperor was re-established. Out of respect for the memory of his cousin, the short-lived Napoleon II* of 6 April 1814, Louis-Napoleon Bonaparte, Emperor of the French, took the name Napoleon III. In every other respect the Constitution of 14 January was maintained intact. The new regime was to be ratified by plebiscite.

This took place on 21 November under the same conditions as those of the preceding year and it produced a result still further improved: 7,800,000 for, 250,000 against.

As we have already mentioned, the schedule chosen made it possible for the official proclamation of the Second Empire to coincide with 2 December, that famous and henceforth quadruple anniversary. But of the four 2 Decembers[15], only the third was subsequently to remain symbolic, known as '*the* 2 December'. That, to some extent, is an indication of the negative side of Bonapartism, just as the Bordeaux speech – a political manifesto as much as a declaration of intent – was an indication of its positive aspects.

It is this combination of aspects (not only of Bonapartism but also of the Republic, or rather the Republics) that we should now, in conclusion, examine.

*In April 1814 Napoleon had abdicated in favour of his son. From a Bonapartist point of view there had thus been a reign of Napoleon II. (In a similar fashion, Louis XVIII (1814–24) adopted that number taking the view that his nephew, the son of Louis XVI, had reigned from 1793 to 1795; it was, of course, a pure fiction, since the child had at that time been a prisoner of the Republic.) 'Napoleon II', who was brought up by his maternal grandfather under the name of duc de Reichstadt, died in 1831.

Conclusion

The democratic Republic eventually imposed itself as the normal political regime of contemporary France. So let us consider what contribution to its evolution and fulfilment was made by the four years of its first trial run that we have been describing.

It is certainly true that the Republic that finally prevailed during the 1870s owed its reappearance in the first place to the failure of the monarchical solutions attempted – that is to both the inability of the Bourbon heirs to adapt to a modern world and the collapse of the last of the Bonapartes, at Sedan. The Republic was reborn when the Second Empire had made itself impossible: too aggressive for the alarmed Europe of the time and too authoritarian for an awakened society.

This is not the place to describe how the Republic of Gambetta and Jules Ferry defined itself in opposition to Bonapartism. Nevertheless, the principal aspects of that antithesis were already discernible in 1851 and 1852: Bonapartism, in this respect an heir to the party of order, drew its strength from docility – docility on the part of the soldiers with their 'passive obedience' and docility on the part of the 'rural population' when faced with the regime's official candidates. The Republic, in contrast, found its supporters in circles of the independently minded – the workers of Paris and Lyons, the intellectuals, even peasants, in the red provinces where the life-style of the villages/*bourgs* was already that of the towns – in other words, its support came from the thinking militants. Bonapartism was the fruit of inadequate political education, the Republic the product of education, awareness and a universal appreciation of civic virtues: that was Jules Ferry's view, but it had also been that of the 'forty-eighters'. It is not difficult to understand how it was that the survivors from the Second Republic, of whom Victor Hugo was merely the most famous, felt perfectly at home with the Third Republic and were quick to become its sponsors.

So the first positive point in the record of the Second Republic, the first lesson learned in the course of this apprenticeship, was the following: the necessity for the masses to receive a complete education ranging from

elementary instruction, which would teach them to read, to democratic political practice, which would make free newspapers, free meetings and free associations possible.

Of course, this record and this apprenticeship of the Second Republic cannot be credited simply to the combination of governments which held power during those four years. They are also in part attributable to the Republic that tried to succeed from February to June 1848 and then to survive from June 1848 to January 1849; and they are above all due to the ideal Republic defined and desired between 1849 and 1851 by the only true republicans of the time, those who were in opposition.

History ought therefore to distinguish carefully between two different records: on the one hand that of this ideal Republic, the regime of all true 'forty-eighters' and of the *montagnards* and, on the other hand, that of the actual, practical Republic of the conservatives who in effect governed.

The Republic of the 'forty-eighters'

This ideal of the Republic was, as we have indicated, associated in the first place with education and universal civic consciousness, which only schooling and liberty can bring.

Secondly – as we have also indicated, in particular in connection with the insurrection of 1851 and the combination of motives behind it – it was regarded as a constitutional form not content with its existing character, but intent upon defining itself further in terms of a popular element. The Republic was not 'the true one', 'the right one', if it was no more than the absence of a monarchy or dictatorship; it was only *the* Republic if the rules for its functioning served a progressive aim.

That aim was the well-being of the people or – to put it another way – socialism. The notions of 'well-being', of 'the people' and even of 'socialism' may be vague, but we must not under-estimate them. Their lack of precise definition does not prevent (is indeed perhaps even a condition of) the strength of the inspiration they provide. The Republic of the 'forty-eighters', of the well-named *démoc-socs*, is a Republic that leads to socialism as naturally as the ideal of the *sans-culottes* of 1793 led them to the *babouvism** of Year IV; and as naturally as, later on, in the speeches of Albi and Jaurès, the initial development (the Republic) leads to the second (socialism) and thence to the third (universal peace) in a progression of moral victories of an increasingly ambitious nature.

But we must repeat that this Republic, with its socialist aims, was also a

*From the name of Babeuf (1764–97), a 'communist' doctrine adhered to by the Jacobins who in 1796 attempted to oppose the 'Thermidorean reaction' with their *Conspiration des Egaux*. (The Thermidorean reaction is the name given to the conservative tendencies of the First Republic after the toppling of Robespierre on 9 Thermidor in Year II.)

Republic of socialism by law. Right from beginning to end – from the days of February 1848, when Lamartine secured the repudiation of everything in the heritage of 1792 that smacked of violence and constraint, through to the days of December 1851, when the insurgents died for 'that scrap of paper', namely article 68 – this was the Republic's most constant feature. The Republic was the reign of law, and violence was no longer justifiable except in defence of the law itself and its authorised representatives. That is why, fundamentally, the workers' June rebellion, which was in other ways so much in conformity with a whole tradition that stretched from the *sans-culottes* down to the communards, was so unusual, so strange and in the last analysis so unique in the political France of those times. The new spirit of the age could see it only as a kind of regression. It is also – and most importantly – why the *coup d'Etat*, with its scorn for the law, inspired such profound repulsion. No doubt Louis-Napoleon would have adhered to the hierarchy of values that a more recent leader expressed as follows: 'Necessity first, politics next and the law, in so far as it is possible to respect it, third.'[1] The essence of the spirit of 1848 was, precisely, revolt against the idea of the law being relegated to third position – if possible – and insistence, on the contrary, on the first place of all for what was later to be described by the hallowed phrase: 'respect for republican legality'.

From their unfortunate experiences, first of 1850 (the Falloux law) and then of 1851–2 (when the clergy supported the regime engendered by the *coup d'Etat*), the 'forty-eighters' also derived a profound anti-clericalism. Too much is made of the conciliatory euphoria of the early weeks and of the Lamartinian Republic that enjoyed the blessing of the priests. After all, it really did not last for very long! And too much is made of those republican syncretisms in which Jesus Christ became a member of the proletariat while God crowned the whole metaphysical edifice, for the tendency has been to overlook the fact that that kind of deism was anathema to true believers. In reality, the men of 1848 must very soon have seen Catholicism as an enemy, although that view must certainly have been tempered by many nuances. Some laid emphasis on the Church's role as a political and social force for conservatism, while others went further and were of the opinion that the very spirit of religion should be resisted as being incompatible with the new education. But they were all in agreement that the Church should at least be driven back from the sphere of temporal and social influence. What was to become the great fighting issue for the Third Republic already figured in the desires of the Second Republic's true supporters.

All these aspirations towards the ideal Republic, the awakening of the masses' political consciousness and sense of civic values, the rights of the people, the reign of law, secularisation, were lived and experienced on a

passionate as well as an intellectual level. That is not the least of the positive points in the record, despite the fact that it is usually considered a subject suitable for lampooning rather than for serious discussion.

The spirit of 1848 was passionate, eloquent, emotional, somewhat wild. We smile indulgently when we speak of those 'old romantic beards' (*ces vieilles barbes romantiques*). The expression is as inaccurate as it is over-used. The fact is that those 'romantic beards' were only truly 'old' under the Third Republic. On the eve of 1848, the non-conformists who allowed their beards (and hair) to grow were chiefly young people who did so in defiance of the close-cropped heads and smooth-shaven faces of all the respectable gentlemen of the time,[2] whether bourgeois or even republican. (Of the eleven members of the provisional government, the only one who was truly bearded was the youngest and poorest of all, the worker Albert. Armand Marrast sported an elegant goatee of a very 'imperial' kind and Flocon had a moustache; the other eight were clean-shaven.)[3] It was only gradually that beards became characteristic of militant revolutionaries, of those in opposition and eventually even of their doctrines, to the point of being banned as such in the university, as we have mentioned above. Was it a question of Romanticism? No doubt it was, to some extent.[4] At the level of educated militants the Romantic influence was clear. These were men whose political convictions had been coloured by their reading of writers such as Lamartine, Victor Hugo, Michelet and George Sand. But there was also a spontaneous, popular kind of Romanticism and that may have been even more important.

We must not forget the speed with which the republican idea won over people who were very poor and very simple, with spontaneous modes of behaviour that certainly could not be termed completely rational. Should we describe them as 'traditional', 'folkloric', 'primitive'? Whatever the correct term may be, the essential point to note is that the way in which the Republic won over the masses was not invariably by submitting their minds to a period of positivist education. Sometimes the conquest was immediate, like the emergence of a new mystique from a veritable conversion. The Republic has often appeared – mainly in country regions, although not exclusively – as some kind of Hope or Sacred Value. In short, it was regarded not as a negation of religion, but rather as a new religion. This emotional and mystic *aura* surrounding the Republic is an essential element. In the first place, it makes it easier to understand the strength and ardour that sustained the republican party from 1849 to 1851. Above all, it helps to explain the intensity of its expressionism and – for example – the importance of the allegorical and figurative element that is part of the heritage left by the 'forty-eighters'. The figure of Marianne was, admittedly, not solely their invention: the first Revolution had certainly made its own contribution. But it was they who in the end defined,

depicted and popularised Marianne. And besides, it was they who baptised her.

This idealism was the factor that Karl Marx failed to foresee and that caused him to make his first mistake in his diagnosis of the situation. He appears to have believed that only monarchies could be 'mystificatory' while in contrast the Republic, which was a depersonalised system of political relations, would, on that account, be perfectly transparent in the matter of class relations. His view was that the rationalisation of political struggles in accordance with purely sociological divisions should thus make for rapid progress once the Republic was established: the class struggle of June 1848 was the normal corollary to February. However, that was not at all the case in reality and for many different reasons, one of which was, perhaps, that the Republic was not nearly as drily abstract as it appeared. Whether or not it was 'mystificatory', it certainly did not deal a death-blow to political idealism but, on the contrary, was well and truly an idealism itself.

The official Republic

The official Republic was, in contrast, 'realistic'. From January 1849 to December 1851 the Republic functioned without republican governors, run by men for whom the regime, undesired but tolerated, was a temporary expedient until such time as circumstances would allow for a monarchical restoration. The restoration that eventually came was, certainly, neither the kind desired by Thiers nor that desired by Falloux; a third party intervened to cheat them of the throne. The fact remains that for three years the forces of the conservative bourgeoisie had governed France without a monarch and had done so without forfeiting either their possessions or their heads.

The involuntary experience of the fact that a Republic could be bourgeois and that such a Republic indeed made it possible for rival partisans of monarchy to work together for the aims they shared, despite the differences that divided them, was surely a discovery that must also be rated as part of this period's historical legacy. It was certainly by no mere chance that Adolphe Thiers, the principal manipulator on the political scene during the conservative phase of the Second Republic, later became one of the founding fathers of the Third. After 1870 Thiers simply accepted as lasting what in 1848–51 he had tolerated as a temporary necessity.

That is certainly not to suggest that Thiers became a *montagnard* in his old age. It was a quite different kind of Republic. The Republic that he eventually accepted differed essentially from the Republic of the 'forty-eighters' in that it truly was a pure constitutional form. It was content to be without either monarch or dictator, more or less beyond reproach from

a legal point of view, but stripped of all populist mystique and all aspirations towards social reform; and it was prudent – very prudent – when it came to the democratisation of civic life.

To sum up, one might say that the Republic of the 'forty-eighters' was a morally conceived Republic aiming for the maximum, while the unwilled Republic of Monsieur Thiers was a Republic conceived purely constitutionally and aiming for the minimum. It is perhaps stating the obvious to remark that these two concepts are ones which are familiar to us today under the respective descriptions of left and right.

So the Second Republic was indeed the common source of the two principal French political traditions of the modern era. Through those unfortunate heroes, the 'forty-eighters', it was the true ancestor of the ideology of the left while, through its *burgraves* and other conservative leaders, it provided a precedent and model for all the centre-rightists of the future.

The Bonapartist dictatorship

However, before the two political wings thus conceived between 1848 and 1851 had the opportunity to confront each other once more, the centre of the stage was, for twenty years, to be occupied by the man of 2 December.

What is the significance of this? We know what the answer of the republican left was: it had proved possible to topple the Republic because the (mainly rural) masses were not yet fully awakened and educated. That is no doubt true. But why Bonaparte rather than the *burgraves*? Why a vaguely demagogic Caesarism rather than an openly bourgeois conservatism? Was it because Bonaparte happened to be on the spot whereas Joinville and Chambord were in exile? Or were there more profound reasons why history needed a new actor?

It was a question that was soon asked, and in particular by socialist thinkers.

In his *Révolution sociale démontrée par le coup d'Etat*, Proudhon accepted the Bonapartist thesis which maintained that Louis-Napoleon was closer to the people than the bourgeois of the Assembly, that he was himself the product of universal suffrage, the result of the advent of the masses upon the political scene. So why not Bonaparte? Perhaps this was a chance to fulfil the socialist desires of the masses. It was on such grounds as these that Proudhon produced the following famous exhortation:

> Let him [Bonaparte] therefore assume his predestined [*fatal*][5] title boldly; let him raise in the place of the cross the masonic emblems of the level, square and plumb-line: that is the sign of the modern Constantine to whom victory is assured: *in hoc signo vinces*! Let 2 December, escaping from the false position created for it by party tactics,[6] produce, develop

and organise without delay the principle that will give it life: anti-christianism, that is to say anti-theocracy, anti-capitalism, anti-feudalism; let him tear the proletariat away from the Church and from its life of inferiority and make men of its members, the great army created by universal suffrage, baptised as children of God and Church, who are deprived of knowledge, of work and of bread. That is his mandate and that is his strength.

To make citizens out of serfs of the soil and the machine; to transform terrified believers into wise men ... that is enough to satisfy the ambitions of ten Bonapartes.[7]

As can be seen Proudhon, with great lucidity, perceived the virtually reformist element of a whole side of Bonapartism, but also the difficulties there would be in accomplishing such progress on account of the conservative and clerical alliance by which Bonaparte was at the same time bound. Only a few months after writing his pamphlet he was to admit in private[8] that the government was leaning in the wrong direction and that 'Orleanism and Jesuitism are in the majority in the Elysée'. So it was not long before he found himself once again in opposition. But the important point is that he put his finger on the major political contradiction of this Bonapartism and on the key to its constant oscillations between alliance with and detachment from the party of order. However, Proudhon seems to have been unable to conceive of anything other than a fundamental alternative between retrograde conservatism on the one hand and social revolution on the other, and that is no doubt why in the circumstances of 1860 people – not all that inaccurately – applied the description 'Proudhonian' to those who were reverting to a belief in social progress through enlightened despotism.

Was there, perhaps, a third alternative: Bonapartism *sui generis*, representative neither of the proletariat nor of the old-style notables?

As is well known, Karl Marx, also at this date, thought he had discovered this to be the case. Immediately after the *coup d'Etat* he too published his analysis [*The Eighteenth Brumaire of Louis Bonaparte*]. In these famous pages he showed that 'Napoleonic ideas' conformed with the desires, needs and preconceptions of the 'peasant smallholder'. The isolated smallholder – the principal element in the French population – 'could not' be republican, 'had to' express himself through Bonapartism. And Marx went on to maintain that what was now 'necessary' was the collapse of Bonapartism, which would dispel men's illusions and open the eyes of the peasant smallholder. The demystification which the 1848 Republic had failed to accomplish would, in short, be the achievement of the next Republic: 'The parody of imperialism was necessary to free the mass of the French nation from the weight of tradition and to reveal in all its purity the antagonism that existed between the State and Society.'[9]

It does not lie within our brief to examine that particular prediction. But, looking no further than this pronouncement written in 1852, we should on the other hand note that, quite apart from the peasants, Marx ascribed to Bonaparte another block of supporters, namely the sub-proletariat. We have several times noted how impressed Marx and Engels had been by the counter-revolutionary role played by the Parisian 'lumpenproletariat'. They (Marx and Engels) were in the last analysis referring to the society of 10 December. Now, boldly extending the concept of the underworld, Karl Marx by analogy included within it distinguished adventurers and worldly politicians who used their inside knowledge to feather their own nests, and wrote: 'Bonaparte appears above all as the leader of the Society of 10 December, as representative of the sub-proletariat *to which he himself belongs*,[10] as do his entourage, his government and his army; and his chief concern is to further his own interests and extract Californian-style lottery tickets from public funds.'[11]

The whole book draws to this conclusion in the style of a pamphleteer. The new governmental personnel is described as 'a bunch of fools, upstarts' from goodness knows where, 'a rowdy, disreputable, grasping lot of bohemians', in short, 'the top layer of the Society of 10 December'. This was in fact also more or less the image of them later drawn by both Hugo in his *Châtiments* and Rémusat in his *Mémoires*.

For Marx, in brief, Bonapartism, representing these two heterogeneous social groups – peasant smallholders on the one hand and parasites of every kind on the other – remained alien to the two fundamental classes, namely the capitalist bourgeoisie and the proletariat. His diagnosis was no doubt distorted both by the passions engendered by the violence of December and also by his lack of historical perspective.

If he had pursued his observations on France with the advantage of a few years hindsight (but he never did return to the subject except in relation to the commune, which he considered from a quite different point of view), Marx would not have failed to notice that the intense business activities of 1852 were not simply a matter of parasitical speculations on the part of shady upstarts 'in yellow gloves'; a whole second generation of French capitalism was involved. Two years earlier Marx had produced some much more useful comments when he observed, at the beginning of *Class Struggles in France*, that under Louis-Philippe only a limited section of the bourgeoisie, a kind of 'financial aristocracy', had reigned and that the 'industrial bourgeoisie', in the strict sense of the term, had been in opposition. Without entering into the details of his identification of these groups – a subject which would lead to lengthy discussion – all we need do is grasp the principle of distinction between already established, conservative, groups of interests on the one hand and innovative, dynamic ones still ill at ease on the other. In terms of historical 'necessity', we

would not wish to deny that Bonapartism brought the jolt that the modern (Saint-Simonian) sector of the bourgeoisie needed to emancipate itself from a timid coalition with the wealthy, who in general found expression through the party of order.

What is so inconvenient, from a moral point of view, is that this kind of economic progressivism did not go hand-in-hand with progressive politics ... But that is a line of thought which would open another series of reflections quite beyond our brief.

As for Marx's analyses regarding the affinities between Bonapartism and the 'smallholders' and the 'sub-proletariat', do they really clash very much with the thesis of a 'Saint-Simonian' empire? Not necessarily. The time would come when Marx's disciples would analyse a certain large political party of the twentieth century, now as the instrument of particular business groups, now as representing the urban and rural middle classes.[12] Were these analyses contradictory? To some extent, no doubt, and it is easy to see in what sense. But at a deeper level they were complementary: one series of analyses of the party in question was concentrating upon the dominant social forces which used it, while the other was seeking the subordinate and more or less mystified social forces which served as its mass basis. The tentative studies devoted in 1852 to the new and disconcerting phenomena that the Republic and plebiscitarian Caesarism represented certainly lie at the distant origins of modern political science.

From that analytical point of view too the history of the Second Republic still has a contemporary relevance.

Appendix: Statistics of the repression of the insurrection of December 1851 (National Archives, BB 30,424.Register)

Definition:

'The number of individuals arrested or charged in France on the occasion of the insurrection of December 1851 was 26,884.'

Classification:

a. *By geographical origin* (departments). The numbers vary across the board from Var (3,147), Seine (2,962), Hérault (2,840), Basses-Alpes (1,669) ... down to Manche (1) and finally Corsica, Finistère, Ille-et-Vilaine and Loire-Inférieure (0). See map 6 above, p. 147.

b. *By profession* (in alphabetical order of trades). See below.

c. *By civil status*
   men: 26,715, women: 169 (Seine 44, Hérault 20, Drôme 19, etc.)
   French: 26,634, foreigners: 250 (no details here)
   married (or widowers): 17,403, bachelors: 9,481
   under 16 years of age: 52 (Seine 35, etc.) – between 16 and 20: 1,253 – 21 to 30: 8,332 – 31 to 40: 9,648 – 41 to 50: 5,873 – 51 to 60: 1,882 – 60 or over: 344.

d. *By destination:* 'These people found guilty were classified by both the mixed and the military commissions as follows' (1st column of figures).
   'But following the measures of clemency, these decisions were modified' ... producing the 'real figure in each category for 30 September 1853' (2nd column of figures).

Category	1	2
Sent or referred to Court Martial	247	244
Cayenne	239	198
Algeria plus	4,549	1,718
Algeria minus	5,032[1]	1,288
Expulsion	980	368
Temporary banishment	640	299
Internment	2,827	1,199
Summary jurisdiction	645	611
Penitentiary	29	6
Surveillance	5,194	7,676
Liberty	5,857	12,632
Returned to Department of Public Prosecution	645	645
	26,884	26,884

Details of the classification by professions

We should remember that these 26,884 individuals arrested or charged *at the time* (*sic*) of the insurrection constitute not so much a list of actual insurgents, rather a list of socialist democrats presumed to be active (arrests were made in almost all departments, not simply in areas where disturbances took place). One might even go so far as to say, in the last analysis, that they are really the statistics of the leaders and militants of the 'republican party'. We can no more give here the full interminable list of professions that appear in the register in alphabetical order than we can reproduce the complete list of departments. We attempt to give the most incontroversial category groupings,[2] indicating in each the professions that figure there most highly.[3] They are classed in descending numerical order.[4]

a. *Upper and middle classes*: total 3,854, i.e. 14 per cent.
    1,570 individuals of private means
    393 liberal professions (legal) (225 *lawyers*, 168 *ministerial officers*)
    472 liberal professions (medical) (325 *doctors*, 92 *chemists*, 3 *dentists*, 52 *veterinary surgeons*)
    83 liberal professions (scientific) (47 *surveyors*, 25 *architects*, 11 *engineers*)
    300 liberal professions (literary and artistic) (106 *painters*, 90 *journalists*, 70 *men of letters*, 34 *musicians*)
    425 teachers (261 *school teachers*, 110 *students*, 54 *professors*)
    44 other civil servants (34 *clerics*, 10 *magistrates*)
    567 big business (427 *wholesalers*, 128 *business agents*, 12 *trade agents*)

b. *Popular milieu (agricultural sector)*: total 7,412, i.e. 27 per cent. 5,423 *agricultural workers*, 1,850 *day workers*, 131 *gardeners*. (We will here include 8 *fishermen* – a frequent economic assimilation.)

c. *Popular milieu (industrial and artisan sectors. There is no way of distinguishing between the two)*: total 12,916, i.e. 48 per cent.
    2,204 in clothing and shoe-making (1,107 *cobblers*, 688 *tailors*, also *clog-makers*, *hat-makers*, etc.)
    1,902 in building (733 *masons*, 271 *carpenters*, also *stone-cutters*, *carriers*, *painters*, etc.)
    1,504 in wood (888 *joiners*, also *coopers*, *turners*, *sawyers*, etc.)
    1,197 in metal (457 *blacksmiths*, 428 *locksmiths*, and others)
    1,032 in textiles (462 *weavers*, also *spinners*, *dyers* etc.)
    1,064 lodging-house keepers and retailers of alcohol (890 *inn-keepers*, and others)
    973 food retailers (415 *bakers*, also *butchers*, *grocers*, etc.)
    853 in other commercial enterprises (616 *salesmen* and various shop-keepers)
    678 in transport and connected trades (191 *coachmen*, 180 *cartwrights*, 138 *sailors*, also 48 *peddlers*, 114 *medal sellers*, etc.)
    855 in various types of manufacture, chiefly leather (238 *tanners*, 156 *saddlers* and many other specialised trades, in particular the 152 *cork-workers* from the Var, etc.)
    402 in fine arts (155 *typographers*, 83 *watchmakers*, 62 *jewellers*, etc.)
    and finally 252 in 'services' (*hairdressers*)

d. *Various marginal occupations*: total 2,685, i.e. 10 per cent.
    soldiers: 103
    servants: 221 (most of them probably already included in b. above)
    vagrants: 9[5]
    other trades: 2,352[6]

Conclusion:

The possible conclusion from all the above might be that the typical victim of the repression of 2 December 1851 was *a man of about thirty years of age, married, French – but from southern France – and employed in a manual profession rather than in agriculture.*

Notes

1. Why the Republic?

1 Biblio. no. 39.
2 Socialism in the wide sense that the word had at the time.
3 Biblio. no. 34.

2. The trial and failure of a kind of socialism (24 February–4 May 1848)

1 What we mean is political and parliamentary reform, the slogan of the opposition – not the newspaper, *La Réforme*.
2 Emile Ollivier has given his own account of this in *L'Empire libéral*, vol. III, pp. 597–615.
3 See Biblio. no. 34, p. 137.
4 The credit for having recently popularised this expression in connection with the Commune should go to J. Rougerie.
5 See Biblio. no. 28, pp. 167–70.

3. The re-establishment of order (May 1848–June 1849)

1 Who had replaced Bedeau and who thus, since March, had held responsibility for both War and Marine Affairs.
2 There is a disturbing resemblance between this trap and the similar one laid on 1 Prairial in Year III. See D. Woronoff's *La République bourgeoise*, p. 28, to be published as *The Thermidorean Regime and the Directory, 1794–1799*, Cambridge University Press, 1984.
3 Biblio. no. 39, p. 325.
4 For instance, one particular Montargis republican who now assembled his squad of National Guardsmen to go to the aid of the government in Paris did exactly the same thing again in 1851 in order to resist the *coup d'Etat*. In both cases it was a matter of 'marching to the assistance of the national representative body' (Ténot, no. 48, p. 8).
5 We are here following Limouzin-Lamothe, whose information is quite convincing. Biblio. no. 59b.
6 Biblio. no. 28, pp. 139 and 143.
7 Sergeants Boichot and Rattier, put forward as candidates by a committee of non-commissioned officers, were elected in the Seine and took their seats on the side of the Mountain. Soon after, Pierre Dupont, in his *Chant des Soldats*, wrote: 'Thinking bayonets ... Let us form a defensive wall around the idea! ... (Baionnettes intelligentes ... Faisons à l'idée un rempart! ...'

4. France faced with the great alternative: order or social democracy

1 See Biblio. nos. 17 and 54.
2 There were many of these for, as well as the Parisian newspapers and those of the large towns (*La Voix du Peuple* at Marseilles, *L'Emancipation* at Toulon, *Le Peuple souverain* at Lyons, etc.), there were many small news-sheets with a departmental circulation.
3 For there were certainly some slanders that were calculated inventions. For example, in *Le Moniteur* that related to the session of 15 May 1848 of the Assembly, which was invaded by the rioters, a famous anonymous invention was inserted later, after the event: 'We need an hour for looting' ... (Seignobos, Biblio. no. 33, p. 103).
4 Seignobos, Biblio. no. 33, p. 103.
5 *Ibid.*, p. 155. Perhaps we may be forgiven if we point out that this all tallies exactly with the stories that we recounted and analysed in our *Republic in the Village* (Biblio. no. 58), end of Part 2.
6 Seignobos was alive to this problem too, observing that for the conservatives the democratic party was, by and large, 'an association of evil-doers'.
7 'Here, slaughtering and butchering take place out of town', unlike in London where the presence of herds of animals in the streets, apart from being inconvenient in other ways, also 'accustoms the people to the idea of slaughter'.
8 In Basse-Provence and the Languedoc, even legitimism easily took on a democratic tinge, since here the type of royalism that supported 'natural rights' (favourable to universal suffrage) found its biggest audience.
9 Biblio. no. 56. Vol. I, pp. 344–5.
10 As for all references to the press, cf. Guiral in Biblio. no. 12.
11 A good description can be found in P. Ariès, *Histoire des populations françaises*, new edn (Le Seuil 1971), ch. 4.
12 Cited by R. Gossez (Biblio. no. 8), p. 316.
13 *Ibid.*, p. 319.

5. Between the conservative order and the Bonapartist order (June 1849–November 1851)

1 Nowadays that theory is challenged. M. Emerit has proposed a different natural father and M. Dansette has supported the thesis of King Louis' paternity, in other words that the birth was legitimate (see Biblio. no. 63).
2 See Biblio. no. 45, p. 175.
3 See *Ibid.*, p. 179.
4 It is perhaps symbolic that Michelet's course of lectures at the Collège de France, suspended by Guizot in January 1848 and re-established by Lamartine's Republic in March 1848, was once again suspended in March 1851 by the Republic of Bonaparte and Falloux.
5 It has been shown (Huard, Biblio. no. 59) that the signatories whose right to vote was not in question far outnumbered those who were threatened with elimination. So people signed on the grounds of their principles, rather than out of any personal motivations.
   Furthermore, the village signatories outnumbered those in the towns. It is already noticeable that democratic propaganda is effectively muzzled when there is strong police surveillance (in the towns) and is not where surveillance is weak (in the villages) or is even non-existent (in small villages with democrat mayors). As we shall see, the situation was very similar when it came to the insurrection of December 1851.
6 See Biblio. no. 28, pp. 293 and 295.

6. Bonaparte's *coup d'Etat* and the republican resistance (2–10 December 1851)

1 The first three were leaders of the intransigent and pugnacious minority of the Mountain and the organisers of a central committee for clandestine resistance which had for the past few weeks been attempting to regroup the loyal militants of Paris. But the police had managed to infiltrate the organisation with an informer and had learned all its secrets. (See Biblio. no. 47.)

2 It is often forgotten that 'A l'obéissance passive' (To passive obedience) is the sad title of the famous passage of *Les Châtiments* on the 'soldiers of Year II'. Its theme, precisely, is the contrast between the civic spirit of the soldiers of Year II and the passivity of the military involved in the *coup d'Etat*.

3 During that morning, the magistrates of the High Court had similarly met in the *palais de justice* and opened proceedings against the president by virtue of the same article. They too were quickly dispersed by the soldiers and did not make a point of resisting.

4 This resistance committee had nothing to do with the one mentioned above. The men to whom we are now referring belonged to the fraction of the Mountain which, up till this moment, had been the most legalistic of all.

5 We are here following Ténot's account (Biblio. no. 48). There is no confirmation available on this particular point, so many historians regard Baudin's remark as apocryphal. But at any rate it had to be cited, as it is so very well known.

6 There is, perhaps, another reason for this collective amnesia where the insurrection of December 1851 is concerned, namely its ambiguity. This insurrectional movement to defend the Constitution was, in the last analysis, legalistic in its ends and revolutionary in its methods. It was impossible for any of the parties to recognise themselves in this unusual combination, neither the extreme socialist left for whom the legalism of the ends was insufficiently radical nor the future staid Republic for which the taking-up of arms was too much so. With its memory thus wiped out by both the 'Guesdistes' and the followers of Ferry, the provincial revolt of December was bound to exert only a short-lived moral influence.

7 Bonny-sur-Loire and Neuvy-sur-Loire, according to Ténot (Biblio. no. 48).

8 Here, and below, we give no exhaustive lists, mentioning only the principal cases.

9 For the details that follow, see in particular our *Republic in the Village* (Biblio. no. 58), last chapter.

10 See Biblio. no. 33.

11 See Biblio. nos. 54 and 58.

7. From the *coup d'Etat* to the Empire (December 1851–December 1852)

1 For the details of this affair, see our *Republic* (Biblio. no. 58). The two peasants in question had their sentences commuted to hard labour for life and died in Cayenne.

2 They had already been arrested and brought to Paris, the two towns being so close.

3 See Biblio. no. 29.

4 Letter to the President of the Legislative Body, cited by G. Weill (Biblio. no. 34), p. 308, note.

5 Cited in the *Encyclopédie des Bouches-du-Rhône* (Marseilles 1929), vol. V, p. 185.

6 Texts cited by Albert Thomas (Biblio. no. 32), p. 39.

7 See Balzac's very Napoleonic novel, *Le Médecin de campagne*. See also, in *Les Misérables*, the figure of M. Madeleine, an even more characteristic philanthropic industrialist. On this point at least, Victor Hugo's 'social' ideas coincided with those of his great enemy, Bonaparte.

8 In this affair, which took place at the beginning of 1850, Lamartine, an expert and convinced supporter of a large-scale railway network, had unsuccessfully pleaded in favour of a unified Paris–Lyons line, this being the solution that was most Saint-Simonian in spirit, most in the interests of the Rothschilds and most agreeable to the Elysée. However, the majority in the Assembly responded in classic style with the liberal opposition reacting against the idea of such a large-scale railway company.

9 J. Bouvier (Biblio. no. 74), p. 157.

10 Biblio. no. 50.

11 Cited by J. Bouvier in *Initiation aux mécanismes économiques contemporains* (Sedes 1969), p. 94.

12 J. Bouvier (Biblio. no. 74), p. 167.

13 According to Charles Warner, 'Le Journal d'agriculture pratique', in *From the Ancient Regime to the Popular Front* (Columbia University Press 1969), pp. 104–5.

14 A. Charles (Biblio. no. 51).

15 1804 (the crowning of Napoleon I), 1805 (Austerlitz), 1851 (the *coup d'Etat*), 1852 (the advent of the Second Empire).

Conclusion

1 Charles de Gaulle, speaking to M. Jean Foyer, a conversation cited by J.R. Tournoux in *Jamais dit* (Plon 1971), pp. 286–7.

2 There is a fine collection of portraits of the age in H. Guillemin, *La Première Résurrection* ... (Biblio. no. 39).

3 Victor Hugo, a serene and clean-shaven bourgeois in 1848, was still clean-shaven in 1851. It was only in exile, in Guernsey, that he grew his beard and even then – it is said – simply to protect his delicate throat from the cold ... That may be the prosaic truth but it was not easy for it to gain the upper hand over the symbolic truth! It is impossible to imagine a beardless author of *Les Misérables* and *La Légende des siècles* or, equally, a beardless Senator Hugo in 1880.

4 The bourgeois publicist Louis Reybaud, the creator of the figure of Jérôme Paturot, thought it amusing, throughout his work of that name, systematically to use the adjective 'long-haired' as an ironic synonym for 'romantic'.

5 i.e. his popular title which was *'fatal'* because necessarily linked (*fatum* = destiny) with the primary origin of his power, namely the vote of 10 December 1848.

6 i.e. the alliance with the party of order, into which he was forced by the resistance of the *montagnards* whom Proudhon blamed for precisely that reason.

7 Cited by G. Renard and A. Thomas (Biblio. no. 32), pp. 35–6.

8 Letter of July 1852 (*ibid.*), p. 37.

9 See Biblio. no. 25, p. 97.

10 Our italics.

11 *Le 18 Brumaire*, p. 98. [*The Eighteenth Brumaire.*] The allusion to Californian lottery tickets refers to the speculations on the stock exchanges prompted by the discovery of gold mines in America – speculations which were making a decisive impact at this time.

12 These two interpretations were both produced by Maurice Thorez and apply to the radical party. This is not the place to discuss how far they are correct. We cite them simply as an example of the ambivalence inherent in the social identification of political phenomena.

Appendix

1 'Although the figure given for those sentenced to transportation is 9,581 (4,549 + 5,032), in actual fact no more than 6,151 individuals were transported.'
2 We give sufficiently full statistics for the reader to compose other groupings if he so desires, in particular so that he may make a comparison with the statistics relating to the Communards of 71 given by Jacques Rougerie in *Paris Libre*, pp. 11 and 259.
3 The italics indicate the *professions* as given in the register.
4 The total included in our regroupings comes to 26,867 instead of 26,884. It is not possible to determine whether the major responsibility for these small inconsistencies lies with us or with the contemporary military records.
5 It has long since been pointed out, from the republican side, how seriously this altogether infinitesimal (official) figure weakens the (official) theory of *jacquerie*.
6 Does this really cover a number of professions each with a tiny number of representatives? Or is it an artifice to make the total 'come out right'? There is no way of knowing.

Bibliography

The tools for our research

We should distinguish between
a. one work in particular
   and
b. other works

a. The Société d'histoire de la Révolution de 1848, founded in 1904, has published a review which has appeared under a number of titles since that date (*Revues* ... and, later, *Etudes* ...). Together, these make up the *Bibliothèque de la Révolution de 1848*. The contents of these publications, from 1904 to 1956 inclusive, are analysed in:

1. L. Dubief, *Tables analytiques des publications de la Société d'histoire de la Révolution de 1848*, Bibliothèque de la Révolution de 1848, XVII, 1957. Since then the following volumes have appeared:
2. Vol. XVIII, *L'Armée et la Seconde République*
3. Vol. XIX, *Aspects de la crise et de la dépression de l'économie française au milieu du XIXe siècle 1846–1851* (general editor: E. Labrousse)
4. Vol. XX, *Le Choléra, la première épidémie du XIXe siècle* (introduction by Louis Chevalier)
5. Vol. XXI, *Les Elections de 1869** (introduction by Louis Girard)
6. Vol. XXII, *Réaction et suffrage universel en France et en Allemagne (1848–1850)* (introduction by Jacques Droz)
7. Vol. XXIII, *La Presse ouvrière 1819–1850* (France and seven other nations) (introduction by Jacques Godechot)
8. Vol. XXIV, *Les Ouvriers de Paris*, I, *L'organisation 1848–1851*, by Remy Gossez

Since volume XXIV, dated 1967, the collection seems to have marked time. On the other hand, in 1948 the PUF produced a 'collection du Centenaire' composed of a number of small volumes, some of which fill an important bibliographical gap. These appear in the list below:

b. other works
9. (collective), *Atlas historique de la France contemporaine 1800–1965*, A. Colin ('U'), 1966

Sic: 1869, not 1849. This volume is devoted to the later reception given to the political problems of the mid-nineteenth century. However, we did not think this excellent work should be excluded from our reference to the *Bibliothèque*.

10. Bourloton, Robert and Cougny, *Dictionnaire des parlementaires*, 5 vols., Bourloton, 1891 (useful in particular for the bourgeois and conservatives who do not appear in the following volumes)
11. J. Maitron (and collaborators), *Dictionnaire biographique du mouvement ouvrier français* (period 1789–1864 in 3 vols.), Editions ouvrières, 1964–6 (fundamental, as most of the forty-eighters were close enough to socialism to be included in this volume, whether or not they were actually workers)
12. (collective), *Histoire générale de la presse française*, II, *1815–1871*, PUF, 1969
13. F. Ponteil, *Les Institutions de la France de 1814 à 1870*, PUF, 1966
14. M. Duverger, *Constitutions et documents politiques*, PUF ('Thémis'), 1957
15. J. Touchard (and collaborators), *Histoire des idées politiques*, II, *du XVIIIᵉ à nos jours*, PUF ('Thémis'), 1962
16. J.–B. Duroselle, *L'Europe de 1815 à nos jours, vie politique et relations internationales*, PUF ('Nouvelle Clio') 1962*

Recent works of synthesis
These themselves incorporate full bibliographies and mention all the most recent discoveries.
17. P. Vigier, *La Seconde République*, PUF ('Que sais-je?'), 1967
18. L. Girard, *La IIᵉ République*, Calmann-Lévy ('Naissance et Mort'), 1968
19. J. Godechot, *Les Révolutions de 1848*, Albin Michel ('Le mémorial des siècles'), 1971
20. J. Sigmann, *1848, Les Révolutions romantiques et démocratiques de l'Europe*, Calmann-Lévy, 1970
21. R. Price, *The French Second Republic, A Social History*, Batsford, 1972

Principal early works used as source material
22. D. Stern (comtesse d'Agoult), *Histoire de la Révolution de 1848*, 3 vols., Sandré, 1850–3
23. L.A. Garnier-Pagès, *Histoire de la Révolution de 1848*, 10 vols., Pagnerre, 1860–71
24. K. Marx, *The Class Struggles in France, 1848 to 1850*, in K. Marx and F. Engels, *Selected Works*, 2 vols., 5th edn, Moscow, 1962
25. K. Marx, *The Eighteenth Brumaire of Louis Bonaparte*, in K. Marx and F. Engels, *Selected Works*, 2 vols., 5th edn, Moscow, 1962
26. A. de Tocqueville, *Souvenirs* (*Oeuvres complètes* vol. XII), Gallimard, 1964
27. Ch. de Rémusat, *Mémoires de ma vie* IV, Hachette, 1962
28. V. Hugo, *Souvenirs personnels (1848–1851)*, Gallimard, 1952
29. J. Michelet, *Journal 1823–1848* and *1849–1860*, Gallimard, 1959 and 1962
A fuller list of works of this kind can be found in L. Girard, cited above (no. 18).

Principal historical classics, still useful
30. P. de la Gorce, *Histoire de la Seconde République française*, 2 vols., Plon-Nourrit, 1887
31. G. Renard, *La République de 1848*, vol. IX of Jaurès's *Histoire socialiste*, Rouff, n.d.
32. G. Renard and A. Thomas, *Le Second Empire*, vol. X in the same collection, Rouff, n.d. (*c.* 1900)
33. Ch. Seignobos, *La Révolution de 1848 et le Second Empire (1848–1859)*, vol. VI of Lavisse's *Histoire de la France contemporaine*, Hachette, 1926

*P. Vigier's study devoted to the social aspects of the period is soon to appear in the 'Nouvelle Clio' collection.

34. G. Weill, *Histoire du parti républicain en France (1814–1870)*, new edn, Alcan, 1928
35. P. Bastid, *Doctrines et Institutions politiques de la Seconde République*, 2 vols., Hachette, 1945
36. (collective), *Actes du Congrès du centenaire de la Révolution de 1848*, PUF, 1948 (in particular E. Labrousse's work which soon became a classic, *Comment naissent les révolutions*)
37. J. Dautry, *1848 et la Seconde République*, Editions sociales, republished 1957
38. G. Duveau, *1848*, Gallimard ('Idées'), 1965

Special studies

1. Principal studies classed by themes, periods or episodes

a. Revolution and resistance
39. H. Guillemin, *La Première Résurrection de la République*, Gallimard ('Trente journées'), 1967
40. A.J. Tudesq, *Les Grands Notables en France, 1840–1849*, vol. II, PUF, 1964

b. June
41. Ch. Schmidt, *Des ateliers nationaux aux barricades de juin*, PUF ('coll. du Centenaire'), 1948

c. The end of the provisional government
42. A.J. Tudesq, *L'Election présidentielle de Louis-Napoléon Bonaparte, 10 décembre 1848*, A. Colin ('Kiosque'), 1965

d. 1849
43. J. Bouillon, 'Les démocrates-socialistes aux élections de 1849', *Revue française de science politique*, 1956–1

e. 1850
44. H. Michel, *La Loi Falloux*, Hachette, 1906
45. A. Prost, *L'Enseignement en France 1800–1967*, A. Colin ('U'), 1968
46. J. Tchernoff, *Associations et Sociétés secrètes sous la IIe République*, Pedone, 1905

f. The final crisis
47. and 48. E. Ténot, *Paris en décembre 1851* and *La Province en décembre 1851*, new edn, Le Siècle, 1876
49. H. Guillemin, *Le Coup du 2 décembre*, Gallimard, 1951
50. L. Girard, *La Politique des travaux publics du Second Empire*, A. Colin, 1952

2. Studies on the various regions

A fuller list, compiled by Gérard Walter, can be found in J. Godechot, cited above (no. 19).
The most important and also most recent works are:

51. A. Charles, *La Révolution de 1848 et la Seconde République à Bordeaux, et dans la Gironde*, Delmas, 1945
52. A. Armengaud, *Les Populations de l'Est aquitain au début de l'époque contemporaine (v. 1845–1871)*, Mouton, 1961
53. G. Dupeux, *Aspects de l'histoire sociale et politique du Loir-et-Cher, 1848–1914*, Mouton, 1962
54. P. Vigier, *La Seconde République dans la région alpine. Etude politique et sociale*, 2 vols., PUF, 1963

55. Ch. Marcilhacy, *Le Diocèse d'Orléans sous l'épiscopat de Mgr Dupanloup 1849–1878*, Plon, 1962
56. Ch. A. Julien, *Histoire de l'Algérie contemporaine* I, PUF, 1964
57. M. Agulhon, *Une ville ouvrière au temps du socialisme utopique, Toulon de 1815–1851*, Mouton, 1970
58. M. Agulhon, *The Republic in the Village*, Cambridge University Press, 1983. First published by Plon, 1970. (The department of the Var excluding the town of Toulon)
59. R. Huard, 'La Défense du suffrage universel sous la seconde République ...', *Annales du Midi*, July–September 1971, pp. 315–36
59a. The manuscript thesis by L. Chevalier: 'Les Fondements économiques et sociaux de la vie politique dans la région parisienne' (1951 Bibl. Universitaire de la Sorbonne)

3. Studies on various personalities (alphabetical order)

We remind the reader that the works nos. 10 and 11, cited above, should also be included under this heading as well as the centenary and PUF collections and G. Walter's bibliography in no. 19.
The other most important works are:
59b. R. Limouzin-Lamothe and J. Leflon, *Mgr D.A. Affre, archevêque de Paris*, Vrin, 1971
60. Ch. Almeras, *Odilon Barrot avocat et homme politique*, PUF, 1951
61. Léo A. Loubère, *Louis Blanc, his Life and his Contribution to the Rise of French Jacobin-Socialism*, Northwestern University Press, 1961
62. G. Geoffroy, *L'Enfermé*, Fasquelle, 1897 (extended more recently by the many studies partially devoted to *Blanqui* by Maurice Dommanget)
63. A. Dansette, *Louis-Napoléon à la conquête du pouvoir*, Hachette, 1961
64. F.-A. Isambert, *Politique, religion et science de l'homme chez Ph. Buchez*, Cujas, 1967
65. F. de Luna, *The French Republic under Cavaignac, 1848*, Princeton University Press, 1969
66. D. Johnson, *Guizot, Aspects of French History 1787–1874*, Routledge & Kegan Paul, 1963
67. C. Pelletan, *Victor Hugo homme politique*, Ollendorff, 1907
68. H. Guillemin, *Lamartine en 1848*, PUF ('coll. du Centenaire'), 1948
69. R. Schnerb, *Ledru-Rollin*, PUF ('coll. du Centenaire'), 1948
70. P. Viallaneix, *La Voie royale. Essai sur l'idée du Peuple dans l'oeuvre de Michelet*, Delagrave, 1959
71. R. P. Lecanuet, *Montalembert*, II and III, Poussielgue, 1898–1902
72. A. Cuvillier, *Proudhon*, M. Rivière, 1937
73. E. Thomas, *Pauline Roland, socialisme et féminisme au XIXe siècle*, M. Rivière, 1966
74. J. Bouvier, *Les Rothschild*, Club français du livre and Fayard, 1967
75. L. Sainville, *Victor Schoelcher 1804–1893*, Fasquelle, 1950
76. H. Malo, *Thiers*, Payot, 1922

Supplementary bibliography

M. Agulhon, *Les Quarante-huitards*, Gallimard-Julliard, 1975
   'La Résistance au coup d'état en province. Esquisse d'historiographie', *Revue d'Histoire moderne et contemporaine*, 21 (1974), pp. 18–26
   Le Cercle dans la France bourgeoise. Etude d'une mutation de sociabilité, A. Colin, 1977

P. Amann, *Revolution and Mass Democracy. The Paris Club Movement of 1848*, Princeton University Press, 1975

Annales historiques de la Révolution française, 87, October–December 1975. This number is devoted to 1848 and includes two useful bibliographical articles by M. Agulhon and R. Gossez

P. Bénichou, *Le Temps des prophètes. Doctrines de l'âge romantique*, Gallimard, 1977

F. Braudel, E. Labrousse (eds.), *Histoire économique et sociale de la France*, III, *L'Avènement de l'ère industrielle, 1789–1880*, Presses Universitaires de France, 1976

T. J. Clark, *The Absolute Bourgeois. Artists and Politics in France, 1848–1851*, Thames and Hudson, 1973

A. Corbin, *Archaïsme et modernité en Limousin au XIXe siècle (1845–1880)*, M. Rivière, 1975

J. Dautry, *1848 et la IIe République*, Les Editions sociales, new edn, 1977

D. O. Evans, *Social Romanticism in France, 1830–1848*, Oxford, 1951 (reprinted Octagon Books, N.Y., 1969)

R. Huard, *Le Mouvement républicain en Bas-Languedoc, 1848–1881*, Fondation nationale des Sciences politiques, 1982

C. Johnson, *Utopian Communism in France: Cabet and the Icarians, 1839–1851*, Cornell University Press, 1974

Y. Lequin, *Les Ouvriers de la région lyonnaise, 1848–1914*, Presses Universitaires de Lyon, 1977

L. Loubère, 'The extreme left in Lower Languedoc, 1848–1851. Social and economic factors in politics', *American Historical Review*, 73, 1968, pp. 1019–51

Radicalism in Mediterranean France: Its Rise and Decline, 1848–1914, Albany, 1974

R. Magraw, 'Pierre Joigneaux and socialist propaganda in the French countryside, 1849–1851', *French Historical Studies*, 20, 1978, pp. 599–640

T. W. Margadant, *French Peasants in Revolt. The Insurrection of 1851*, Princeton University Press, 1979

D. C. McKay, *The National Workshops*, Harvard University Press, 1933

P. McPhee, 'The seed-time of the Republic: society and politics in the Pyrénées-Orientales, 1848–1851', *Australian Journal of Political History*, 22, no. 2, 1976, pp. 195–213

J. Merriman, *The Agony of the Republic: Repression of the Left in Revolutionary France, 1848–1851*, Yale University Press, 1978

B. Moss, *The Origins of the French Labor Movement*, University of California Press, 1976

R. Price (ed.), *Revolution and Reaction*, Croom Helm, 1975

C. Renouvier, M. Agulhon, *Manuel républicain de l'homme et du citoyen (1848)*, Garnier, 1981

W. H. Sewell, 'La Classe ouvrière de Marseille sous la seconde République', *Mouvement social*, 76, July–September 1971, pp. 27–65

P. Sussel, *La France de la bourgeoisie, 1815–1850*, Denoël, 1971

J. Vidalenc, *Le Peuple des campagnes, 1815–1848*, M. Rivière, 1970

Le Peuple des villes et des bourgs, 1815–1848, M. Rivière, 1973

P. Vigier, *La Vie quotidienne en province et à Paris pendant les journées de 1848*, Hachette, 1982

E. Zola, *La Fortune des Rougon*, Gallimard, Bibliothèque de la Pléiade, 1960

Index of names